EX LIBRIS

COLLEGII DAVIDSONIENSIS

Given in memory of

ALBERT WERTHEIM, Ph.D.
Professor of English
Indiana University

by his wife
Mrs. Judith B. Wertheim

Money & Politics in
Ibsen, Shaw, and Brecht

Money & Politics
in Ibsen, Shaw, and Brecht

Bernard F. Dukore

University of Missouri Press

Columbia & London, 1980

Copyright © 1980 by
The Curators of the University of Missouri
Library of Congress Catalog Number 79-5380
Printed and bound in the United States of America
University of Missouri Press,
Columbia, Missouri 65211
All rights reserved

Library of Congress Cataloging in Publication Data

Dukore, Bernard Frank, 1931–
   Money & politics in Ibsen, Shaw, and Brecht.

   Bibliography: p. 167
   Includes index.
     1. European drama—History and criticism.
2. Money in literature. 3. Politics in literature.
4. Ibsen, Henrik, 1828–1906—Political and social
views. 5. Shaw, George Bernard, 1856–1950—Political
and social views. 6. Brecht, Bertolt, 1898–1956—
Political and social views. I. Title.
PN1851.D83   809.2'9'3   79-5380
ISBN 0-8262-0294-2

To Margi and Joan

Acknowledgments

For having read all or part of this book in an earlier form, and especially for having engaged in lively debate about its contents, I am more grateful than I can say to Oscar Berland, Charles A. Carpenter, Dennis Carroll, Margaret Mitchell Dukore, Joseph Maltby, and Myron Matlaw. While they are not responsible for the final product, and may not agree with all of it, it is better after having passed through their hands than it otherwise would have been.

Contents

Introduction: The Apostolic Succession
—Ibsen, Shaw, and Brecht, xi

1. "How Much?"—Money, Survival, and
   Independence, 1
   *A Doll House, Pygmalion, Mother Courage and
   Her Children*

2. The World as Brothel—Exploiter and Exploited, 27
   *Ghosts, Mrs. Warren's Profession, The Good
   Person of Szechwan*

3. "Special, Chosen People"—Society and the Professional
   Classes, 50
   *The Master Builder, The Doctor's Dilemma,
   Life of Galileo*

4. Society's Crumbling Foundations—Potential
   Destruction, 75
   *Pillars of Society, Heartbreak House,
   Puntila and Matti, His Hired Man*

5. "Scrap It"—Money and Morality, 100
   *An Enemy of the People, Major Barbara,
   Saint Joan of the Stockyards*

6. The Prospect of Revolution—Reactionaries,
   Liberals, and Radicals, 134
   Rosmersholm, On the Rocks, The Mother

7. Money and Politics in Ibsen, Shaw, and Brecht, 160

Bibliography, 167   Index, 171

Introduction

The Apostolic Succession—Ibsen, Shaw, and Brecht

Almost any list of major modern dramatists would include the names Henrik Ibsen, Bernard Shaw, and Bertolt Brecht. Representing three successive dramatic generations, each of the two younger men was influenced by, or at least drew upon, the plays of the older man who immediately preceded him.

In 1891, Shaw wrote the first book in English on Ibsen, *The Quintessence of Ibsenism*.[1] Despite the fact that Shaw did not complete his first play, *Widowers' Houses*, until the end of the following year, numerous critics claim that Shaw's critical study of Ibsen should really be called *The Quintessence of Shavianism*.[2] Far from discouraging such observations, Shaw heralded them. A self-proclaimed disciple of Ibsen, he called many of his dramatic works "discussion plays" along the lines initiated by the Norwegian master, and he applied such terms as *realism* and *idealism*, which he used to analyze Ibsenite drama, to his own. Indeed, more than one of Shaw's plays reveals a little touch of Henrik in the night, and some—particularly *Candida*—reveal a great deal. Indebted to *A Doll House*,[3] *Candida*—according to Shaw himself—intends to demonstrate that in modern society, it is the husband, not the wife, who is treated as a doll.[4] As other critics have pointed out,[5] *Candida* also owes a debt to Ibsen's *The Lady from the Sea*, for in both plays a husband agrees to let

---

1. See Bernard Shaw, *Major Critical Essays*.
2. Even as recently as 1971, by Michael Meyer, in *Ibsen: A Biography*, p. 457; and 1972, by Michael Egan, in his Introduction to *Ibsen: the Critical Heritage*, p. 21. As late as 1977, Ronald Gray calls *The Quintessence* "more about Shaw than about Ibsen" in *Ibsen—A Dissenting View*, p. 205.
3. See my *Bernard Shaw, Playwright*, pp. 54–60.
4. See Stephen S. Stanton, ed., *A Casebook on* Candida, p. 158.
5. For example, Arthur H. Nethercot and Jacob H. Adler, in ibid., pp. 234, 258–67.

his wife decide freely whether to remain with him or to go off with another man.

While Brecht was not a Shavian to the extent that Shaw was an Ibsenite, he nevertheless acknowledged the importance of Shaw, whose plays he studied.[6] When Max Reinhardt produced Shaw's *Saint Joan* in Berlin's Deutsches Theater in 1924, Brecht attended rehearsals.[7] Two years later, in a tribute called "Three Cheers for Shaw," Brecht proclaimed that Shaw's drama dwarfed that of his contemporaries.[8] Moreover, *Saint Joan of the Stockyards*, which may be one of Brecht's major works, draws heavily on two works by Shaw, *Saint Joan* and *Major Barbara*.[9]

Ibsen, Shaw, and Brecht all challenged established social values of their times; all wrote from viewpoints of the radical left. Together, they form an apostolic succession of radical dramatists. If their affinities in this respect are not immediately evident, they may become so if one takes several unidentified statements and attempts to assign them to their most likely author. For instance:

> (1) How the old ideas will come tumbling about our ears! And it is high time they did. Up till now we have been living on nothing but crumbs from the revolutionary table of last century, and I think we have been chewing on that stuff long enough.
>
> (2) I am, and have always been, and shall now always be, a revolutionary writer, because our laws make law impossible; our liberties destroy all freedom; our property is organized robbery; our morality is an impudent hypocrisy.... I am an enemy of the existing order....

Although each statement has its own tip-off, or authorial signature, one could attribute each to any of the three playwrights. However, the first is by Ibsen, in a letter to Georg Brandes.[10] The tip-off is the reference to the French Revolution, in the eighteenth century (although Shaw wrote his early plays in the late nineteenth century, he fed his radical appetite with that century's

---

6. Karl-Heinz Schoeps, "Epic Structures in the Plays of Bernard Shaw and Bertolt Brecht," in Siegfried Mews and Herbert Knust, eds., *Essays on Brecht: Theater and Politics*, pp. 28–29, 43.
7. Bertolt Brecht, *Brecht on Theatre*, trans. John Willett, p. 13.
8. Ibid., pp. 10–13.
9. See my "Brecht's Shavian Saint," *Quarterly Journal of Speech*, pp. 136–39; and Eric Bentley, *Theatre of War*, pp. 201–4.
10. Evert Sprinchorn, ed., *Ibsen: Letters and Speeches*, p. 106.

socialism; Brecht, who was youngest, dined on both nineteenth-century Marxism and twentieth-century Leninism). The second is by Shaw, in his preface to *Major Barbara*.[11] The tip-off is his distinctive rhetorical style.

Or take these. The first centers on a dramatic rather than societal issue; the second, on both.

(1) A theatre that can't be laughed in is a theatre to be laughed at.
(2) As to pity and terror, if people's souls could only be set going right by pity and terror, then the sooner the human race comes to an end the better. You cannot pity unless you have misfortunes to pity. . . . I do not want there to be any more pity in the world, because I do not want there to be anything to pity; and I want there to be no more terror because I do not want people to have anything to fear.

Shaw might have written the first; Brecht did, in *The Messingkauf Dialogues*.[12] If this aphorism contains an authorial tip-off, it is extremely subtle (the very symmetry suggests Shaw). Although the anti-Aristotelianism of the last statement immediately points to Brecht, who might have written it, Shaw did, in a talk on actors and acting.[13] The tip-off is the reference to the end of the human race, a Shavian but not Brechtian motif. In brief, Ibsen, Shaw, and Brecht—each in his own way a radical, left-wing writer who challenges established societal values—have strong affinities to each other.

While noting their affinities, however, one should also stress their differences. Just as Ibsen, Shaw, and Brecht represent three successive dramatic generations, so too do they span three successive generations in the history of European capitalism. Since capitalism changes with changing times, it appears differently in their drama. Not only because of the nature of the individual playwrights, then, but also because of the nature of the world around them, the essential qualities and thrust of their social criticism differs, as does their projection of an alternative relationship between the individual and society, and the segment of society on which they place their hopes for social regeneration.

11. Bernard Shaw, *The Bodley Head Bernard Shaw: Collected Plays with Their Prefaces*. All quotations from Shaw's plays and prefaces are from this edition and will be cited, by work, in the text. Other quotations will be footnoted in the usual manner.
12. Bertolt Brecht, *The Messingkauf Dialogues*, trans. John Willett, p. 95.
13. E. J. West, ed., *Shaw on Theatre*, p. 197.

Each is radical in his own way, which in important particulars is not always the way of the others.

Ibsen's radicalism was individualistic—at times, to the point of anarchy. The revolution he called for was of the human spirit. To improve society, he believed, one must first improve oneself. To Ibsen, who had no use for politics or politicians, liberals are even worse enemies of freedom than absolute despots, for liberals provide the illusion of freedom without the actuality, while such absolute despots as the Czar of Russia provoke, by their very despotism, fervent dedication to freedom.[14] "The state must be abolished!" Ibsen told Georg Brandes, and his explanation of that anarchic sentiment reveals its romantic, individualistic basis: "Undermine the idea of the state; make willingness and spiritual kinship the only essentials for union—and you have the beginning of a liberty that is of some value. Changing one form of government for another is merely a matter of toying with various degrees of the same thing—a little more or a little less. Folly, all of it."[15]

What was Ibsen's response to socialism, which was the major radical movement in the nineteenth century? On 18 August 1890, one month to the day after Shaw read to the Fabian Society a paper that he would revise and publish the next year as *The Quintessence of Ibsenism*, Ibsen expressed his satisfaction with Shaw's lecture (or what newspapers reported of it) and declared:

> I did not . . . say that I have never studied the question of socialism. The fact is that I am much interested in the question and have endeavored to the best of my ability to acquaint myself with its different aspects. I only said that I have never had time to study the extensive literature dealing with different socialistic systems. . . . I was surprised that I . . . should, without consciously aiming at it, have arrived at some of the same conclusions as the social-democratic moral philosophers had arrived at by scientific processes.

And yet, in the same letter: "I have never belonged, and probably never shall belong, to any party whatsoever." To Ibsen, it was "an absolute necessity . . . to work quite independently and to pursue my own course."[16]

---

14. Sprinchorn, *Ibsen: Letters and Speeches*, pp. 106–7, 114, 122.
15. Ibid., p. 109.
16. Ibid., p. 292.

Ibsen's contemporaries, particularly those more conservative than he, regarded him as a dangerous radical. In his early twenties, he barely escaped arrest for seditious writings; in his early forties, his radicalism prompted Georg Brandes to call it more extreme than that of Marat and Proudhon.[17] Max Nordau called Ibsen "an anarchist" who was "in a state of constant revolt against all that exists" and who had "only one longing—to destroy it."[18] To the doctrinaire socialist, Ibsen's individualistic form of radicalism was merely well-intentioned bourgeois futilitarianism, for Ibsenite drama failed to reflect the major revolutionary trend of his time, which provided solutions to those social problems which the playwright only saw through a glass darkly.[19]

Among Ibsen's contemporaries was one of socialism's founding fathers, Friedrich Engels. In an undoctrinaire letter written a month before Ibsen's statement on socialism that I have just quoted, Engels observed:

> At a time when throughout all Europe the victory of Napoleon spelled a victory of reaction over revolution . . . Norway was able to secure a constitution far more democratic than any constitution in Europe at that time. . . .
> The Norwegian peasant has never known serfdom, and this fact gives an altogether different background to the whole development of the country. . . . The Norwegian petty bourgeois is the son of a free peasant, and for this reason he is a *man* compared to the miserable German philistine. . . . And whatever the weaknesses of Ibsen's dramas, for instance, they undoubtedly reflect a world of the petty and the middle bourgeoisie, but a world totally different from the German world, a world where men are still possessed of character and initiative and the capacity for independent action. . . .[20]

In this sympathetic analysis, Engels perceived the individualistic

---

17. Meyer, *Ibsen: A Biography*, pp. 78, 339.
18. Max Nordau, *Degeneration*, pp. 396, 399. See also Clement Scott, quoted in Shaw, *Major Critical Essays*, pp. 14–16; Brian W. Downs, *Ibsen: The Intellectual Background*, pp. 2, 134; Robert Brustein, *The Theatre of Revolt*, pp. 37–38.
19. For example, George V. Plekhanov, "Ibsen, Petty Bourgeois Revolutionist," in *Ibsen*, ed. Angel Flores, pp. 52, 69; Anatol Lunacharsky, "Introductory Note," ibid., pp. 8–9; John Howard Lawson, *Theory and Technique of Playwriting*, pp. 71–72.
20. Flores, *Ibsen*, pp. 22–24.

independence at the heart of Ibsen's thought as well as the possibility of social regeneration through individualistic action.

So, for that matter, did Shaw. In passages of his 1890 lecture to the Fabians, excluded from the published *Quintessence of Ibsenism*, he explicitly stated that Ibsen belonged to no socialist party and, preaching defiance of society and social duties, the only creed he would probably accept would be laissez-faire, for Ibsen distrusted societal and governmental interference in individual conduct.[21] Another contemporary socialist, Karl Marx's daughter Eleanor, greatly admired Ibsen. In 1888, she provided the first English translation of *An Enemy of the People*, which she called *An Enemy of Society*. Five years earlier, in her Bloomsbury drawing room, she played Nora in a reading performance of *A Doll House* (in Henrietta Frances Lord's translation, called *Nora*). On that occasion, her friend Shaw acted Krogstad.[22]

Whereas Ibsen refused to affiliate himself with any political party and remained uninvolved in political action, Shaw became a Fabian socialist and political activist. Fabian socialism pervades the Shavian dramatic canon, to the consternation of many Marxist critics, who castigate the Fabian rejection of much Marxist dogma. Among the Marxist assumptions repudiated by the English Fabians is the idea that a revolutionary working class will reconstruct society along socialist lines.[23] As Shaw admitted, the Fabians were entirely members of the middle class who believed that they and people like them would, by persuading Englishmen to democratize and socialize their laws, create the conditions for a socialist society. He delighted in pointing

21. "Discarded Pages," fols. 27–28.
22. Under William Archer's editorship, in the eighth volume of his *Collected Works of Henrik Ibsen*, she retitled it *An Enemy of the People*. Eleanor Marx-Aveling, as she signed her name, was married to Edward Aveling, who served as model for Dubedat in *The Doctor's Dilemma*. See Yvonne Kapp, *Eleanor Marx*, 2:99,103; James Walter McFarlane, ed., *The Oxford Ibsen*, 6:426; and Archibald Henderson, *George Bernard Shaw: Man of the Century*, p. 669.
23. Shaw might have, but as far as I know did not, cite Friedrich Engels in support of this view. In 1888, four years after the formation of the Fabian Society, Engels—in a letter to Margaret Harkness, an Englishwoman who wrote novels under the pseudonym John Law—declared that "nowhere in the civilized world are the working people less actively resistant, more passively submitting to fate, more *hébétés* [dazed, stupefied] than in the East End of London." See my *Dramatic Theory and Criticism*, p. 804.

out that Marx and Engels themselves were well-educated sons of the bourgeoisie, not poor laborers.[24] No matter, according to Marxists, Fabianism is not true socialism but a socialism diluted and thus distorted by bourgeois values and attitudes. When Shaw "abandoned Marxism for Fabianism," says Alick West, a Marxist critic, he "reduced socialism to a series of practical legislative measures."[25] Why practicality constitutes reduction, West does not say. As early as 1908, however, Shaw mocked this sort of statement as romantic. Prosaic success, he asserted, was better than heroic defeat.[26] A dozen years before, speaking for the Fabians, he implored socialists in search of a sensational historical crisis to join another society, not theirs.[27] Still earlier, though, in 1890, he revealed his recognition of the limitations of exclusive reliance on Parliamentary methods and argued that Fabianism should not become "an excuse for not fighting. I am afraid some of our recently acquired middle class vogue is due to an impression that we have found out a way of making socialism an excuse for exhorting the working class not to do anything rash." Members of Parliament, he continued, will pass measures favorable to the working classes "only when they are convinced that otherwise a worse thing will befall them; and nothing can convince them of that except the determination of the workers to resort to force if Parliament fails."[28] Note, however, the word *if*. As he maintained in 1904, the year before he wrote *Major Barbara*, the Fabian methods and the barricades methods are not mutually exclusive. Since capitalism will not submit meekly to its own destruction, Parliamentary action is but the first stage of civil war. According to Shaw, "The mistake made by our wildcat barricaders is not in believing that the revolution will be effected by force, but in putting the fighting at the wrong end of the process." Only after years of parliamentary activity will Englishmen be ready to storm the barricades.[29] Fol-

---

24. *Report on Fabian Policy: Fabian Tract No. 70*, p. 3; *The Intelligent Woman's Guide to Socialism, Capitalism, Sovietism, and Fascism*, pp. 185–86.
25. Alick West, "*A Good Man Fallen Among Fabians*," p. 44.
26. Bernard Shaw, *Essays in Fabian Socialism*, p. 292.
27. Bernard Shaw, "Socialism at the International Congress," *Cosmopolis*, p. 669.
28. Louis Crompton, ed., *The Road to Equality*, pp. 101–2.
29. Quoted in Eric Bentley, *Bernard Shaw 1856–1950*, pp. 11–12. As Bentley says, Sidney Webb's famous phrase "the inevitability of

lowing the Russian Revolution of 1917, Shaw became more impatient with parliamentary methods and wondered, in nondramatic statements as well as in plays like *On the Rocks*, whether the time might then be ripe.

At the start of his career, Shaw's more conservative contemporaries regarded him as an author of socialist tracts thinly disguised as plays. According to his Marxist critics, Shaw's plays reflect his Fabianism, which is all talk but no action—a variation of that apolitical cliché about his plays—and therefore lack artistic as well as political value.[30] Since he achieved fame, Shaw has often been regarded as a humorist whose wit is so great that it dominates all other aspects of his plays, including the political. As commentators frequently phrase this notion, the clever Shaw puts lots of sugar-coating around the bitter pill he serves audiences, but the cleverer audiences lick the sugar-coating without swallowing the pill.[31] In 1925, when he was almost seventy, he received the Nobel Prize for Literature, and soon began to outlive most of his contemporaries. Partly for these reasons, but also because the Nobel Prize reflected general critical and public consensus as to the quality of Shavian drama, he became institutionalized, and how radical is an institution?

To Marxist critics like West, Christopher Caudwell, and E. Strauss, Shaw is a bourgeois playwright who is not as radical as he thinks. Before and after 1917, they denounced his Fabian-inspired plays as unsocialistic, for they fail to dramatize the class struggle, vilify capitalists, applaud the moral preeminence of the working class, and present exemplary socialists with whom audiences of workers might identify.[32] On Shaw's part, such omis-

---

gradualism" was not coined until 1923, meant "only that deep social changes take time," was "no blanket endorsement of parliamentary methods," and did not exclude violence except at tactically wrong times (pp. 10–11).

30. For example, Christopher Caudwell, "George Bernard Shaw: A Study of the Bourgeois Superman," in Wilbur Scott, ed., *Five Approaches of Literary Criticism*, p. 150; E. Strauss, *Bernard Shaw: Art and Socialism*, pp. 22–23; Lawson, *Theory and Technique*, p. 111.

31. According to Eric Bentley (*Theatre of War*, p. 205), Egon Friedell first said this. Friedell did so in *A Cultural History of the Modern Age*, 3:434–35. Although his observation is devastating, as Bentley says, Friedell may not have intended such devastation, for he dedicated his three-volume book to Shaw.

32. West, "*A Good Man*," pp. 51–54, 164; Caudwell, "Bourgeois Superman," pp. 151–53, 158; Strauss, *Art and Socialism*, pp. 19, 53–54, 95.

sions were deliberate. Conflicts between obvious absolute good and obvious absolute evil are the stuff of crude melodrama, he stated in his preface to *Plays Pleasant*. Their relationship to real life is not established and their cheapness is not enriched when the good is embodied in a socialist hero and the evil in a capitalist villain.[33]

Engels commented on Ibsen, Lenin on Shaw. Unfortunately for Shaw, Lenin employed a clever phrase that Marxist critics adopted to plague the playwright. West uses it as the title of his book: "a good man fallen among Fabians." His emphasis is on *fallen*. But what is the context of this quotation? "Shaw is a good man fallen among Fabians," said Lenin, who added, "and a great deal further left than his company." When someone called Shaw a clown, Lenin objected: "He may be a clown for the bourgeoisie in a bourgeois state, but they would not think him a clown in a revolution." In fact, Lenin appreciated and applauded Shaw's satiric exposure of capitalism. To him, Shaw was primarily a *good* man who was a valuable fighter for socialism.[34]

Whereas Shaw was a Fabian, Brecht was an outright Marxist. The conception of class warfare was central to Brecht. Society, he believed, could be restructured along socialist lines only by means of a revolutionary working class; not at all by the middle class, Fabian or otherwise. Clearly a radical playwright, Brecht took as his goal Marx's famous statement—"The philosophers have heretofore *interpreted* the world in various ways; the thing, however, is to *change* it"—and, as Eric Bentley points out, substituted the word *playwrights* for *philosophers*.[35]

Yet as Martin Esslin reminds us, "Brecht's case defies . . . simplifications."[36] Apparently, he joined no country's Communist party either before or after his decision to reside in East Berlin. While few doubt his intention to dramatize his Marxist commitment, the extent to which his plays succeed in fulfilling his purpose is an open question. "This play is just communist propaganda!" a student of mine once said of *The Good Person of Szechwan*, whose propagandistic themes he proceeded to sum-

33. Bernard Shaw, *Our Theatres in the Nineties*, 2:192.
34. Vladimir Scherbina, *Lenin and Problems of Literature*, pp. 90–91.
35. Bentley, *Theatre of War*, p. 206. Marx made the statement in his *Eleventh Thesis on Feuerbach*.
36. Martin Esslin, *Brecht: The Man and His Work*, p. xvi.

marize. Minutes later, another student argued that the play's structure and themes were not obvious or even clear-cut, and he extemporized how a hack propagandist would change the play to make it conform more closely to a communist viewpoint. To the first student, Brecht realized his intentions perfectly—too perfectly, in fact, and for that reason the student condemned the play. Although the second student praised the play for its ambiguities and indirection, East German and Soviet critics often feel uneasy about Brecht's drama in general for precisely these same reasons. More than once, East German authorities asked Brecht for revisions in order to make the Marxist themes of his plays more specific, thus more clearly propagandistic.[37] Here in the West, criticism tends to focus on Brecht's ideas about epic theatre, not on the Marxism that informs his radical plays, and those productions I have seen usually minimize or neutralize Brecht's Marxist views. As partial corrective, this book contains no further reference to epic theatre.

Each in his own way, Ibsen, Shaw, and Brecht are radical playwrights. This book examines their different treatment of similar social themes and issues. Except for the concluding chapter, each of the following chapters focuses on a particular social subject that involves money, politics, or both. Each isolates a particular viewpoint through which these playwrights treat capitalist society. The first chapter centers primarily on money, the last primarily on politics—crucial areas of concern among radical dramatists of the left who criticize the status quo. Both subjects form lesser or greater parts of the chapters between, each of which has a different primary viewpoint. Chapters 2, 3, and 4 move progressively up the social ladder. The focus of the second chapter is on the exploited—particularly the lower classes and women (of various classes); the third, on the professional classes; the fourth, on the upper classes, which are usually considered the pillars of capitalist society. The fifth chapter, subtitled "Money and Morality," emphasizes a key aspect of the first chapter; it concerns several social classes, including those which are a primary focus of each of the three intervening chapters; and it anticipates a principal concern of the penultimate chapter, "The Prospect of Revolution." For two reasons, a chronological approach seems inappropriate. First, the order in which the

---

37. Ibid., pp. 232, 243.

playwrights selected their subjects was determined by artistic as well as—or instead of—social reasons. Second, while the work of any one writer might be discussed chronologically, his chronological development differs from that of the other two.

In all of the chapters except the last, I have selected a play by each dramatist that appears most clearly to exemplify the particular social issue that is the chapter's concern. The chapter that explores the relationship among money, survival, and independence deals with *A Doll House*, *Pygmalion*, and *Mother Courage and Her Children*. Exploitation is the focus of chapter two, which examines three plays that employ prostitution as both theme and symbol of such exploitation: *Ghosts*, *Mrs. Warren's Profession*, and *The Good Person of Szechwan*. In *The Master Builder*, *The Doctor's Dilemma*, and *Life of Galileo*, Ibsen, Shaw, and Brecht dramatize the relationship between one of the professional classes (in Shaw's case, two) and the society of which it is a part. Capitalism is the form of society in which the authors lived (in Brecht's case, lived most of his life). In *Pillars of Society* (written long before the first world war), *Heartbreak House* (written during that war), and *Puntila and Matti, His Hired Man* (written after the war, and after the Russian Revolution of 1917), each writer explores capitalist society's foundations, which might collapse, how they might collapse, and—in the plays of Ibsen and Brecht—what might replace them. The relationship between money and morality—which may but does not necessarily involve religion—is an integral element of *An Enemy of the People*, *Major Barbara*, and *Saint Joan of the Stockyards*. Although many of these plays—particularly the last trio—deal with politics as part of the social issue, the penultimate chapter examines these playwrights' dramatization of the spectrum of politicians, from reactionaries on the extreme right, to liberals, to radicals on the extreme left. Ibsen wrote *Rosmersholm* well before the 1917 revolution; Shaw composed *On the Rocks* after he returned from a visit to the Soviet Union; Brecht's *The Mother* concerns the Russian revolution. The succession of plays in each chapter implies neither radical, more radical, most radical, nor good, better, best; and no direct corollary exists between the degree of radicalism and the quality of the play.

At this point, I should deal forthrightly with Ibsen's well-known and apparently clear-cut statement in a speech he delivered in 1898, after he wrote all the plays I analyze in this book:

"Whatever I have written has been without any conscious thought of making propaganda. I have been more the poet and less the social philosopher than people generally seem inclined to believe."[38] "Apparently" clear-cut. Ibsen does not claim that his plays contain no propaganda, much less that they have no radical viewpoint about society. He says he has not consciously written them from this viewpoint, which is an altogether different matter. Similarly, he does not claim to be a poet rather than a social philosopher. What he says is that he is more a poet and less a social philosopher than his contemporaries generally seem to think, which is also quite a different matter. When Ibsen made this statement, audiences and critics talked and wrote so much about his radical viewpoint that they said relatively little about other aspects of his art. Today, the reverse seems to be the case. Now, one requires a reminder that Ibsen's plays shocked his contemporaries, and the same is true of many of Shaw's plays. To the contemporaries of both, of course, the shock was all too apparent.

Whether or not Ibsen had Shaw in mind when he made his 1898 assertion, Shaw himself was conscious of his restrictive approach to Ibsenite drama in *The Quintessence of Ibsenism*. At the conclusion of his 1891 preface to the book is "a reminder that it is not a critical essay on the poetic beauties of Ibsen, but simply an exposition of Ibsenism."[39] Although Shaw is neither unaware of nor impervious to Ibsen's poetic beauties, he limits his book to a different subject. I should like to use Shaw's statement as a reminder to readers of this book. Although I am alert to the poetic beauties of Shaw and Brecht as well as those of Ibsen, and although I am also aware that their plays deal with subjects other than money and politics, this book does not explore those beauties or other subjects.[40] Instead, I have restricted it to various societal themes and issues that are among the major but often neglected concerns of these three writers.

38. Sprinchorn, *Ibsen: Letters and Speeches*, p. 337.
39. Shaw, *Major Critical Essays*, p. 12.
40. Deliberately, it avoids such considerations as mysticism and metaphysics. It therefore neglects, for example, the white horses of *Rosmersholm* and it pays little attention to those areas of Rebecca West's persona which are not germane to this book's subjects, to which it tries to stick.

1.

"How Much?"—Money, Survival, and Independence
A Doll House, Pygmalion, Mother Courage and Her Children

While money may talk, characters in plays do not always talk about money. Those in Ibsenite, Shavian, and Brechtian drama do—notably, in *A Doll House, Pygmalion*, and *Mother Courage and Her Children*—for money is a major factor in the societies these plays reflect and criticize. The absence of money means inability to survive. In the case of Torvald Helmer, lack of money—some years before the start of *A Doll House*—meant nonsurvival in the most literal sense of the term: he might have died. To acquire money, people could borrow, as his wife did; and they could sell: flowers and speech lessons in *Pygmalion*; food, drink, clothing, military supplies, as well as male and female bodies in *Mother Courage and Her Children*. While the acquisition of money may enable one to survive, money does not necessarily make one independent, no matter how large the amount, for independence is a more complex matter.

In these plays, Ibsen, Shaw, and Brecht link money to the question of survival, and they employ it to raise the subject of independence. In *A Doll House*, money is part of the atmosphere of that house. Its need and its permeation in society create the conflicts that inform the play. It sustains or fails to sustain the home, a societal institution suggested by the title. Dependence upon money creates questions about independence from it as well as from individuals and social conceptions of which it is a part. In *Pygmalion*, money means survival, and more of it is a means to higher status, which characters try to reach or maintain. Certain things money can buy: lessons in language and behavior, for example. However, higher status guarantees neither survival nor independence—as the Eynsford Hills demonstrate. Status without money makes survival difficult, independence impossible. In this play, Shaw examines the relationship between money and these social issues. All but two of the characters in *A Doll House* are middle-class: a nurse and a maid. While those of *Pygmalion* span the social spectrum, from poor flower girl and garbage collector to wealthy colonel and society matron, its ambience is upper-middle-class society. In *Mother Courage and Her Children*, all but a few of the characters are lower- or lower-middle-class, and the play's social atmosphere is that of the lower echelons of society. Here too, money is the dominant thread of this play's fabric. As in *A Doll House*, lack of it may mean death. In all three plays, it is necessary for survival. However, while each playwright treats the subject of independence differently, money is their plays' chief link. In each, it is a critical problem. Were it not, there would be no play.

※   ※   ※   ※

At the start of Ibsen's play, Nora Helmer enters the titular doll house; at the end, she leaves it. Between start and finish, entry and departure, Ibsen dramatizes the nature of that house, which by extension represents middle-class society. Among the foundations of this house and of middle-class society is money. But while survival is at stake, so is independence. Nevertheless, the relationship between independence and money does not form a simple one-to-one equation. Financial independence helps create individual, emotional independence, since without it, dependence and insecurity are likely to result. Yet, financial security is neither a necessary nor a sufficient cause of such independence. In *A Doll House*,[1] Ibsen dramatizes the complex relationships among money, survival, and independence.

1. Although the title is usually rendered in English as *A Doll's House*, translator Rolf Fjelde notes that Ibsen's title, *Et dukkehjem*, lacks the possessive (Henrik Ibsen, *The Complete Major Prose Plays*, p. 121). As Fjelde's reason for his break with tradition indicates, he is very much concerned with fidelity to Ibsen's Norwegian, which is the chief reason I use his translations of Ibsen's plays throughout this book. Another is his concern with contemporary, spoken American English. Nevertheless, I have also consulted other reputable translators: (in alphabetical order) William Archer, Una Ellis-Fermor, Eva Le Gallienne, James Walter McFarlane, Otto Reinert, R. Farquharson Sharp, and Peter Watts, who are likewise concerned with fidelity. Although no two translations of any passage are always identical—good spoken English (American or British) does not necessarily result from a literal translation of good spoken Norwegian—the sense of Fjelde's translations does not essentially differ from those of the others I have cited. In key passages, differences are often inconsequential or nonexistent. For ex-

Perceptively, Elizabeth Hardwicke points out that "almost the first line of the play is, 'How much?'"[2] To be exact, the question occurs at the end of the play's first, three-line speech. The heroine, Nora, addresses a delivery boy, who has just carried in a Christmas tree. Not only does Ibsen establish the subject of money at the very start, he also establishes its social function: payment for services rendered. Although the fee is fifty öre, Nora gives the boy a crown (one hundred öre) and tells him to keep the change—an action that is less frivolous than festive, in harmony with the holiday season. In this five-line scene, Ibsen suggests themes of money and financial independence.

The next scene modifies the impression of financial independence. From the adjoining room, the voice of Nora's husband, Torvald Helmer, asks whether *his* little lark and *his* little squirrel has returned. Later, he calls her beauty "mine, mine alone—completely and utterly." Belonging means dependence, not independence. But if Helmer considers Nora his property, as he apparently does, Nora encourages him to do so. To him, she calls herself *his* little squirrel and *his* lark. When she pleads, "I can't get anywhere without your help. . . . Yes, take care of me, Torvald, please!" he responds in kind: "Gladly, if it's what you want." Do both desire the type of relationship in which she is dependent upon him? So it would seem.

Nora's early response to her husband returns the subject to money, and the dialogue that follows relates money to the question of independence. She invites him to see what she has bought. "Can't be disturbed," he immediately responds, a set-up for his comic entrance: "*(After a moment he opens the door and peers in, pen in hand.)* Bought, you say?" Underlying the humor that derives from the stereotyped image of the flighty wife injudiciously spending money earned by her hard-working husband, who calls her purchases "throwing money around again," the scene firmly establishes the themes that the immediately preceding scene implied: money and financial independence. At the same time, it reverses the play's initial suggestion that those who dwell in this house are financially independent. In this house,

---

ample, of these translators who have rendered *A Doll House* into English, all but one employ the phrase I take for the title of this chapter. The exception, Watts, has "How much is that?" The same holds for the phrase I use as the title for the third chapter, "Special, Chosen People." The exception, McFarlane, has "specially chosen people."
2. Elizabeth Hardwicke, *Seduction and Betrayal*, p. 38.

matters are not necessarily what they seem to be, particularly such matters as money and independence.

As money and lack of it are among the preoccupations of the society in which they live, so are they major concerns of the Helmers. Until this Christmas, Nora reminds her husband, they have had to economize. Now that he has acquired a well-paying job, they need not skimp but can spend freely, an appropriate way to celebrate this holiday. Since he will not actually have his higher salary in hand for another three months, he argues, they should not imprudently squander money. To use a stock-exchange image, Nora is speculating on a futures commodity. Independence, in other words, has not yet arrived. No matter, suggests she, they can borrow money. A great matter, he counters, for if they were to borrow, she to spend, and he to die, she would be entirely without resources, and her person and property would be dependent upon the wills of moneylenders. Explicitly, Helmer links money, dependence, and independence: "No debts! Never borrow! Something of freedom's lost . . . from a home that's founded on borrowing and debt."

It is appropriate to observe how economically Ibsen sets up these themes of the importance of money and its relationship to other aspects of life. Primarily money, but also indebtedness, dependence, and independence, are established within the first two pages of the play.

Helmer is a decent man, not a miser. Why did he and Nora lack money for so long? Although he used to be a lawyer, he refused to take unjust cases. As a result of such principles, he failed to earn a good or steady income. Now, matters are different, for Helmer has what Nora calls "a safe, secure job" with "a huge salary and lots of commissions." She looks forward to "stacks of money and not a care in the world." To her, stacks of money will indeed result in a life that is independent of care. To emphasize the importance of money and its relationship to independence, Ibsen gives Helmer not just any job but a job as manager of a bank. Appropriate to his new position and to the play's theme, Helmer uses financial images. He says Nora earned the applause given her tarantella, and he calls her "his richest treasure." At parties, he sends her what he terms "a stolen look."

In their society, financial independence for them means dependence for others. As Nora recognizes, "everyone who works in the bank [is] dependent now on Torvald." By contrast, their former lack of money is a direct cause of Nora's present dilemma, dependence upon the wishes of a blackmailer. Because Helmer did not earn much money at law, he had to take on extra jobs which, according to Nora, occupied him morning and night, and wore him down until he fell deathly ill. His doctors declared it essential that he travel south. His health ruined by lack of money, his health could only be restored by money— 4,800 crowns, the cost of the trip. Then, independence was not even an issue; survival was, and its price was money. To raise it, Nora acted independently. Forging her father's name on a promissory note, she borrowed the sum. Paradoxically, while Nora had depended for her money on Helmer's wages from his jobs, the cure for his ill health that was a consequence of those jobs depended on her independent acquisition of money. Paradoxically too, while her ability to repay the debt is dependent upon Helmer's salary, the consequences of this better-paying job—firing one of the bank workers now dependent on Helmer, Krogstad, who had lent Nora the money—make her, and, therefore, her husband, dependent on the man who is apparently dependent on Helmer.

The matters of money, survival, dependence, and independence become more complex. As these money-related paradoxes suggest, both Nora and Helmer are in different ways dependent upon each other. While Helmer treats Nora as a doll, she treats him as a doll. As a bank manager, he manages money. Though not a bank manager, she does too. True, she lacks complete understanding of business jargon. "In the business world there's what they call quarterly interest and what they call amortization," she says, "and these are always so terribly hard to manage. . . . These accounts, you know, aren't easy to figure." Nevertheless, she has business competence. Although she found it difficult to do so, she met her payments on time. Apparently a dependent doll in a doll house, Nora is an independent businesswoman who manages her household money so as to siphon off enough to pay her debt without skimping on her husband and children. She manages her domestic economy secretly and independently of her husband, who for that reason and in that sense is a doll in the house she runs.

Other characters in the play parallel Nora and Helmer. Krogstad, who lent Nora the money she needed, once committed the same crime as Nora: forgery.³ Like Nora, Krogstad—to whom Nora is in debt—is dependent on Helmer for money: she receives it at home, he at the bank. To Krogstad, his job means more than a salary; it means survival. Potentially, it also means a life that makes him independent of his reputation as a forger, and affords a means to achieve a higher position that will enable him to demonstrate such abilities as to supplant Helmer. The financial security and independence Helmer apparently enjoys, he plans to acquire.

With Mrs. Linde, money has always been a concern. Survival, for herself and her family, has been her goal. Because she had to support a helpless mother and two small brothers, she dropped the penniless Krogstad, whom she loved, and married the apparently well-off Linde. As she puts it, using the third person, she "sold herself." But Linde's business, which turned out to be shaky, collapsed after he died. Mrs. Linde and Nora discuss her widowhood in terms of profit and loss: "And he left you nothing?" "No." "And no children?" "No." "Nothing at all, then?" "Not even a sense of loss to feed on." To Mrs. Linde, who understands the necessity of money in order to survive, independence is not invariably reducible to monetary terms. Now independent of everyone on whom she either depended or who depended on her—husband and mother dead, brothers grown up—she finds her life empty. Armed with a job (Krogstad's old job, in fact), she needs "someone to work for," but this does not mean someone to be dependent upon her money as Nora is dependent upon Helmer's. It means someone who needs her affection and understanding as much as she needs his. "We both need each other," she tells Krogstad, who agrees. Acknowledging such need, they transcend financial conceptions of dependence. With (her) wages that will enable them to survive and give him the strength to try again for a foothold in society, their emotional interdependence and mutual love, candor, and sense of responsibility supersede the question of independence.

Ibsen provides other suggestive parallels and contrasts. As Helmer used to be, Rank is in ill health. Whereas the restoration

---

3. Apropos, as the antifeminist August Strindberg aptly observes in one of his attacks on this play, it is not at all unreasonable for Helmer, refusing his wife's request, to fire from a job at a bank a man known to have been a forger and, agreeing to her earlier request, to hire in place of the forger a woman with business experience. See Strindberg, *Getting Married*, trans. Mary Sandbach, pp. 34, 36.

of Helmer's health depended upon a response to the question "How much?" and the cash at hand to purchase it, the wealthy Rank cannot buy his health. Even so, in the society in which he lives—a society based on buying, selling, and borrowing—he is accustomed to discuss even health in terms of money: "These past few days I've been auditing my internal accounts. Bankrupt." Financially independent, his external accounts bear no relation to his internal accounts.

Among the lower classes, money means survival, and considerations of independence are irrelevant. To Anne-Marie, the nurse of Nora's children and the nurse of Nora when she was a child, money is necessary to survive, and that is all there is to it. When she had an illegitimate child, she gave it to strangers. Why? She had to, for she needed a job, and the position offered by Nora's parents was too good for a poverty-stricken fallen woman to pass up. Unlike Nora at the end of *A Doll House*, Anne-Marie did not abandon her child in order to fulfill herself as a free, independent human being; and she did not leave the child with its father ("That slippery fish," she calls him, "he didn't do a thing for me"). She gave her child to others because she could not afford to do anything else.

Before the famous final scene between Nora and her bank-manager husband, the Helmers' lives link survival, dependence, and independence with money. During this scene, the issue for Nora is solely independence. She begins with financial imagery appropriate to his position. They are, she says, reaching a final settlement, closing accounts. Although money figures at the start of her description of her life—"I'd lived here as a beggar"—it soon becomes apparent that it is no longer the vital issue it had been. Significantly, the only reference to money beyond the initial allusions is an aborted one, in which Helmer begins to offer her some and she interrupts him before he can speak the word aloud. Though unspoken, a view of life in financial terms underlies their discussion. More pressing than what society insists she owes her husband and children, she makes clear without using such terms, is her debt to herself. Nora insists that she learn for herself what life really is, what ethics really are. No longer should Helmer feel bound to her, or she to him. Symbolic of the end to their dependence upon each other, a trade seals their separation. In a reversal of the transaction that first bound them, each returns the other's wedding ring.

Independent of bank-manager Helmer, Nora uses language

that is independent of banking terms. What of her debt to her children? In the second act, Ibsen makes clear that Anne-Marie will be present to care for them. Why does not Nora prudently put money in her purse before she leaves? In the first act, she does, forty crowns, which Helmer extracts from his wallet (a visually emphatic action) so that she may purchase something for herself, not the house, during the holiday season. This, she does—though not in the way he (or she) imagines at the time. With the money, she presumably can return to her home town to start a new life. Independent at the end of the play, free of her debt to Krogstad and of her tie to her bank-manager husband, Nora no longer speaks in images that connect her to either. To Nora, money, survival, and independence become her private, personal concerns—not those of her husband.

But Nora at the end of the play is not essentially different from Nora at the beginning. She is only different from what she seemed to be.[4] Earlier, she managed the household finances and was skillful enough to manipulate money in order to meet her payments when they came due. Why imagine that she will be less skillful in future? At the end of the play, Nora acts not only independently but unconventionally as well. Here too, she is no different from what she was previously, when she managed to go it alone to borrow a large sum of money and to commit forgery in order to secure the loan. The presence of Anne-Marie notwithstanding, does Nora lack consideration for her children? Perhaps, though here too Nora at the end of the play is no different from the earlier Nora. "But didn't you ever consider that this [forgery] was a fraud against me?" asks Krogstad. Nora's response: "I couldn't let myself be bothered by that. You weren't any concern of mine." Then and now, when Nora establishes a priority, she considers all other values unimportant. What is different at the end of *A Doll House* is that Nora acts for herself alone. For her self-fulfillment, she requires independence.

In the middle-class society depicted by Ibsen, survival, dependence, and independence relate to money, and Ibsen dramatizes these relationships. But they are neither simple (one-to-one) nor constant. Although he links them verbally when they are organically connected to each other, he verbally dissociates them from each other when he stresses the dissociation of an exemplar

---

4. Compare Hardwicke, *Seduction and Betrayal*, pp. 42–44.

of independence from the criterion of money, and from one of its exemplars. Ibsen regards individual fulfillment as primary, but its nature varies according to the individual. To Mrs. Linde and Krogstad, survival requires money, but ultimately, emotional independence demands a mutually dependent, candid, and responsible relationship between wife and husband. To Nora, plagued for years by a dependence upon money, independence demands an initial dissociation from considerations of money and from ties associated overtly and covertly with money. At the end of *A Doll House*, leaving husband and house, she achieves emotional independence.

*   *   *   *

In *Pygmalion*, Mrs. Higgins says that Liza Doolittle is Higgins's and Pickering's "live doll." She complains that her son treats Liza as an object, like "a lost umbrella," and his attitude and behavior toward Liza confirm her observations. In this respect, he resembles the Pygmalion of myth who created a statue, which one might call a large doll.[5] The Pygmalion of myth came to perceive Galatea, his creation, as a woman. At first, Higgins boasts that he has created "this thing," but later he says he created a woman.

Higgin's second boast is inaccurate. Galatea was a "thing" turned into a woman by a goddess; Higgins's "thing" turns herself into a woman—as Nora does, and like Nora she becomes an independent woman. As Ibsen does in *A Doll House*, Shaw in *Pygmalion* dramatizes themes of money, survival, and independence. But Shaw's major concerns include the impermanence of the class system, a bastion of capitalist society, and the fact that members of the lower classes can both change their classes and have them changed by others.[6] He therefore treats these themes more explicitly than Ibsen does. In this play, *explicitly* does not mean *simplistically*. In their initial appearances, the lower-class daughter and her lower-class father try to sell. "How much" does each require for independence? As the play demon-

---

5. For a comparison of the play and the myth, see Charles A. Berst, *Bernard Shaw and the Art of the Drama*, pp. 200–202.
6. This point, as well as several others that are developed below, is treated differently in my *Bernard Shaw, Playwright*, pp. 60–64, 286–89.

strates, the relationship between money and independence differs for each. For Liza, the ability to earn more money promises to give her more independence. For her father, however, whose social class also changes between the beginning and end of the play, a small amount of money creates an independent spirit, whereas a large sum of money saps that spirit's independence.

As the play begins, the Eynsford Hills, caught in a sudden downpour, are dependent upon a taxi for safe journey homeward. By the end of the short, expository first act, a taxi becomes a symbol that links money and independence. For this reason, their inability to obtain one hints at their straitened financial circumstances. While Mrs. Hill and Clara depend on Freddy to find a taxi, Clara complains that he has insufficient enterprise to do so, and his mother calls him helpless. He may say he cannot get a cab "for love or money," but he has little money, and the cabs, all occupied by people with money, are unavailable. Agreeing to try once more, he complains he will get soaked "for nothing."

Whereas this first scene develops the money theme metaphorically, the second scene, which begins with the entry of Liza, who collides with Freddy, develops it explicitly. After Liza calls him by name, Mrs. Hill's investigation takes the form of an economic exchange. Although Liza begins with a loss—two bunches of violets dropped in the mud—she ends with a greater profit than if she had sold them. Her first speech to Mrs. Hill concludes with a demand for money: "Will ye-oo py me f'them?" To survive, she must sell her flowers. Since all concerned know the price—"a penny a bunch," Clara soon says—no one inquires, "How much?" Instead, Mrs. Hill asks her daughter for pennies. When Clara says she has nothing smaller than sixpence, Liza—adept at business matters and apprehensive that she might receive nothing—promptly offers to provide change. While Clara urges her mother to take the change, Mrs. Hill tells Liza to keep it, a fourpenny windfall for the clever flower girl. Upon Mrs. Hill's discovery that Liza does not know her son, Clara notes their financial loss: "Sixpence thrown away!" Their straitened finances, treated symbolically at first, are clear at this point. A few moments later, Shaw stresses them further when Pickering, like Mrs. Hill, gives Liza a tip—though unlike Mrs. Hill, who purchases information, he does not want her to give him anything in return (except to stop pestering him for money), and unlike Clara, who pinches pennies, he is indifferent to a small sum of money.

Since money is a crucial aspect of capitalist society, it is a crucial element of every act in this play. In the first act, which presents a spectrum of society and which lays the groundwork for the remainder of the play, it is part of every scene. When both Higgins and Pickering, who can afford to live where they like, tell Liza she may live where she pleases, the socially aware Sarcastic Bystander comments, "Park Lane, for instance." When Liza claims to be short of money for her rent, Higgins calls her a liar and reminds her she said she could change half a crown. Soon, church bells prompt him to be charitable, and he drops a handful of money, including a half-crown and a half-sovereign, into her basket. When Freddy arrives with a taxi, she takes it (thereby relieving him of his obligation to pay the driver and perhaps foreshadowing her later suggestion that she will support him) and orders the driver to take her to Buckingham Palace (perhaps foreshadowing her later social rise). Of chief importance is the fact that Freddy, who has little money, surrenders the cab for this reason and that she, who can afford to splurge because of Higgins's unexpected largesse, takes it.

Higgins understands the socioeconomic aspects of his profession, teaching speech. Because lower-class capitalists on the make succeed in moving to a higher social class, but betray their lower-class origins, his is a lucrative profession. "Men begin in Kentish Town with £80 a year, and end in Park Lane"—where, one recalls, the Sarcastic Bystander mocked the notion that Liza might live—"with a hundred thousand. They want to drop Kentish Town; but they give themselves away every time they open their mouths." He teaches them how to avoid giving themselves away. No sooner does Higgins provide this explanation that connects money, mobility from one social class to another, and speech, when he explicitly relates these ideas to Liza. Whereas he teaches the nouveaux riches to change their diction after they have acquired money, he brags he can teach this working-class girl better English so that she will then acquire more money through a better-paying job with higher status. The boast is not lost on Liza, who soon tries to take him up on it.

In act 1, Liza offers to sell; in act 2, she offers to buy. As a customer, she behaves more independently than as a seller. To get a better job (better conditions for survival through higher wages), she wishes to purchase speech lessons from Higgins, and she threatens to go elsewhere if he does not consider her money good enough. Aware that money makes a difference in how people are treated, she responds to one of Higgins's insults, not with the temperamental yet impotent abuse she employed after she tried to sell him flowers in the first act, but with an assertion of what she knows to be her rights as a customer: "I wont be called a baggage when Ive offered to pay like any lady."[7] Higgins, who would sell what she would buy, now asks the critical question: "How much?" And he asks it twice. She computes the value in terms of a similar purchase. Since a friend of hers paid one and a half shillings per hour to learn a different language, which Liza believes should be more expensive than learning how to polish her own, she offers a shilling per hour. Computing her offer in terms of her income, Higgins concludes that a shilling to her is what sixty to seventy guineas would be to a millionaire. Although money is the basis of both Liza's and Higgins's professions, they do not directly form a financial relationship with each other. Just as Liza does not sell Higgins flowers in act 1, Higgins does not sell her speech lessons in act 2. Remembering Higgins's other boast—that in three months he could palm off the guttersnipe as a duchess at an ambassadorial party—Pickering bets the expenses of the experiment and the cost of the lessons that Higgins cannot do so. Higgins accepts the wager.

Paradoxically, when Liza, poor as she is, offers to spend her own money, she is independent (unless Higgins treats her decently, she claims she will leave). But when it turns out that Pickering or Higgins will foot the bill (depending on who wins the bet), and thus permit Liza to save her money, she becomes dependent. What she wants Higgins to teach her differs from what Pickering and Higgins want to teach her. Upon her agreement to participate in the experiment, she no longer calls the tune, for she does not pay the piper; they do. Subtly, Shaw links money to independence. Higgins orders a bath for Liza. Naked, she will come into a new world, since he orders her old clothes burned; her new clothes will be those provided by Higgins, on whom she begins to depend for such necessities. At the start of her new situation, she becomes more dependent than before.

7. Shavian quotations follow Shaw's idiosyncratic omission of apostrophes, variations of spelling, and use of spaces rather than italics for emphasis.

Apparently, he recognizes the social consequences of the wager, which will result in Liza's entry into a "new station in life." Later, he describes his actions in terms of social consequences. He is changing a human being "into a quite different human being by creating a new speech for her. It's filling up the deepest gulf that separates class from class and soul from soul." But his understanding is only superficial. Although he proposes to "help her to prepare and fit herself" for her new class, he does not actually do so. Instead, he teaches her external characteristics of that class: how to speak, what to say, and rudiments of deportment. These are insufficient preparations for membership.

What neither he nor Pickering understands is that the social transformation they prepare to create is different from, and far more radical than, the one proposed by Liza. Mrs. Pearce understands. Twice, she asks the key questions: "Is she to have any wages? And what is to become of her when youve finished your teaching?" The first concerns money, the second survival. Dismissing the obvious basis of the first question as inconsequential, and disregarding the implications of the second, Higgins conjures a fantasy whose points of reference unwittingly form analogies to what will become Liza's problem. She will ride around town every day in a taxi (that is, she will become incapable of earning wages, only of living idly) and will marry the son of a marquis (that is, sell herself to a rich man in order to survive in comfort—a notion Higgins actually suggests later). At the end of the experiment, he forecasts, she will go to Buckingham Palace (where—though he is unaware of this fact—she herself first ordered the taxi driver to take her), which is the home of socially unproductive parasites whose survival depends on the esteem and financial support of the nation (as Liza will become fit only to be esteemed, therefore supported, by another).

Liza goes to Higgins's home to buy; Doolittle comes to sell. His commodity is Liza, his customer Higgins. A "*revolted*" Higgins explicitly asks whether Doolittle would really sell his daughter. The father replies affirmatively. He cannot afford morals, he admits, and adds, "Neither could you if you was as poor as me." To Doolittle, the money he requests does not mean survival; it means a luxury, a binge (paralleling Liza's splurge when she rides in a taxi after she too receives money from Higgins). When Higgins offers Doolittle more than he asks, Doolittle rejects it, for it would make him prudent and less carefree—that is, no longer independent of conventional attitudes toward money. Later, when Higgins is morally beggared by Liza's refusal to remain dependent upon him, he insists that she does not "belong to" Doolittle. "I paid him five pounds for her."

Later too, the audience learns that Higgins is as socially irresponsible with Liza's father as he is with Liza. Without bothering to inquire of Doolittle's wishes in the matter (nor had he done so with Liza), Higgins mentions him favorably to an American millionaire, who dies and leaves him an enormous sum of money. Like his daughter, Doolittle gets something different from what he requests; likewise with social consequences that neither he nor Higgins foresees.

Though it is sometimes submerged, independence inheres in Liza's being. Despite her intimidation in the first act, she pleads for her rights; and when she discovers she need not fear, she is so aggressive she tells her social better he should be stuffed with nails. Independent in spirit at the start of the second act, she is gradually made dependent upon Higgins. But he does not crush her spirit. Although Liza performs like a wind-up doll during Mrs. Higgins's at home in the third act, and prompts Mrs. Higgins to call her a doll, her independent spirit enables her, within the rigid confines established by the man who has made her dependent upon him, to perform with a surprising amount of originality. Higgins gives her "strict orders . . . to keep to two subjects: the weather and everybody's health—Fine day and How do you do, you know—and not to let herself go on things in general." While she keeps to the two subjects prescribed by her mentor, she goes considerably beyond his two examples. Health leads to a commentary on alcoholism and on a death that may have resulted from murder, not illness.

What Mrs. Pearce drops in the second act, Mrs. Higgins picks up and develops in the third. She presses her son on the question of what is to be done with Liza after the experiment. When Higgins attempts to dismiss the subject by referring to the advantages he has given her, his mother, alluding to Mrs. Hill, exclaims, "The advantages of that poor woman who was here now! The manners and habits that disqualify a fine lady from earning her own living without giving her a fine lady's income!" Giving Liza disadvantages rather than advantages (money), he has created social conditions wherein Liza will have difficulty surviving and will be made dependent, not independent.

The fourth act begins with a portent of things to come. "Money-lender," says Higgins of the one piece of mail he examines. Only after Liza's success at the ambassadorial garden party does she recognize the problem raised by the two other women in Higgins's life. What is to become of her now that she can no longer return to her former way of life and is unfit, for lack of money, to function in her new social class? Without money, without the prospect of employment appropriate to her new way of life, she is desperate. In order to survive, she might marry, Higgins advises, proposing a situation wherein she will be dependent. But he pegs the advice lower than his previous fantasy about the son of a marquis. "I daresay my mother could find some chap or other who would do very well." Rejecting this proposal, Liza contrasts herself, in terms of money, with what she used to be: "I sold flowers. I didnt sell myself. Now youve made a lady of me I'm not fit to sell anything else." He then suggests she run a flower shop. "Pickering could set you up in one: he has lots of money." Perhaps because its establishment would involve dependence upon the generosity of Pickering, she does not respond.

Whereas act 4 resolves the question of whether Higgins will win his bet, act 5 resolves the question of Liza's future. As she herself recognizes, her physical survival requires money; her emotional survival, independence. "Oh! if I only c o u l d go back to my flower basket!" she tells Higgins. "I should be independent of both you and my father and all the world! Why did you take my independence from me? Why did I give it up? I'm a slave now, for all my fine clothes." When Higgins offers to adopt her as his daughter and settle money on her, she refuses to respond. Money alone is insufficient. She must earn it, independently. Significantly, for it reveals independence, Higgins does not solve her problem; she solves it herself. Using the principles she learned from him, she can do to others what Higgins did to her: teach phonetics to people who want to improve their diction. "You cant take away the knowledge you gave me.... I'll advertize it in the papers that your duchess is only a flower girl that you taught, and that she'll teach anybody to be a duchess just the same in six months for a thousand guineas." Far from becoming angry at her independent spirit, Higgins is filled with admiration: "I like you like this." Basically, Liza had always been independent. Doolittle admits he took no trouble to raise her. Before she submits to Higgins's lessons, she demonstrates her independence. In the midst of her studies, when she follows her mentor's orders, she displays independence. At the end of *Pygmalion*, she regains and increases her independence through the possibility of a larger income. Capable of earning more money than before (better conditions of physical survival), she becomes both financially and emotionally independent of Higgins.

What of the perennial question that dogs *Pygmalion*, romance between Higgins and Liza? What of the play's subtitle, "A Romance in Five Acts"? According to Shaw, the subtitle means that the play "is the story of a poor girl who meets a gentleman at a church door and is transformed by him, like Cinderella, into a beautiful lady."[8] Because this may not settle the matter, one should look into what the play contains. One should also consider what it does not contain. In so many words, Higgins declares himself to have always been impervious to the supposed charms of his female students, who "might as well be blocks of wood. *I* might as well be a block of wood." Twice, he calls himself a confirmed bachelor. "I cant be bothered with young women," he tells his mother, and since he admits to a mother fixation as well, "some habits lie too deep to be changed." The usual marital arrangement, says he, is commercial, for which he expresses his "righteous contempt"; he adds that he thinks more of Liza for throwing his slippers in his face (an independent gesture) than for fetching them (a dependent one). In contrast to Doolittle, moreover, as he explicitly declares, he is unintimidated by middle-class society's view that a man should marry. As for Liza, at no point does she say she wants to marry him. Just the reverse: "I wouldnt marry you if you asked me." To those who regard this statement as the angry response of a spurned woman who really wants to marry Higgins, one might point out first that Liza has not been spurned and that, far from rejecting her, Higgins has been imploring her to return; second, that if she wanted to marry him, she would explicitly say she would return, and Shaw might hint that she would try to make Higgins more dependent on her than he is. Furthermore, she talks of love only in connection with Freddy, and she explicitly asserts she does not want Higgins to feel romantically about her.

8. Quoted in Archibald Henderson, *George Bernard Shaw: Man of the Century*, p. 616.

What the play does not contain is a scene of wooing between Liza and Higgins, or even a scene of flirtation. When he tells her, "I like you like this," he refers to her independence. As Shaw makes clear, Liza also likes herself this way: she could kick herself, she says, for not recognizing earlier how to avoid being trampled by him. Why on earth should they marry?

But why should she marry Freddy? Apart from her normal romantic inclinations, to which she admits, Freddy is closer to her age (she is between eighteen and twenty, Higgins is middle-aged). Moreover, in contrast to marrying Higgins, marrying Freddy would increase rather than decrease Liza's independence. "I'll marry Freddy, I will," she declares, "as soon as I'm able to support him." In their marriage, she will have both money and independence. Freddy will be dependent upon her—in contrast not only to the conventional arrangement, but also to the first-act situation, which had the women in his family dependent upon him (for a taxi). Like the play's first speech, which alludes to an offstage Freddy, the final speech alludes to an offstage Freddy. In that last speech, Higgins acknowledges that Liza is "going to marry Freddy."[9]

Like Ibsen, Shaw is not simplistic. Whereas Liza's changed social status results in increased independence and (presumably) more money, Doolittle's changed social status results in still more money, but no independence. To the contrary, he becomes, as he puts it, a slave to middle-class morality, dependent upon what others might think of him. In addition, his newly acquired wealth makes him dependent upon the services of doctors, servants, and even people like Higgins, since he predicts he will consider himself obliged to learn to speak middle-class English. Liza's marriage to Freddy will make husband dependent on wife and will (she imagines) make her happy, but her father's marriage to his mistress will accomplish the reverse. An unmarried woman, says Doolittle, is more independent than a married woman. While he is not married to the woman he lives with, he complains to Higgins, he has no hold on her, must be agreeable to her, and is obliged to give her presents. Though one would

---

9. To those who find it difficult to believe that an attractive, independent young woman would marry an attractive ninny of a man who adores her, one can point to the ease with which they can believe that an attractive, independent man would marry an attractive ninny of a woman who adores him.

think that marriage to her would therefore make him happy, the circumstances of their marriage at the end of the play fail to do so. Evidently, he likes her independence. At the end of the play, middle-class morality claims her as well as him: "poor woman! respectability has broke all the spirit out of her. . . . She's been very low, thinking of the happy days that are no more." As this quotation hints, Shaw treats the crestfallen Doolittle in comically exaggerated terms.

What Liza gains is what Doolittle loses: independence. This makes the difference in the resolution of their stories. Money without independence is barren, as Doolittle's circumstances demonstrate. But so-called independence without money is a sham, as Mrs. Hill's circumstances demonstrate. Unlike Mrs. Hill, to whose way of life Liza is bred, she learns how to afford to live it. Although life is good when money and independence join, *Pygmalion* dramatizes, the acquisition of one does not necessarily result in the acquisition of the other, and indeed may result in its loss.

*   *   *   *

In the current edition of *Bartlett's Familiar Quotations* is a quotation from *Pygmalion* that today's readers and audiences of the play might find unfamiliar. "Independence?" asks Henry Higgins indignantly, "Thats middle class blasphemy. We are all dependent on one another, every soul of us on earth." When Shaw revised *Pygmalion* for its 1931 publication in the standard edition of his works, he deleted the speech, and except for editions that reprint the earlier text (such as Dodd, Mead's widely used *Complete Plays*, still in print in the 1960s), publishers follow Shaw's revised version. Although the passage is catchy enough to merit inclusion in *Bartlett's*, its omission from the play is artistically sound, for Shaw distinguishes between personal or emotional independence and social interdependence. To let the statement stand would confuse Shaw's issue in the scene, the fifth-act argument between Liza and Higgins. To expand and explain it, however, would constitute a digression and impair the scene's dramatic momentum.

But Higgins's deleted statement befits *Mother Courage and Her Children*, which derides the notion that one can be independent, either personally or socially, in capitalist society. In one respect, the figures of Brecht's play resemble Anne-Marie and

Mrs. Linde in *A Doll House*. Like them, survival is at issue, and consequently the need for money to survive. Independence is beyond their realistic expectations. "How much" for independence? To Anne-Marie, Mrs. Linde, and the characters in Brecht's play, the price is more than anyone in their social classes could possibly afford. As the prostitute Yvette bluntly puts the matter: "Pride isn't for the likes of us. If we can't put up with shit, we're through."[10]

In "The Song of the Great Capitulation," which is central to the play,[11] Mother Courage, who had forgotten that independence was not for the likes of her, recognizes anew this dispiriting factor of societal existence. When she was young, like the young soldier she teaches to capitulate, she considered herself sufficiently above the common lot that she could act independently. "No common peddler's daughter, not I," says she, "no second best for me. . . . the rules are for somebody else!" She learned otherwise. "In step" she had to march, on cue to sing. "On my ass and knees I was when they were through"—though not, presumably, at the same time. Instead of independence, her goal is simply to acquire money enough for survival, though its acquisition, and thus survival, are not simple matters. As she later expresses it, "My aim in life is to get through, me and my children and my wagon." Her wagon, she explicitly says, is her livelihood, and its merchandise, she also says explicitly, is what she lives off. Although she probably has no alternative to capitulation, or to buying and selling merchandise, audiences might object to a world without alternatives to them. As she sings "The Song of the Great Capitulation," she realizes that to assert her independence by complaining to the authorities would be a luxury she cannot afford if she and her children are to survive. When she walks, she must do so in step; when she does not, her position must be on ass or knees.

Not war, but buying and selling—business and monetary transactions—comprise the chief business of this play that is only apparently about war. What is war, really? In so many words, Mother Courage tells us: "It's business." Where business is, there she goes. Why did she leave Bamburg for Dalarna? "I

10. Quotations from this play are from the translation by Ralph Manheim in Bertolt Brecht, *Collected Plays*, ed. Ralph Manheim and John Willett, vol. 5.
11. See Eric Bentley, *Theatre of War*, p. 171.

couldn't wait for the war to kindly come to Bamburg." The war, she predicts, will probably continue for another five years. "With a little planning ahead, I can do good business if I'm careful." To earn a living, to survive, she cannot be independent of war, on which her business depends. Business metaphors permeate the play. Every scene but one (the tenth, in which Mother Courage and Kattrin listen to a voice inside a peasant's house sing about a rosebush) contains monetary transactions and references to business.[12] Even in that exception, one sees Courage's wagon, her traveling shop, with some of her wares hanging on its outside. But Courage is only a small businesswoman, not a major capitalist. As such, she is a surrogate for capitalists, who do not appear in the play. As small businesswoman, moreover, she occupies a dual role: she is exploited by and dependent upon the larger economic forces that control her destiny; and, in turn, she exploits her customers, who depend upon her, as she, for that matter, does upon them for her livelihood. For both small-scale business and large-scale capitalism, the essence is the same: buy or make the commodity as cheaply as possible, sell it as dearly as possible.

The first two scenes establish these themes. The play begins with an officer and a sergeant discussing their business, recruitment. Money figures in the first speech, wherein the officer complains of the type of person who gets the better of him in a business transaction. He buys alcohol for a potential recruit, who willingly imbibes, listens to the recruiter's sales pitch, then leaves while the officer pays for the drinks. In war years, as in certain times of the business year, one takes inventory of the stock: in wartime, men and horses. When Courage and her children are asked to identify themselves, her response is literally accurate and thematically pointed: "Business people." The very "Song of Mother Courage," sung in the first scene and repeated in several later scenes, indicates the primacy of business over war and links business with death, even with damnation. How unthinkable, she sings, for soldiers to march off to death before they purchase boots or schnapps from her, or to hell before she sells them food.

As business determines her life, so it determines her name,

12. To emphasize money and business, actress Helene Weigel, the dramatist's wife who played the role under his direction, audibly snapped shut a leather moneybag she wore around her neck every time she completed a sale. Brecht, *Collected Plays*, 5:346.

which she acquired "because when I saw ruin staring me in the face I drove out of Riga through cannon fire with fifty loaves of bread in my wagon. They were getting moldy, it was high time, I had no choice." Despite her statement—whose accuracy is questionable, since it is designed to persuade soldiers that though she has no license she is a legitimate businesswoman—she had a choice: possible financial ruin and possible life, or possible profit and possible death. Despite her professed motive, a coward does not drive through cannon fire. What her speech reveals is not that Mother Courage is uncourageous, but that business rather than honor or virtue motivates her courage. While a spectator or reader might laugh at her explanation, the laughter is not at cowardice mistakenly called courage, but at Brecht's ironic transvaluation of values that unconventionally links courage, a virtue, and business, a profitmaking activity.

References to money and business abound. If she does not reach Moravia, "it's a total loss." Her dead horse "cost fifteen guilders, but not out of my pocket, glory be." The intelligence Eilif inherited from his father consists of that man's ability to steal from peasants. Courage tries to sell merchandise to the recruiting officer and his sergeant, who try to buy her sons for the army. As inducements to enlist, says the recruiter listing them in order of importance, "There's profit . . . and glory." A businesswoman, Mother Courage recognizes business when she sees it. Inadvertently revealing her limited, small-scale understanding of larger business matters, she says the recruiting sergeant will receive five guilders for Eilif (he will get more). Unintentionally equating business with theft, she tells Swiss Cheese that the soldiers are trying "to steal" his brother. While she bargains with the sergeant over the price of a belt buckle, the officer simultaneously bargains with Eilif over enlistment. "Half a guilder," says Courage. "A bonus of ten guilders," says the officer. At the same time, they conclude their business transactions. Not only do war and business parallel each other, but the play has the business of war begin as a business deal (recruitment), in which Eilif sells his independence for money, an action that diminishes his mother's chance of survival, though she simultaneously concludes another business deal, but one that involves less money.

Scene 2 starts with the same activity that concludes scene 1, haggling over the price of merchandise, a dominant motif throughout the play. Courage and the Cook argue about how much he will pay for a capon she wants to sell him. "This is extortion," says the Cook, frustrated. Literally inaccurate but figuratively apt, he calls it "highway robbery." Eilif accomplished his heroic deed, which wins the General's applause and prompts him to demand good food for his guest, by business negotiations—the same means Courage uses in selling that food to the Cook, whose survival depends on both General and merchant. When peasants were about to kill Eilif and his men, Eilif quickly recognized that if he could not purchase survival with money, he might do so with the idea of money (a stratagem to disconcert): "I'm bargaining. Twenty guilders is too much for that ox, I say, how about fifteen? Like I'm meaning to pay. They're flummoxed, they scratch their heads. Quick, I reach for my sword and mow them down." He then actually commits what the Cook accuses his mother of, "highway robbery": he steals the peasants' oxen. Like father, like son; and like mother, like son.[13] Father and son steal from peasants; mother and son profit through a different type of robbery; war and business interlock; war employs methods of business, business of war.

The play continues these themes and metaphors. When Eilif sends for money from his mother, she says he is speculating on mother love. Brecht also treats the subject explicitly. Neither Catholic nor Protestant soldiers are concerned with a merchant's religion, says Mother Courage, "all they want to know is the price." Whereas her wagon—with its food, clothing, and bootleg ammunition—is her means of support, of survival, Yvette's commodity is herself, which she sells at a higher or lower price, depending upon demand, competition, and the merchandise's perceived or reputed quality. When Courage sees that her daughter Kattrin has stolen Yvette's red shoes, a sign of her trade, she expresses not maternal but business concern: Yvette "ruins herself for money, that I can understand." But Kattrin wants "to do it free of charge, for pleasure." Through the characters' discussions, Brecht expands the social framework to reveal the financial factors that underlie war. Since the war "cost [the Swedish king] a fortune," says the Cook, he had to levy a tax that "cost the poor people a fortune." The "big wheels," says Courage, are "making war for profit. If they weren't, the small fry like me

---

13. Brecht himself points out the parallel between mother and son: Brecht, *Collected Plays*, 5:334.

wouldn't have anything to do with it." Although she understands the activities of the big wheels and perceives that she is small fry, she mistakenly identifies herself with the big fry, since like them she exploits peasants, townspeople, and soldiers. What she fails to understand is that her business operation is too small to succeed and that the big wheels exploit her as well.

War is a form of business, business of war. Each has its casualties; their interdependence creates casualties. Mother Courage's business activities directly cause the death of one of her children, and she engages in business activities while the others are killed. In the case of two of these children, their own concern with money or business relates to their deaths.

Swiss Cheese is not just a soldier, he is a paymaster, and enemy soldiers want the cash box that had been entrusted to him. When he confesses he threw it in the river, they kill him. Without money one dies. When Mother Courage tries to bribe a sergeant to save Swiss Cheese, she haggles too long over the price. Without enough money, and on time, one dies. But she is neither entirely nor chiefly to blame. To sell her wagon to obtain the full sum of the bribe would leave her, her daughter, and the son she would save with nothing to live on, for they depend on the wagon (her business) for survival. What good is life that is doomed to starvation? Yet life clearly has greater value than money. Brecht's point seems to be that socioeconomic conditions leave Courage no solution. By stressing the social conditions that create her dilemma, he refuses to permit total pity or total blame for the individual Courage, who—both part of them and victim of them—does not represent them in their entirety.

Previously Eilif pretended to bargain with peasants before killing them and stealing their cattle; now he eliminates the bargaining phase. For this business transaction, which occurs during an interval of peace, he is killed. While this happens, his mother is in town, selling her wares before prices drop. Although she does not cause his death, as she partly caused Swiss Cheese's death, and in fact does not even learn of it, her actions are similar on both occasions: she haggles over price. Earlier, she tried to buy, as cheaply as possible; now, she tries to sell, as dearly as possible. Her trading activities therefore link with Eilif's death.

For the same reason, they connect to Kattrin's death. Whereas Courage goes to town to sell when Eilif is killed, she goes to town to buy when Kattrin is killed. Once more, she haggles. While a peasant tells her, "Maybe it wouldn't have happened if you hadn't gone to town to swindle people," *maybe* is a long way from *surely*. Even so, her business actions relate to the wartime deaths of her three children.

Courage has limited insights. Through the death of Swiss Cheese, she recognizes the importance of giving her children's survival first priority. Thus, when the Cook offers to take her but not Kattrin to live and work in a tavern in Utrecht, where they would be independent of the war, she refuses to abandon her mute daughter, who is utterly dependent upon her.[14] At one point she understands, "Victory and defeat don't always mean the same thing to the big wheels up top and the small fry underneath. . . . On the whole, you can say that victory and defeat cost us plain people plenty." Yet she fails to act on her insight, which is transitory. While she says, "God damn the war" at the end of scene 6, she says, "Stop running down the war" at the start of scene 7.[15] At the conclusion of the play, Courage still thinks she can profit by war. Hitching herself to her wagon—that like Mother Courage herself is older, more damaged, and with fewer provisions than before—in order to join a passing regiment, she drudgingly insists, "I've got to get back in business." In the end, as in the beginning, she cannot wait for the war (which her business requires) to come to her, but instead hastens to join it. Small businesswoman Courage is dependent on war for business, thus for survival.

Whereas Mother Courage fails to learn, another character succeeds, though only partially: the Chaplain. In scene 3, he announces that to die in battle is "a blessing" because "This is a war of religion. Not a common war, but a war for the faith, and therefore pleasing to God." In scene 6, however, he blames those who start wars, since they are responsible for dredging up people's lowest instincts. In scene 9, he chastises Mother Cour-

---

14. Thus, Robert Brustein errs when he says that Mother Courage "*invariably* chooses the most selfish, ignominious, and profitable course" (my emphasis). See Robert Brustein, *The Theatre of Revolt*, p. 269.
15. Brecht's production emphasized the superficiality of her insight even at the end of scene 6. According to Manfred Wekwerth (a director at Brecht's Berliner Ensemble), when Helene Weigel cursed the war, she simultaneously let flour run through her fingers as she tested its commercial quality. See Manfred Wekwerth, "Brecht Today," p. 120.

age for living off war and tells the Cook he can no longer preach to people.

But if the play demonstrates that war does not give big profits to little people, what of the one lower-class person who makes a big profit, the prostitute Yvette? What is noteworthy is that Yvette prospers not from two-bit prostitution but from marriage into the aristocracy. She has become the Countess Stahremberg.[16] It is as one of the big people that she profits.

Emphasizing both the theme and the failure of the play's characters to understand it, a regimental chorus sings the play's finale: "Our food is swill, our pants all patches/The higher-ups steal half our pay/And still we dream of God-sent riches./Tomorrow is another day!" With such understanding, let them dream on. The audience learns what the higher-ups do and understands that the tomorrow of these commoners, under the same social conditions as their today, will be the same as that today. Although they gripe, they—like Mother Courage—still dream of riches. In the concluding two lines, the soldiers sing enthusiastically as they march, "And if by chance you're still alive/It's time to rise and shake a leg." *If by chance* notwithstanding, the lyrics and the beat are good for morale.

* * * *

In *A Doll House*, *Pygmalion*, and *Mother Courage and Her Children*, money is a major theme and motif. The answer to the question "How much?" involves more than a statement about crowns, pounds, or guilders, though it usually involves such a statement as well. To some characters—Mrs. Linde, Liza Doolittle, and Mother Courage, for instance—money is necessary to survive. But survival is not all they want. Among Mrs. Linde's other desires is a relationship of mutual dependence with a man; among Liza's, independence. At the start, Nora's need is solely money; at the end, solely independence. Yet money does not necessarily buy survival or independence. It cannot purchase Rank's health, and it robs Doolittle's sense of independence. Clearly, the relationships among money, survival, and independence are complex. Just as clearly, Ibsen, Shaw, and Brecht dramatize those complexities.

16. In Brecht's production, as he notes, the actress playing Yvette spoke thereafter with the accent of Austrian aristocracy. See Brecht, *Collected Plays*, 5:373.

At the end of Ibsen's and Shaw's plays, the heroines achieve emotional independence, and in the latter, the heroine also discovers how to earn money that will enable her to become financially secure. At the end of Brecht's play, as at the beginning, the heroine pursues business, the acquisition of money. She renounces independence as a goal that is unattainable for someone in her class. Survival alone is her aspiration.

Despite Brecht's political persuasion and didactic aims, *Mother Courage and Her Children* is far from a cut-and-dried tract about money and capitulation (the renunciation of independence), business and war. Furthermore, its themes are less explicit than those of either *A Doll House* or *Pygmalion*. What Brecht enables the audience to perceive, he either does not permit his characters to perceive, or gives them at most only partial perception. Both statements hold for Ibsen and Shaw, neither of whose plays is a cut-and-dried tract.

As these three plays indicate, like the trios in succeeding chapters, the chronologically successive works of Ibsen, Shaw, and Brecht do not necessarily correspond to categories of good, better, and best (most critics would be hard put to divide this trio into such categories). Nor do these plays necessarily represent a progression from lesser to greater radicalism: the Marxist Brecht does not dramatize an alternative to capitulation to the status quo; the Fabian Shaw demonstrates a method to begin the dissolution of class distinctions; one might conclude from the individualist Ibsen that one has the right to repudiate all social duties if they hinder one's personal development. Instead of radical progression, might not one perceive radical regression? The point is neither progression nor regression, for all three dramatists offer different views and criticisms of society. Rather, their different insights and critiques employ different stratagems that elucidate similar themes.

2.

The World as Brothel—Exploiter and Exploited
Ghosts, Mrs. Warren's Profession, The Good Person of Szechwan

"Sell when you can," Ganymede advises Phebe in Shakespeare's *As You Like It*; "you are not for all markets." Since Ganymede puts the matter banteringly rather than crassly, and the tone of the play is comic, the admonition is funny. Nevertheless, what the advice amounts to is that Phebe take up prostitution, which is the appropriate term when one sells or rents oneself, either for marital security or for a short-term business exchange.

With this viewpoint, which is a jest but not a theme in *As You Like It*, the world is a brothel. Prostitutes permit the exploitation of their bodies for payment. Yet, as Shaw put it in a Fabian lecture, the term *prostitution* is not restricted to the sale of one's body, because when one accepts only the monetary incentive for any type of work, and sells one's soul according to commercial principles of supply and demand, that person too is a prostitute.[1] Whoever pays, either a fee or wages, exploits the prostitute, whose wares, abilities, time, and labor he uses for his own gratification or benefit, not the prostitute's.

In the world dramatized by Ibsen, Shaw, and Brecht, exploitation is endemic. Characteristic of a world dominated by business, exploitation also props the homes of businessmen and their workers. One exploits or is exploited, both in business enterprises and at home.

Symptom and symbol of that world is prostitution. *Ghosts, Mrs. Warren's Profession*, and *The Good Person of Szechwan*[2]

---

1. Bernard Shaw, "Notes for a Fabian Lecture," fol. 15.
2. The most familiar English translation of this play's title, by Eric Bentley, is *The Good Woman of Szechwan*, which sounds better in English than *Good Person*. Unfortunately, it is less accurate (*Mensch* is the German word).

treat the capitalist world as a brothel. Not only is prostitution a metaphor in these plays, it is also an activity. As the dramatic focus of each of these plays differs from that of the others, the activity of prostitution itself, vis-à-vis prostitution as metaphor, differs. In *Ghosts*, whose locus is the home, prostitution is a metaphor for marriage and the activity that will literally occur, after the final curtain, in another "home" that, to reverse the cliché, will really be a house. Prostitution is the profession to which Shaw's title alludes, and the focus of his play is on profession—not only the mother's profession (formerly, prostitute; at present, procuress), but also the daughter's (actuary, plus—as she puts it—"law, with one eye on the Stock Exchange"), which is also, and more obviously, related to capitalism. While the protagonist of Brecht's play begins as a prostitute, she becomes a businesswoman early in the play. Focusing on business activities, Brecht demonstrates its affinities to prostitution, and he dramatizes exploitation in a brothellike world of business.

* * * *

As later analysis will elaborate, a linchpin of *Ghosts* is the memorial Mrs. Alving plans to give her late husband, an orphanage, appropriate to this whoremonger who peopled the world with bastards in need of such a home, and who is one of the titular ghosts. When the orphanage burns down, the ground will be used for the establishment of what will become a thinly disguised brothel, another ghost. Furthermore, each of the play's five characters relates directly to both exploitation and prostitution.

At the play's start, Ibsen presents a striking visual image: a pretty young girl, Regina, tries unsuccessfully to prevent the entry of a deformed man, Engstrand, into a respectable house. During this activity, verbal imagery of exploitation and prostitution reinforces the implication of deformed human relationships and the presence of deformity in what is apparently respectable. To provide a respectable aura for himself, Engstrand, who was on a binge the previous night, exploits and thereby deforms God's name and scriptural phrases; for instance, "nobody's going to say about Jacob Engstrand that he can't put temptation behind him."[3] In the society depicted in *Ghosts*, hu-

---

3. For an analysis of Engstrand's language, see John Northam, *Ibsen: A Critical Study*, pp. 78, 96.

man relationships are deformed, and no character successfully avoids or prevents such deformation.

A major dramatic question in the scene that follows his entrance is who will exploit whom. Engstrand has saved money from working on Alving's memorial orphanage (an appropriate memorial for Alving, it is equally appropriate for Engstrand, who years before turned a profit because of an unmarried woman Alving impregnated—still another ghost from the past). With that money, Engstrand aims to open "a sort of hotel for seamen." When he invites the girl, whom he called a slut a few minutes before, to join him in running the establishment, it becomes clear that this hotel will be a brothel: "But there've got to be women on the premises, that's clear as day. Because we want a little life in the evening—singing and dancing and that sort of thing." Undaunted by her refusal, he tries to persuade her much the way a pimp might try to persuade a girl to become a prostitute. If she joined him, she would have "dresses to burn." If she learned how to show off her good looks, she might nab a ship's officer as a husband. When she protests that she will not marry a sailor, Engstrand is unfazed: "Then forget about getting married." The other way "can pay just as well." Her mother, who he claims was no better looking than she, obtained three hundred dollars from an English yachtsman. Like mother, like daughter, according to Engstrand, who profited from the mother's prostitution and wants to profit from the daughter's. More ghosts, it turns out—revenants of prostitution and exploitation. But Regina, at least at this point in the play, will have none of Engstrand's scheme. If things go the way she plans, she tells him, she could do better where she is. Instead of enticing several men chiefly for his profit, thus permitting him to exploit her, she hopes (it later becomes clear) to entice one man for her own profit.

With Pastor Manders, Regina's behavior creates an ambience that suggests a combination of bourgeois and bawdy-house parlor. Urging him to sit in an armchair that she moves toward him, she slips a footstool beneath his feet, arranges his comfort, and points out that since he saw her last she has "filled out." After she manages to make him consider her in sexual terms, she exploits his friendly attitude by trying to persuade him to find her a job in town in the house of a gentleman whom she could "care for and look up to, almost like a daughter. . . ." *Almost* like a daughter? If Manders succeeds in helping her—and he promises to remember her if he hears of a suitable position—he may become almost like a pimp.

When Mrs. Alving tells Manders the truth behind the planned Captain Alving Memorial Home, in which she plans to give Regina a position, she reveals the appropriateness of her tribute to her late husband and of Regina's position in the establishment. As dissolute at the end of nineteen years of marriage as he was before its beginning, Alving was a whoremonger who carried his extramarital sexual activites into their home: he impregnated Joanna, whose role as servant in the house prevented her from stopping the master's exploitation of her in the role of woman as well. To preserve their reputation, Mrs. Alving prostituted herself by continuing to live with him. She even behaved as a prostitute behaves with a client. At night, she became "his drinking companion as he got sodden over his bottle," and she forced herself to listen to "his jokes and toasts and all his maundering, abusive talk. . . ." By day as well, she permitted herself to be exploited. Alving benefited from her labors: "All the additions to the property, all the improvements and technical innovations that Alving got fame and credit for—do you think those were *his* doing? *He*, sprawled all day on the sofa, reading old government journals! No . . . it was I who had to pull the whole load when he fell back in his old wild ways or collapsed in groveling misery."

What to do with Joanna? To prevent any recurrence of adultery in her own home, and also to hush up the affair and its consequences, Mrs. Alving exploited her. She bribed Joanna with three hundred dollars—a large sum to Joanna, a pittance to Mrs. Alving. With this money as bait, the pregnant Joanna acquired a husband, Engstrand, whom she had previously spurned because he was physically repulsive. She prostituted herself to become what society calls an honest woman; he prostituted himself for the money. In this case, mutual exploitation proved mutually advantageous. While Mrs. Alving may not technically have been a procuress, she at least enabled Joanna to become her own pimp. Although Engstrand later claims he did not touch a penny of Joanna's money, and although Manders believes him, why should the audience? Mrs. Alving does not credit Engstrand's assertion, and because Manders does, she considers the pastor "a big baby," that is, an innocent, gullible fool.

When Manders calls Joanna's marriage immoral and declaims against a man who marries a fallen woman for three hundred dollars, Mrs. Alving asks his opinion of herself, since she married a fallen man. The respectable Manders insists there was a world of difference between the two cases, but she corrects him: "Much less than a world, I think. There was a considerable difference in price—a paltry three hundred dollars as against a whole fortune."[4] Her mother and aunts, she adds, "wrote up my bill of sale. Oh, it's amazing how neatly they figured it out, that it would be stark madness to turn down an offer like that." Like Joanna, she was a prostitute. In a more clear-cut way than she acted with Joanna, her family acted as her procuress. The money Mrs. Alving contributed to the whoremonger's memorial orphanage is exactly "the amount that made Lieutenant Alving such a good catch at the time. . . . It was my selling price." It is, in other words, conscience money.

When Mrs. Alving overhears her son Osvald make a pass at Regina—yet another ghost from the past—she confesses to Manders that the servant is the daughter of her former servant. Although Regina herself later presses this point, one might recognize now that Regina, who is Alving's daughter as well as Joanna's, is not her half-brother's social equal in the house of her natural father, but a maid, and therefore exploited by her father's wife. To prevent Osvald and Regina from doing what their father and her mother did, Mrs. Alving aims, ghostlike, to do with the daughter something similar to what she did with the mother.[5] Although her action would again involve exploitation and prostitution, class differences give her action a different shape. Working-class Joanna got three hundred dollars to fend for herself, but Regina has Alving's bourgeois blood. Mrs. Alving herself therefore intends to see that she is established in a decent marriage. Formerly a respectable prostitute, Mrs. Alving aims to become Regina's respectable procuress, and to do with Regina what her own mother and aunts did with her.

As his early scene with Regina hints, there is something of the pimp in Pastor Manders, who concurs with Mrs. Alving's proposal for Regina's future. To the society he represents, unpal-

---

4. Compare John Howard Lawson, *Theory and Technique of Playwriting*, pp. 72–73.
5. Compare Northam, *Ibsen: A Critical Study*, pp. 87–88.

atable truths that might expose its nature are better kept quiet than told. His participation in society's conspiracy of silence about prostitution is another specter from the past. Years before, when he persuaded Mrs. Alving not to leave her husband or to reveal the truth about their marriage, he inadvertently became Alving's pimp. Now, he joins Mrs. Alving as partner in procuring, and in preventing the revelation of truth.

Although Regina would not object to the form of prostitution Mrs. Alving has in mind—marriage for money—she aims to act in her own behalf: to profit herself, not her employer. She hopes to persuade wealthy Osvald to marry her. On his last trip home, he had delighted her when he casually asked if she would like to visit Paris. This time, the same day he arrived, she unhesitatingly and unsubtly takes the initiative to remind him of his proposal. Osvald describes her as "standing there as if her arms were simply waiting to take me in." No doubt they were. Recognizing her market, Regina displayed her wares.

When the orphanage burns to the ground, Engstrand exploits Manders. Prostituting his own reputation to preserve Manders's, Engstrand agrees to take the blame. Although Engstrand's reputation is not particularly high, the commercial principles of supply and demand increase its value in this particular situation. His price is Manders's help in establishing the seamen's home. Manders pays the prostitute. He gives Engstrand the land that was to have been used for the orphanage. Engstrand proposes to name his "house for wayfaring seamen . . . 'Captain Alving's Home,' yes. And if I get to run that house after my own devices, I think I can promise you it'll be truly worthy of that great man's memory, bless him." This promise, one can be sure, he will keep. His whorehouse will be a tribute even more appropriate than the orphanage, a ghost with lively reenactments of Alving's past.

Once Mrs. Alving tells Regina and Osvald the truth about their father, Regina recognizes that she has been exploited: "You know, Mrs. Alving, you could have raised me as a gentleman's daughter—and I would've been a lot better off." Although the statement is vindictive and self-serving, it is nonetheless accurate. She had wanted to exploit Osvald, but she refuses to help him when she learns about his health: "I really can't stay out in the country and run myself ragged for invalids. . . . A poor girl's only got her youth; she'd better use it—or else she'll find herself barefoot at Christmas before she knows it." In Ganymede's phrase, she recognizes she must sell now. Upon learning that Manders knows everything, she leaves to catch up with him before the boat sails, since she believes she can exploit him as her stepfather did, perhaps get some of the money Engstrand got from her mother. "And if things really go wrong, I still know a house where I'll do just fine. . . . In 'Captain Alving's Home.'" So she can, for Engstrand promised to have a place open for her should she change her mind about working there. Exploitation and prostitution, in one form or another, are very likely in her future.

Osvald too is an exploiter. While Regina planned to exploit him, he planned to exploit her. A syphilitic, he would have enjoyed her youth and beauty, and—perceiving her lack of selflessness—understood that once his disease reached the terminal stage, "She soon would have gotten tired of tending an invalid like me." Thus, she would have given him the overdose of morphine pills he will want. As he explains this to his mother, he drinks champagne while she keeps him company—a ghostly reminder of what she did while his father drank. Unable to exploit Regina, he now wants to exploit his mother. "You can be especially useful to me," he tells her, "now that I'm ill. . . . I can't be concerned very much with others; I have enough just thinking about myself." Like his father, he is self-centered and self-indulgent. Like his mother—a point at which Ibsen hints but does not stress—he is a coward who delays action as long as possible. He wants to live as long as his precarious health permits, and though he could take the morphine pills himself before the final attack occurs, he does not do so. Ghosts of both parents reside in him.

Will Mrs. Alving give him the overdose when the terminal attack arrives at the end of the play? Ibsen's point is that her previous actions have boxed her into the insoluble dilemma of killing him or of watching his disease slowly and painfully destroy him. If she chooses the latter, her existence will bear a ghostlike resemblance to her existence with his father: she will become her son's drinking companion, sit alone with him as he babbles incoherently, drag the helpless man to bed, until one of them dies. Exploited by her husband, she would be exploited by her son.

Ultimately, *Ghosts* suggests, though Ibsen does not use such terms as capitalism and social classes, the blame lies in a society that regards all actions in terms of money, duty, and respectability, and whose moral codes push people toward marriages based on monetary considerations, then keeps them there regardless of circumstances. Under such social conditions, exploitation is a way of life. Such a world is a brothel where people buy others and sell themselves.

* * * *

In *Ghosts*, Mrs. Alving is a marital type of prostitute who would become a pimp. In *Mrs. Warren's Profession*, the title character is a conventional type of prostitute who becomes a pimp. Much more explicitly than *Ghosts*, *Mrs. Warren's Profession* links prostitution with capitalism in an exploitative world that resembles a brothel.[6]

Mrs. Warren, whose titular profession revolves around prostitution, echoes Mrs. Alving's comment on herself: "What is any respectable girl brought up to do but to catch some rich man's fancy and get the benefit of his money by marrying him?—as if a marriage ceremony could make any difference in the right or wrong of the thing!" Although her own daughter Vivie is a respectable girl, Mrs. Warren did not raise her to catch a rich husband. No need: she has money enough to make such an enterprise unnecessary for her child.

But as Samuel Gardner, the clerical father of Vivie's young suitor Frank, does not have much money, he gives his son the same sort of advice Ganymede gives Phebe, and Regina gives herself: to turn his good looks to account by marrying a woman with money. Instead of portraying a woman who would become a matrimonial prostitute, Shaw portrays a man who would become one. By making the source of this advice a clergyman—who, moreover, used to be one of Mrs. Warren's customers—Shaw foreshadows the play's later revelation of the complicity of all parts of society in prostitution, which in this play is a metaphor of capitalism, a link to capitalism, and capitalism itself.

Still, Mrs. Warren, who is part owner and manager of a chain of brothels throughout Europe, does not leave her business hab-

---

6. Whereas Ibsenite criticism has scanted this metaphor in *Ghosts*, Shavian criticism has noted it in *Mrs. Warren's Profession*; for example, in the last dozen years: Charles A. Carpenter, *Bernard Shaw and the Art of Destroying Ideals*, p. 52; Martin Meisel, "Shaw and Revolution," in *Shaw: Seven Critical Essays*, ed. Norman Rosenblood, p. 117; my *Bernard Shaw, Playwright*, pp. 77–78.

its in her business house, or houses, when she enters her home. Upon learning that Frank has no money, she refuses to entertain the prospect of his marriage to her daughter. To her, a matrimonial suitor is like a potential customer.

Whereas Frank lives off his father, Vivie's other suitor, Sir George Crofts, lives off his workers. Since they are socially kindred spirits, Frank objects to Crofts on personal, not social, grounds. He sees no reason for people to work when they can afford not to. He only wishes he were lucky enough to be in their financially advantageous position. What he objects to is Crofts's lack of style.

Apart from their personal differences, there is a social difference between Vivie's suitors. If Frank were to marry Vivie, he would become her matrimonial prostitute. If Crofts were to marry her, she would become his. A business partner of Mrs. Warren, Crofts treats the proposed marriage as if it were a business deal at one of their establishments. In dealing with Mrs. Warren, he treats her as much as a procuress as a mother—appropriate behavior, actually, for she is both. He proposes to give Vivie his property, his title (a baronet), and a sizable inheritance.[7] He also offers a commission for the pimp: "if you want a cheque for yourself on the wedding day, you can name any figure you like—in reason." When he broaches the subject of marriage to Vivie herself, he declares, "what I value I pay hard money for," then restates the business terms he discussed with her mother. Like Mrs. Warren, Vivie abusively turns him down. To mother and daughter, his response to such rejection is the same—"Damn you!"—as if they were to blame for refusing a good offer from a rich customer.

Like her business partner, Mrs. Warren proposes that Vivie live with her as an idly rich young lady. She offers Vivie what she might offer a young woman she would lure to one of her houses: new dresses, fine gentlemen, good meals, and the like. As Vivie recognizes, "You must have said all that to many a woman, mother, to have it so pat." Linking her mother and her mother's business partner, she says that this offer represents "the Crofts philosophy of life." Vivie refuses to prostitute herself for the gratification of Mrs. Warren's sense of motherhood, which

---

7. As Charles Berst points out, Crofts's proposal is partly a parody of Victorian marriage transactions. See *Bernard Shaw and the Art of the Drama*, p. 8.

the daughter's presence would display for her mother's guests. Like her mother, and unlike Crofts and Frank, Vivie is a workaholic who cannot abide a life of idle luxury. Whereas Mrs. Warren's sister, Liz, left the profession once she acquired a fortune, Mrs. Warren remained. Work, she says, suits her.

If Vivie were to marry Frank, she would not live idly, as she would with Crofts or her mother. Instead, she would have to work to support him, since he is incapable of earning a living. But Vivie refuses him, too. What of Crofts's charge, in the third act, that they are half siblings? Mrs. Warren says they are not, Frank's father claims he does not think they are, and Crofts has no way of knowing. What seems dramatically important about the accusation is not that it may be accurate, but that it forces Vivie to recognize she does not want a sexual relationship with a man. In the second act, before Crofts makes his charge, Vivie finds Frank's romancing "very tiresome" and she determines "to get rid of him. . . . " Crofts's allegation clinches the matter. A sibling relationship, she tells Frank, is the only male-female relationship she cares for. Her statement recalls one made by her prostitute-mother, that sex is "not work that any woman would do for pleasure," and it hints that Vivie, in her own way, may be a part of the brothellike world of which her mother's profession is symbolic.

When Vivie's mother decided to become a prostitute, as Shaw points out in his preface to the play, she chose not immorality over morality, but one type of immorality over other types. Her alternatives were various forms of exploitation that would degrade her far more than prostitution. Of her unmarried mother's four daughters ("She called herself a widow," says Mrs. Warren of her mother), two were respectable. Their respectability led one to death by lead poisoning, the result of having been exploited as a worker in a whitelead factory: twelve hours a day for a paltry nine shillings per week. It led the other, who fared little or no better, to marry a worker on whose salary of eighteen shillings a week she had to keep them and their three children, until he became an alcoholic. Respectably selling herself to one man rather than unrespectably renting herself to several, the married sister made a bad bargain. Mrs. Warren herself was exploited—first as a scullery maid, then as a waitress-dishwasher who worked fourteen hours a day for four shillings a week plus board.

When she saw the contrasting prosperity of her sister Liz, a prostitute, who reprimanded her for ruining her health and beauty for the profit of others, she quickly recognized Liz was right in her choice of job and that her own respectable work would leave her a worn-out drudge before she turned forty. After she entered Liz's profession, she and her sister became self-employed, small-business partners. Through the social virtues of thrift, industry, and sound business judgment, the socially disreputable sisters (in contrast to Frank's socially upright father, a worthless clergyman incapable of writing his own sermons) saved enough money to purchase their own brothel, where they hired prostitutes to work for them. True, Mrs. Warren admits, thrift and good management would succeed in any business, but in no other business could she and Liz acquire money to save. Their only initial capital was "our appearance and our turn for pleasing men. Do you think we were such fools as to let other people trade in our good looks by employing us as shopgirls, or barmaids, or waitresses, when we could trade in them ourselves and get all the profits instead of starvation wages?" Rather than be exploited by others, she chose to reap the profits herself. Although prostitution gave her no pleasure, it was far better than any other work she could obtain—work that would also give her no pleasure.

While Mrs. Warren's defense of her original choice is valid, as Shaw says, it is at the same time specious, as he also says, for it does not apply to her remaining in business after she earned enough money to quit (as her sister did). In her present capacity as part-owner and manager of brothels in many major European cities, Mrs. Warren exploits others. She, not any of her workers, reaps the substantial profits of their industry. Instead of blurring his picture of the nature of capitalism by making worker and capitalist the same person, as Shaw's Marxist critics charge,[8] he sharpens the picture. Under capitalism, *Mrs. Warren's Profession* reveals, one has limited choices: exploit or be exploited. Such a world, this play suggests, is a brothel.[9]

Not only is prostitution an extremely lucrative business organized as a corporation for the profit of capitalists, the play dem-

---

8. For example, Alick West, "*A Good Man Fallen Among Fabians*," pp. 63–64.
9. Compare my *Bernard Shaw, Playwright*, p. 272.

onstrates, it is not essentially different from other capitalist enterprises. As Crofts points out, the church owns and collects income from property whose tenants include a variety of sinners, and a scholarship at Vivie's school is a gift of Crofts's brother, a member of Parliament whose wealth derives from a factory that exploits its female workers by paying them so little for their manual labor that they seek additional income by letting Mrs. Warren exploit them for their sexual work. At the end of Vivie's second scene with her mother, she calls Mrs. Warren "conventional." She is right—though also in a way she does not understand. Mrs. Warren and her profession embody and exemplify the socioeconomic convention of capitalism.

The main targets of Shaw's attack, however, are his audiences. As he says in his preface, "the guilt of defective social organization does not lie alone on the people who actually work the commercial makeshifts"; it also lies with the entire citizenry, whose views and actions can eliminate Mrs. Warren's profession by creating "a humane industrial code and a 'moral minimum' wage." Although Shaw does not take Mrs. Warren, Crofts, Crofts's brother, or their like off the hook—since guilt lies on them—he puts every member of society on the same hook, for together they are capable of changing a world of exploiter and exploited, a world that is a brothel.

Play as well as preface makes this clear. "I believe I am just as bad as you," Vivie tells Crofts when she learns the source and connections of the money that has raised her. So she is, but all she does is let off steam by name-calling: "you and my mother! the unmentionable woman and her capitalist bully. . . . "

Herself a product of prostitution and capitalism, Vivie reveals at the start of the play that she is both a prostitute and a capitalist trainee. Not for enjoyment of the work itself, which she disliked, but solely for the money her mother promised her, she competed for mathematical honors at Cambridge, and succeeded in tying for third place. Her major complaint, though, is that her mother did not pay her enough to make it worth her while. She does not refuse to do such a thing again; she merely refuses to do it for the same price. Not only did Vivie prostitute herself, her procuress mother—adept at her profession—persuaded her to do it and underpaid her.

Like her mother, although the audience is not yet aware of her mother's business at this time, Vivie plans to use her experience in this type of prostitution to her own advantage. Like her mother, she will have her own business that will derive from her type of prostitution. She intends to go into business (like her mother, in partnership with another woman) in London's financial center, where she will use her mathematical skills to work at insurance and annuity premiums, dividends, deeds, leases, property titles and transfers, and similar matters, while on the side she invests or speculates on the Stock Exchange.

At the end of the play, she does what she plans. Despite her name-calling, she takes no actions to alter the conditions that permit Crofts and her mother to operate. Shaw's description of her in his stage directions is accurate: a *"sensible, able, highly-educated young middle-class Englishwoman."* What does such a person do? Work at an aspect of capitalism in which she is skilled. In so many words, Mrs. Warren tells Vivie the aim of education in England: "to keep the cowardly slavish common run of people quiet." Vivie may be sensible and able, but in accordance with this aim she is highly educated. With her, the final act demonstrates, the educational goal succeeds.

In *Ghosts*, a clergyman and a mother hush up the truth about sexual relationships in middle-class society. Shaw goes further than Ibsen. Early in *Mrs. Warren's Profession*, he hints that a public conspiracy of silence perpetuates that profession and all it stands for. In the first act, Vivie reveals that her mother refuses to talk about her life, and she suspects it "wont . . . bear being talked about." As Catherine in *Arms and the Man* hypocritically says to her husband and Sergius, so Mrs. Warren, by failing to tell her daughter the truth, says to her, in effect, "If such women exist, we should be spared the knowledge of them." Only when Vivie forces her to do so late in act 2 does Mrs. Warren tell her about her life. When Mrs. Warren dares Reverend Gardner to tell his congregation about her, she effectively silences him. At this point, early in the second act, the silencing of the clergyman is comic. At the end of the play, the silencing of the others is not comic. "I am sure," declares Vivie in the fourth and final act, "that if I had the courage I should spend the rest of my life in telling everybody—stamping and branding it into them until they all felt their part in its abomination as I feel mine." Note the word *if*. Vivie lacks the courage. Crofts is right when he says, in act 3, "As long as you dont fly openly in the face of society, society doesnt ask any inconvenient questions; and it makes precious short work of the cads who do."

Vividly, Shaw dramatizes the conspiracy of silence. One may

discuss capital and capitalists, and Vivie gives Frank and Praed, an architect, details about the amount of capital, chief shareholder, manager, and locations of her mother's business. But not only will she not speak aloud the two words that describe her mother, she and the two men either destroy or hide the words once they are written. After Vivie writes the words for them, she tells them not to read the paper, retrieves it, and tears it to pieces. Frank, who has managed to see the words before she tears the paper, "*takes a card from his pocket; scribbles the two words on it; and silently hands it to Praed, who reads it with amazement, and hides it hastily in his pocket.*" Shaw was not too prurient to use the words. When Ellen Terry, upon reading the play's page proofs, inserted a slip of paper to ask Shaw what the two words were, he readily wrote "Prostitute and Procuress."[10] And he uses such words often enough elsewhere—in the play's preface, for instance. But in this scene, the failure to speak the words aloud is a dramatic point that Shaw makes by visual rather than verbal means. Through silence, he shows the conspiracy of silence that perpetuates Mrs. Warren's profession.

Early in the play, a clergyman remains quiet. Later, a capitalist explains that people in his circle do not discuss the subject. In the final act, members of the middle and professional classes join the conspiracy of silence. The play ends with an image of Vivie sucked into the system that embraces and causes what had filled her with loathing: "*she goes at her work with a plunge, and soon becomes absorbed in its figures.*"

A master of dialogue, Shaw demonstrates in the last act of *Mrs. Warren's Profession* that he is a master of stage pictures as well. These pictures provide dramatic emphasis to his exposure of prostitution as an aspect and symbol of capitalism, of a society of exploiter and exploited, of a world whose members in one way or other prostitute themselves, prostitute others, and by silence instead of action maintain the status quo.

* * * *

As in *Ghosts* and *Mrs. Warren's Profession*, the same woman is prostitute and procuress in *The Good Person of Szechwan*, though in Brecht's play her disguise makes her appear to be a

---

10. "Mrs. Warren's Profession," in *Shaw: An Exhibit*, ed. Dan H. Laurence, no. 205.

procurer. Like Shaw's play, Brecht's explicitly links prostitution and exploitation to capitalism.[11] Although Brecht does not stress the widespread nature of such links as clearly or as strongly as Shaw does, he depicts more forcefully than Shaw the nature of the exploitation that underlies all facets of capitalism. Both playwrights urge that a poor woman who chooses prostitution over other forms of employment available to her (thereby permitting herself to be exploited by others in a socially condoned manner) or over unemployment, is not blameworthy. Echoing Mrs. Warren, Shen Teh's alter ego Shui Ta says that to be a pauper is worse than to be a prostitute. Like the Fabian Shaw, the Marxist Brecht makes exploited and exploiter the same person. To both, capitalism offers no other alternative. Yet, in significant respects, the plays are unlike each other. Shaw is more explicit about the relationship of prostitution to capitalism; Brecht stresses economic exploitation more than he does prostitution, and Brecht is more explicit in his effort to implicate and involve the audience. Even so, both plays differ greatly from the run-of-the-mill socialist or communist propaganda play. While both urge an alternative to the system that creates the social problems they dramatize (Brecht's more clearly than Shaw's), neither specifies what that alternative might be. Does anyone join a socialist or communist party? Neither play even mentions them.

Before *The Good Person of Szechwan* is a few minutes old, Brecht establishes major themes: capitalism (selling), exploitation (the turning of what is part of nature—water in Wang's case, love in Shen Teh's—into a commodity for sale, and the fluctuation of price based on supply and demand), poverty (the result of exploitation and capitalism), and ignorance as to its cure (the supposition that only the gods can help). In the play's first sentence, Wang tells the audience that he sells water. When it is plentiful, he says, he gets nothing for it, and his statement implies that when water is scarce he charges an exorbitant price (later, he dreams of the power a drought can give him). The entire province, moreover, "is plagued by bitter poverty. Everyone says that only the gods can help us."[12]

11. Compare Karl-Heinz Schoeps, in *Essays on Brecht: Theater and Politics*, ed. Siegfried Mews and Herbert Knust, p. 34.
12. All quotations from this play are from Ralph Manheim's translation, in Bertolt Brecht, *Collected Plays*, ed. Ralph Manheim and John Willett, vol. 6.

With the arrival of three gods, Brecht establishes the irrelevance of religion to social welfare. Wang's explanation of the floods that beset the province of Kwan is that the people lack piety. The second god corrects him: "It's because they've let the dam fall apart." Later, he refutes the contention that only the gods might rescue Szechwan from poverty: "We can't meddle in questions of economics." For two thousand years, they have heard complaints "that the world can't go on as it is, that no one can live in it and remain good." Note the phrase, *go on as it is*. The gods are unconcerned with the creation of different social conditions. The choices they present are to keep the commandments in the world as it is, or to eliminate the world entirely. At the end of the play, however, Brecht urges consideration of another alternative: to change the world.

Apparently, the prostitute Shen Teh qualifies as that rare phenomenon, a good person in the world as it is. Despite her fear that the landlord will throw her out the next morning if she lacks money for rent, she gives charity and devotion (providing shelter to the gods) a higher priority than business (she turns down a customer in order to do so). Shen Teh also has the virtue of modesty. Though praised by the gods for her action, she protests she is unpraiseworthy because she sells her body. At least, she tries. Because Szechwan's widespread poverty has created a glut on the market, she can barely earn enough to keep alive.

Like Shen Teh, the gods consider prostitution to be immoral. Like the audience, they condemn Shen Teh's business. But they fail to condemn Wang's, even though both sell what in the moral world is nonsalable, a gift of nature. What the gods condemn in Wang's activities is "dishonest business methods" (his water cup has a false bottom), not the business itself. After all, such business is part of the world as it is. Nor do they find fault with the salesman's pitch Wang employs to try to find the gods a lodging: "don't miss this chance. Such an opportunity doesn't come twice. Invite the gods to your home before someone else snaps them up." His technique is part of the world as it is. While the gods are technically unable to interfere in economic questions, they devise a subterfuge so that Shen Teh may quit her immoral profession. With the thousand silver dollars they give her as payment for their lodging, she buys a tobacco shop, and thus sells commodities other than her body. At no point do the gods consider that the two activities are alike, in that both operate according to commercial principles of supply, demand, and selling. By shifting from the prostitute as prostitute to the prostitute as businesswoman, Brecht dramatically calls attention to their relationship and reveals similar principles at work in both activities.

In business matters, as in prostitution, exploitation prevails. When she sells Shen Teh the tobacco shop, Mrs. Shin exploits her ignorance, for Shen Teh does not know—and Mrs. Shin does not tell her—that the people in the neighborhood are too poor to buy anything. A married couple and their nephew, members of a family who were Shen Teh's first landlords when she came to Szechwan from the country but who turned her out when her money was gone, are now poor. When they ask Shen Teh to shelter them, they exploit her generosity by bringing five more relatives. The only people who do not exploit Shen Teh are an old couple who run a small business nearby. Without demanding security or a binding legal document, they lend her the money she needs. In doing so, they prepare the conditions of their own exploitation. Since they do not exploit, Brecht demonstrates, they are exploited. Furthermore, their kindness is an individual gesture that operates within rather than alters the social conditions that create its necessity. It is therefore futile, at best only a stopgap measure.

Notwithstanding her tolerance and permissiveness toward the family that exploits her, Shen Teh is no fool. She understands that the poverty in Szechwan is so great that no single person can possibly relieve it. While she wishes to help rather than exploit people, she recognizes that if she continues, others will exploit her to the point that she will no longer be able to help people. She therefore masquerades as a fictitious male cousin, Shui Ta, under whose guise she exploits as much as necessary to save her business, then disappears in order to permit Shen Teh to commit good deeds. Shui Ta's first action is to dispossess the family who exploits Shen Teh and thus threatens her business. Her next action is to exploit a carpenter whose custom-made shelves are useless in any shop but Shen Teh's. With a wife and four children to support, the carpenter agrees to cut his price eighty percent, since the alternative is no money at all. Significantly, the family who exploited Shen Teh, themselves former business people, approve Shui Ta's action, for it is standard business practice. But since Shen Teh is only a small businesswoman, she is exploited by those with more capital and power, and she can exploit only those lower than her in the economic scale. Within such a system, the only means of survival, which is itself inadequate, is to acquire more capital—that is, the means to exploit more people and thereby to lessen the number of people who exploit you.

Before the old couple offers to lend Shen Teh money to pay six months rent in advance, a policeman advises Shui Ta how she might obtain it. "Don't imagine the authorities are without feeling for the struggling small businessman," says the policeman. Previously, he continues, Shen Teh earned a living as a prostitute. He knows she did this in order to pay her rent, but he calls her occupation unrespectable. As he explains, "love shouldn't be for sale, for then it becomes mercenary love," and "it's not respectable with someone who pays you, but only with someone you love." Although he fails to recognize this to be the case, his solution to the problem of raising six months rent for her shop is the same as her solution to pay the rent for her room, mercenary love: "we need capital. . . . All right, we marry a little money." In this scene, Brecht dramatizes several points: the complicity of business (the economic status quo) with the police (enforcers of that status quo), the prostitution that underlies business and permits it to function, the policeman and businessman as pimps (with the irony that Shen Teh—as Shui Ta, an exemplar of business—is one of her own pimps).[13] Although Brecht gives no character an explicit speech similar to Mrs. Alving's and Mrs. Warren's, that a respectable marriage for money is no different from prostitution, or similar to Sir George Crofts's, that the business of prostitution is no different from other types of business, he does not have to do so. If the policeman's bright idea, which immediately follows his description of Shen Teh as prostitute, does not clarify these notions, his composition of an ad for a husband does: Wanted is a "respectable" man "with a small capital," who wishes to marry "into promising tobacco shop." As enticement, the policeman adds, "Attractive appearance." The appearance—of both Shen Teh and the sexual-economic relationship—is indeed attractive.

---

13. John Fuegi points out that in Brecht's earliest sketch of this play, he explicitly states that the prostitute becomes her own pimp. See "The Alienated Woman," in *Essays on Brecht*, ed. Mews and Knust, p. 195.

In answer to Shen Teh's need of a man with capital comes the barber Shu Fu, to buy the respectable businesswoman as he would buy the unrespectable prostitute. A businessman, he exploits her financially desperate situation. Although he tries to convince himself that he is acting decently, the very terms he employs give him away: "Miss Shen Teh's charm resides not in the solvency of her shop but in the goodness of her heart." To permit her to continue her good work of sheltering the poor, he places at her disposal his houses behind the cattle yard. He does not need to be explicit. As one businessman talking to another, he knows that Shui Ta understands what underlies his apparent generosity. As in *Ghosts* and *Mrs. Warren's Profession*, they conspire in silence. Later, Brecht has one of the tenants reveal that this gesture costs Shu Fu nothing. The barber gave Shen Teh the houses, whose floors were rotting, because the dampness made the soap he had stored there get moldy. When Shu Fu adddesses the audience, requesting confirmation that his action is decent rather than businesslike, he cannot avoid disclosing the true state of affairs: "Could anyone be more unselfish? More sensitive? More farsighted? . . . No, there will be no exploiting of an unfortunate situation, no taking advantage of a disillusionment." By using such terms as *farsighted*, *exploiting*, and *taking advantage*, Shu Fu reveals that he thinks of the situation in business terms. Whereas Shen Teh hides the better part of herself under the mask of a businessman, the businessman Shu Fu hides the worse part of himself (partly revealed by his inhumane treatment of Wang) under the mask of one who admires Shen Teh's humane qualities.

Later, still under the guise of unselfishness, he exploits Shen Teh's unhappier circumstances so that she might more favorably consider marriage to him. "I want no assurances, no promise to accept my help!" he exclaims. "But here *(he pulls out a checkbook and signs a check which he lays on the cart)* I'm giving you a blank check, you can write in any sum you like. And now I leave you, happy and serene, asking nothing in return, on my tiptoes, reverently, without a thought for myself." By stating that he asks nothing in return, he reminds Shen Teh that she might give him something in return. By declaring he thinks not of himself, he implies that she might think of him. Emphasized visually by his presentation of a check, and verbally by his exaggerated rhetoric, which comically juxtaposes *on my tiptoes* and *rever-*

ently, these factors indicate that the businessman Shu Fu uses business methods to promote what he may have convinced himself is a love match.

When Shen Teh becomes pregnant, she determines that her child will not have to forage in garbage cans, as she sees a hungry boy do. Disguised as Shui Ta, she turns the situation of helping the poor for the sake of charity into helping them for something in return; that is, exploiting them for business purposes. Instead of distributing food free of charge, Shui Ta gives the poor a chance to earn the money for food by working in Shen Teh's tobacco factory. Although Shui Ta does not say so, wages will barely suffice for food. Shui Ta also exploits the prostitutionlike engagement between Shen Teh and Shu Fu. He fills in the blank check for ten thousand silver dollars—ten times the amount the gods gave Shen Teh. Businessman and procuress are one, like Mrs. Warren, though Brecht's protagonist is disguised as a procur*er*.

Early in the play, Shen Teh's fiancé, Sun, tries to exploit her, but he succeeds only to a limited extent. Though Shen Teh gives him some money to get a job as pilot, the amount is insufficient. When the pilot job falls through, he squanders the money in two days. With Shui Ta in command, Sun receives the alternatives of jail or a job in the factory, from which Shui Ta will deduct, in installments, the money Shen Teh lent him. Sun considers himself a professional pilot rather than an ordinary laborer, but since he has little choice, he prostitutes himself by accepting the factory job.

Once Sun understands the system that makes one who does not exploit others exploited himself, he decides to join the exploiters, whose income is larger. To get the foreman's job, he exposes the foreman's practice of overpaying the workers, a practice which is to the firm's disadvantage. Instead of the bonus Shui Ta offers, Sun proposes he be given the foreman's job and the opportunity to demonstrate that his brains are more valuable to the firm than his muscles are; in other words, he can exploit the workers to the firm's advantage. This he does, thereby achieving success in business. After he rises to an executive capacity, he proposes something like prostitution for himself. Since the firm needs new shacks to store its tobacco, he suggests he visit the landlady—"tickle Mrs. Mi Tzu's fat knees"—and thereby "get the place for half the price." Working for Shui Ta, who is Shen Teh, Sun works at both of Shen Teh's professions, business and prostitution, which—in a brothellike world of exploiters and exploited—are one. In the final scene, Brecht points up the contradiction between the social values of man-as-lover and man-as-businessman. Because the man Shen Teh loves is a scoundrel who exploits people, they separate; because he is a scoundrel who exploits people, Shui Ta advances him in the firm.

When Sun learns that Shen Teh may be pregnant, he concludes that Shui Ta exploited him, and he decides to use this information to exploit Shui Ta. The hat Shui Ta gave him is insufficient bonus, he decides, and he tells Shui Ta he wants full control of the business. Shen Teh's other suitor, Shu Fu, also concludes that Shui Ta has exploited him. Payment is due for his matrimonial investment. In future, he will discuss business only with Shen Teh, the object of his financial and romantic devotion. But she has unaccountably disappeared.

As various people charge, Shui Ta ruined, swindled, and exploited people. Because such business dealings are not illegal, the police do not act. When a business person disappears, however, the law enters.

In the trial to determine whether Shui Ta has kidnapped Shen Teh, the three gods preside. Shui Ta reveals the truth, that he himself is Shen Teh. In others words, *The Good Person of Szechwan* has no title character. Despite theatrical appearances that hide the truth, from the audience as well as from the characters on stage, the "good" Shen Teh and the "wicked" Shui Ta are the same person. One cannot, and Shen Teh does not, excuse herself because she is different. Under the social conditions dramatized in this play, one cannot be a good person, and appearances notwithstanding, Shen Teh is not a good person. She is Shui Ta, a ruthless exploiter of human beings. Under capitalism, says Brecht, one cannot be a good person—in Szechwan or anywhere else. The usual excuses are ridiculous, and Shen Teh knows it: "Condemn me: all my crimes/Were committed to help my neighbors/To love my beloved and/Save my little son from want." According to Brecht, she is right to call for condemnation, since her actions were, as she admits, criminal. Because social circumstances demand that she exploit others in order to accomplish her objectives, she nullifies whatever goodness one might ordinarily attribute to them. How can one help one's neighbors when one exploits them? Is love possible in an acquisitive and exploitative world, which is a brothel wherein people sell and are sold? When Shui Ta pleads that he acted for Shen Teh's child, the carpenter whom he swindled pointedly asks, "What about my children? What have you done to my children?" But Shui Ta has no reply.

At the end of the play, Shen Teh tries to make the gods understand that she could not at the same time be good to others and to herself, for the person who tries to help another is crushed in a world wherein one must exploit in order to survive. "Are we to admit that our commandments are fatal?" ask the gods. "Are we to give up our commandments? *(Stubbornly)* Never! Is the world to be changed? How? By whom? No, everything is in order." Of the phrases that are not questions, one is reasonable (never give up commandments to virtue), but others are not. Clearly, the play reveals, goodness can be fatal *because* everything is not in order. One cannot remain good in the world as it is. Their effort to find a person who could do so fails. Although the gods are unable to answer how and by whom the world might be changed so that one can do good and survive, their inability to do so suggests that while the world should be changed, human beings, not gods, must effect this change. In the face of the gods' response, Shen Teh's last word in the play constitutes a crucial admonition to the audience: "Help!"

*   *   *   *

In *Ghosts*, Ibsen condemns a society in which marriage is no different from prostitution. In *Mrs. Warren's Profession*, Shaw condemns a society in which prostitution is a business enterprise no different from other business enterprises, and linked to them as well as to apparently noncommercial institutions, such as churches and universities. In *The Good Person of Szechwan*, Brecht employs a protagonist who early in the play is a prostitute, later a businesswoman, but who in both professions must operate according to principles of supply, demand, and exploitation. Thereby, he links prostitution with capitalism, which he condemns. In all three plays, exploitation is necessary for survival, and in all three—more clearly in the last two than in the first—characters face the alternatives of being exploited by others or of exploiting others. All three are radical denunciations of the society that is their setting.

Ghosts concludes with the revelation about and then advent of a hideous disease, the result of society's self-perpetuating conspiracy of silence concerning prostitution and the exploitation of human beings. At the end of *Mrs. Warren's Profession*, Shaw visually portrays the conspiracy of silence that perpetuates her profession, which he explicitly reveals to be a part of capitalism. Yet he permits the audience to infer their complicity in such a conspiracy and the need to change the situation. In respect to the latter, Brecht does more than imply. In an epilogue to *The Good Person of Szechwan*, he directly asks the audience for their solution to the situation. After rejecting the idea that the play's gods or different gods might resolve it, the epilogue concludes that the audience themselves should ponder the problem until they find "The ways and means and measures tending/ To help good people to a happy ending./Ladies and gentlemen, in you we trust:/The ending must be happy, must, must, must!" Like *Mrs. Warren's Profession*, however, and like *Ghosts* as well, *The Good Person of Szechwan* offers no explicit, prepackaged solution to the problem of an exploitative society that resembles a brothel. What is more explicit in this play than in the others is the need for the audience to find a solution.

3.

"Special, Chosen People"—Society and the Professional Classes
The Master Builder, The Doctor's Dilemma, Life of Galileo

Halvard Solness is a self-made man. Having begun life "as a poor boy from the country," he stands, at the start of *The Master Builder*, as "the top man in [his] field." As a consequence of so spectacular a rise to eminence, he considers himself, particularly in contrast to members of his profession who fell from prominence while he rose, one of those "special, chosen people who have a gift and power and capacity to *wish* something, *desire* something, *will* something—so insistently and so—so inevitably—that at last it has to be theirs." Often, this is how successful members of the professional classes regard themselves, especially if they are self-made men.

However, not all of the members of the professional classes in *The Master Builder, The Doctor's Dilemma,* and *Life of Galileo* are self-made men. Nor are they all successful. Apart from membership in a professional class, what they—and the plays in which they are characters—have in common includes the view that members of their class are in some way special people. In addition, all three plays portray the actions and attitudes of members of a professional class in terms of or in relation to the society of which it is a part. But the importance of this portrayal in the total thematic and structural fabric of each play differs from the others.

* * * *

Note that Solness calls himself a master builder, not an architect. "Never went through the training," he explains. Presumably, the impoverished country boy could not afford formal education. "Almost all I know I've had to find out for myself." Although knowledge and ability were necessary requirements in his rise to the top of his profession, they were not sufficient. Ambition and ruthlessness also played roles. Very likely, they had to, for those in the profession would probably be unready to help a lower-class upstart compete for their share of the market. "Pushed your way up," says the architect Brovik, who now works for Solness. "Cut the ground out from under me—and so many others." As Solness admits, "I . . . broke him. . . . I had to have room for myself." To Solness, as to Brovik, for that matter, the alternatives were *him* or *me*. In capitalist society, the methods Solness uses to rise to the top of his profession are commonplace.

Not only ability, ambition, and ruthlessness, but also opportunity and the alertness to seize and exploit it, are requirements for self-made success. Consider what gave Solness the chance to make his name as a house builder: the accidental burning of his wife Aline's house. However, this fire indirectly contributed to the death of their two children. The death of youth—little boys, in fact, rivals to the father—suggestively links to Solness's professional powers and hints at his fears. Obsessed by the horrible memories associated with the fire and its consequences, Aline does not want to live in a new house on the same land as the old. Since an enormous garden adjoined the house, Solness thereby acquired a large piece of property. The shrewd builder then subdivided it into small lots. (Aline, who with Solness evidently lives on the edge of the old estate, complains the lots are so small that strangers can sit at their windows and look at her.) On these lots, he built houses, which he sold. Thus, he broke what was in effect a monopoly held by trained architects and gained a reputation as a builder of homes that people could afford.

Although the lots are small, Solness does not churn out cheap tract homes. He is a self-made *master* builder, proud of his craft and anxious that the houses reflect favorably on his name. When a young couple, impatient to move into their own home, press him to work more quickly on it, he explodes with indignation: "So they'll make do with anything—any kind of a—a roost. Just a peg to hang their hats. But not a home. . . . I'll have nothing to do with strangers." The homes Solness creates are designed for particular individuals whom he would get to know before designing the environment in which they will live.

For his success in the marketplace, he has, he admits "paid . . . a price," his inner peace. Not only does he feel indebted to his wife, since his good fortune resulted from her ill fortune, but he fears that rivals might supplant him as he supplanted Brovik and other architects. Based on his own career and his understanding of the competitive conditions of the marketplace, this is realistic, not paranoiac. While he has no monopoly on house building, he clings to as large a corner of the market as he can. To do so, he keeps down potential rivals. Emblematic of this action, Brovik's son Ragnar, a draftsman in training under Solness, has "*a slight stoop.*" In order to prevent Ragnar from striking out on his own, thereby becoming his competitor, Solness uses his sexual charms to persuade Kaja, Ragnar's fiancée who also works for Solness, to remain with him and to persuade Ragnar to stay as well. Before Ragnar, others studied with Solness, but according to him, "none of them ever came to much." Because of his treatment of Ragnar, one wonders whether none of the others failed to come to much as a result of Solness holding them down too.

Success notwithstanding, Solness is clearly insecure. With younger people constantly entering the competitive marketplace, he has good reason to be. Once he climbed a high tower, both a real steeple and a symbol of his professional ladder, on which he had become "the top man." His fear of falling from the real tower reflects his terror of falling from the professional ladder. The reason for his fear, he admits, is that "someday things have to change...." As he recognizes, the change will come from the young. "Someone or other will set up the cry: Step back for *me!* And all the others will storm in after, shaking their fists and shouting: Make room—make room—make room!... Someday youth will come here, knocking at the door—... Well, then it's the end of Solness, the master builder."

No sooner does Solness express this fear, than youth literally knocks at the door: Hilda Wangel, who is in her early twenties. Ibsen points up the connection between Solness's fear and Hilda's action: "Youth *did* come along, knocking at your door," says a doctor who is with him when she arrives. As if to underscore the accuracy of the doctor's perception, Ibsen has Solness propose that Hilda stay in one of the house's nursery rooms and then say "you can be the child here for a while."

Young Hilda is ambivalent toward Solness. Attracted by his sexual charm and his aura of success, she tells him—in a "*half serious, half laughing*" tone that suggests her ambivalence— "Nobody but you should have a right to build.... Have the field to yourself." Candidly, he admits that in his solitude he has thought so too. Despite their apparent agreement on this issue, however, youth sides with youth. Young herself, Hilda sees nothing to fear from youth. "Pooh!" she sniffs, and she proposes that he open his door to the young and bid them enter as friends. Understandably, Solness is skeptical of such advice. Later, when he lets Ragnar believe he considers the young man's drawings worthless, Hilda calls his treatment of Ragnar mean and cruel. When Solness reminds her that she herself had told him no one but he should be allowed to build, she can only retort, "*I* can say that—but *you* mustn't."

Just as youthful Hilda is ambivalent toward middle-aged Solness, so is he ambivalent toward her, and the youth she represents. "You, Hilda, are youth," he tells her. "Youth that you're so afraid of?" she asks. "*Nodding slowly*," he replies, "And that, deep within me, I'm so much hungering for." Indeed, she embodies both aspects.

Not only does young Hilda rejuvenate him, she also causes his downfall—first, from his position on the professional tower, then from an actual tower. He confides to her that if he gives Ragnar—the embodiment of all his younger professional rivals—the slightest chance to rise, he would "break me—same as I broke his father. . . . He's all the youth that's waiting to come thundering at my door—to do away with master builder Solness." Nevertheless, she persuades him to write words of encouragement on Ragnar's drawings and to give him the opportunity to design and build the house commissioned from Solness by the couple mentioned earlier. Once Solness agrees to permit Ragnar to supplant him in this job, he seems to resign himself to his professional demise. Earlier, he had spoken of mystic "helpers and servers" over whom he had power and on whom he depended for success. At this point, one of his real helpers and servers lies dying, and he dismisses the other two from his employ. "What are you building next?" Hilda asks later. His answer: "Don't think I'll build much more now." All he plans to construct are "castles in the air" for Hilda.

But as Solness recognizes, what has happened is "inescapable." He is already being edged out of his eminent position by a changing marketplace that wants the different type of house a younger generation can design. Before Solness resigned his commission in favor of Ragnar, Ragnar had shown the couple, who had commissioned Solness, drawings he made on speculation. According to Brovik, they liked his son's designs, which they considered "completely new and different," and they intended to ask Solness to give up the commission.

After Solness gives Ragnar his chance, the young man demonstrates the accuracy of Solness's professional prediction. Ragnar is as merciless to him as Solness had been to Ragnar's father. When Hilda tells Ragnar he should have thanked Solness for having given him his opportunity, Ragnar exclaims, "Thank him, when he's held me down year after year!" And he concludes that Solness recognized his abilities but was afraid of him. Ragnar explicitly connects the climbing of the tower with professional status. Aware that Solness is now afraid to climb as high as he builds, Ragnar calls Hilda's attention to a group of young students who has come to watch Solness avoid climbing the tower of the house he has just completed: *"(with seething scorn)* He's kept us down so long—now we're going to see him have the pleasure of keeping himself down."

But a few minutes before, Hilda successfully persuaded Solness to climb the tower, thereby overcoming his fears, reasserting his professional skill, and—recalling his glorious triumph a decade ago—rejuvenate himself. Responsible for the beginning of Solness's professional downfall, symbolic of death, Hilda is also responsible for his actual death. To Ragnar's surprise, Solness climbs the tower. But he falls. Ragnar concludes that in the final analysis "he really couldn't do it." Youth invades Solness's life; youth invades his profession; youth grabs his corner of the marketplace; youth causes his death.[1] Though one of the "special, chosen people," Solness is not the only one. The competitive marketplace has other such people to replace him. The fall of one means the rise of another. As Solness replaced Brovik, whom he destroyed, so Solness, who destroys himself, will be replaced by another—perhaps by Brovik's son Ragnar.

*   *   *   *

If a man whose profession is to build houses can consider himself among "special, chosen people," what of a man whose

---

1. Solness, who is no longer young, dies—as Ibsen indicates—on the night of 20 September, which in Scandinavia in 1892, when Ibsen wrote *The Master Builder*, was the end of summer and the eve of autumn. For this information, I thank Mr. George Bunton, astronomer and director of the Science Center of the Bishop Museum, Honolulu.

profession revolves around matters of life and death? Is not such a professional man more special? A doctor might consider himself to be a god.[2]

So, in fact, does Sir Colenso Ridgeon, the most capable medical man in *The Doctor's Dilemma*, consider himself—though he is unaware he does so. Whereas Solness may be among the chosen, the godlike Ridgeon does the choosing. He refers to the ten people whose tuberculosis he intends to cure as "chosen cases." In selecting each of his chosen people, he admits, with a hint of pseudodivinity, "I have had to consider . . . whether he was worth saving." Of the fifty who applied to be his patients, he has staff and facilities to treat only ten. If a patient is worth saving, Ridgeon will see to it that he "shall be saved." Though powerful, this god is not all-powerful. For the chosen, says he, life (a far cry from eternal glory, but good enough); for the "condemned," death (a far cry from eternal damnation, but bad enough). With a tinge of irony, his colleague Sir Patrick Cullen calls him "Mr Savior of Lives." The artist Dubedat's view of Ridgeon is as Manichaean as Ridgeon's view of himself, though Dubedat reaches a different conclusion. Ridgeon's voice, says he, "sounded devilish." At the end of the play, Jennifer recognizes that Ridgeon does consider himself "a little god."

Ridgeon is not the only member of the medical profession in the play who unconsciously considers himself a god. The others do so as well, and in the first draft of the play Sir Patrick says so explicitly.[3] But Shaw does not set up straw men to knock down. Although the other members of this profession consist of two fools, two frauds, and a hypocrite (as is Ridgeon himself), they believe in the effectiveness (or relative effectiveness) of the cures they propose, they sincerely desire to cure, and the three most important medical practitioners in the play—Ridgeon, Cutler Walpole, and Sir Ralph Bloomfield Bonington ("B.B.")—offer their services without fee to impecunious cases (these gods are merciful, though their social mercy is selective). In fact, B.B. and Walpole consider themselves so socially conscious that they even agree to minister gratis to Dubedat, a patient whose social attitudes they condemn, and whom B.B. calls a borrowing rather

---

2. Compare my *Bernard Shaw, Playwright*, pp. 64–70, 257–61. For a full treatment of Shaw and the medical profession, see Roger Boxill, *Shaw and the Doctors*.
3. Bernard Shaw, "The Doctor's Dilemma," Notebook B.

than a paying patient. Furthermore, as often as not, their foolish or fraudulent cures succeed. Shaw presents the medical profession at its best, which is bad enough.

The fools are the modish B.B. and the fashionable surgeon Cutler Walpole. B.B. attributes the ills of mankind to people's unstimulated phagocytes. Any kind of antitoxin will do to stimulate them to cure any bacteriological disease, he believes, as long as one injects it three times daily, fifteen minutes before meals. Although he once accidentally injected a tetanus antitoxin into a patient with typhus and a typhoid antitoxin into a patient with tetanus, both patients recovered. In total ignorance of Ridgeon's discovery, the opsonin index which informs the doctor at what point a serum should be injected (at the right stage, it cures; at the wrong stage, it kills), B.B. injected Ridgeon's serum into an ailing prince of the realm. By chance, he injected it during the right stage and cured the little prince. The result was a knighthood for Ridgeon.

As their colleague Sir Patrick puts it, Walpole (the other fool) and his like have discovered that people's bodies are filled with useless organs that one can remove without leaving them too much the worse for the operation. For all the difference it makes, however, patients "might as well get their hair cut." Walpole's discovery is a useless organ called the nuciform sac, which he sincerely believes is detrimental to health. Because he considers its removal more important than vaccination, he wishes the operation were compulsory. Nonetheless, he is a fool. When an opera singer came to him to remove a growth from her vocal cords, force of habit prompted him to remove her nuciform sac. Inexplicably, however, she regained her voice and, as a result, she considers him the greatest living surgeon. By a similar fortuitousness that saved the typhus and tetanus victims and the ailing prince entrusted to the care of B.B., Walpole succeeded. Through such astonishing successes, based on chance, Shaw condemns the medical profession perhaps more devastatingly than he does through its failures.

By fraudulent advertising, Loony Schutzmacher has made enough money to retire. The advertisement consisted of two words, "Cure Guaranteed." While only God can guarantee any cure—and a godlike doctor cannot—Schutzmacher's treatment, he claims, succeeded oftener than ninety percent of the time. As he explains, "most people get well all right if they are careful and you give them a little sensible advice." No matter what the case, his sensible prescription was phosphates, which he takes himself when he feels run down. Nevertheless, *most* and *if* differ from a guarantee; and sincerity, demonstrated by his self-prescription, differs from scientific knowledge and professional expertise.

A far less successful doctor, Blenkinsop has a poor practice that barely enables him to make ends meet. Although he has not opened a medical book since he received his degree thirty years earlier, cannot afford to subscribe to medical journals, and has forgotten what science he used to know, he uses experience and, like Schutzmacher, common sense. Since the poor workers who are his patients cannot afford the type of treatment that might cure them, he prescribes what they can afford and what, at worst, can do them no harm: "a pound of ripe greengages every day half an hour before lunch." The fifth act reveals what this prescription does at best: it cures.

While Sir Patrick cynically exposes the professional incompetence of his colleagues, he hypocritically places the blame for the shocking state of the medical profession not on those colleagues, but on their patients: "When you know as much as I know of the ignorance and superstition of the patients, youll wonder that we're half as good as we are." Apparently, it does not occur to him that the patients' ignorance and superstition derive from the medical men's inflated, godlike announcements or advertisements of their curative powers: choosing people, guaranteeing cures, removing nuciform sacs, stimulating phagocytes, and whatnot.

Like the doctors, the artist Louis Dubedat considers himself above the common herd. A professional man like master builder Solness (and the doctors), he regards himself the same way Solness does. According to the Jewish doctor Schutzmacher, Dubedat, hinting that he was Jewish, called himself "one of the chosen people" and cited his artistic faculty as evidence. Although Dubedat unscrupulously cheats people in order to obtain money that will give him the leisure to practice his art, he scrupulously practices that art. As he is dying, he honestly boasts that in art, he has never denied his faith or been untrue to himself. His belief "in Michael Angelo, Velasquez, and Rembrandt; in the might of design, the mystery of color, the redemption of all things by Beauty everlasting" is sincere. As Shaw observes, "no man is scrupulous all round. He has, according to his faculties and interests, certain points of honor, whilst in matters that do not interest him he is careless and unscrupulous. . . . [Dubedat] had his faith, and upheld it." In the same passage, however, Shaw condemns those who "offer a high order of talent as an excuse for a low order of conduct. . . . "[4] As he says in his 1907 preface to *The Sanity of Art*, written a year after *The Doctor's Dilemma*, "It is idle to demand unlimited toleration of apparently outrageous conduct on the plea that the offender is a genius . . . and no honorable artist would plead on his behalf that misappropriating trust money is one of the superiorities of that very loosely defined diathesis which we call the artistic temperament."[5] In short, the artist, special though he may be in one respect, has the same social obligations as anyone else.

Just as Dubedat would sacrifice anyone to his art, so would the superficially appealing Jennifer. She regards Blenkinsop as ordinary, therefore fit to immolate for the special, chosen human being, Dubedat. When Ridgeon tells her that he will take Blenkinsop, not Dubedat, as his patient, her immediate response, which Shaw underscores with a stage direction, "*attaching no importance whatever to Blenkinsop*," is to dismiss him as elderly and silly.

She also attaches no importance to art critics, except insofar as they can serve Dubedat. She regards them as ordinary people, useful only to puff his paintings. "*Indignantly*," she calls two bad reviews of them "disgraceful" and "infamous." According to her, the critics owe her a good review of her late husband's paintings, particularly because they accepted her bribes of cigars, sandwiches, and drink on press day. What other purpose have they? Do their bad reviews mean that Dubedat is not a genius? Possibly, though no one mentions other reviews, which presumably are favorable, and those doctors who can afford to be connoisseurs of art regard Dubedat's paintings highly. Two reviews notwithstanding, Jennifer basks in Dubedat's reflected glory—not only because he was her husband but also because she is the subject of many of his paintings. The ridiculously sentimental title of her biography of Dubedat, "The Story of a King of Men. By his Wife," reveals that she regards herself very much

4. Bernard Shaw, *Sixteen Self-Sketches*, pp. 103–4.
5. Bernard Shaw, *Major Critical Essays*, p. 289.

as Dubedat regarded himself, a special person. If she calls Dubedat a King, one knows the regal title of his wife, who becomes as special a person as he.

What of the dilemma of Shaw's title, and Dr. Ridgeon's solution to it? To begin with, Shaw states the dilemma four different ways, in this sequence: (1) Considering that Dubedat is an artistic genius, should Ridgeon drop another patient in order to take him on? (2) Because Blenkinsop, an honest man, also has TB, should Ridgeon try to cure him rather than the dishonest, socially reprehensible Dubedat? (3) Since Ridgeon loves Jennifer, who he believes will marry him if Dubedat dies, should he allow his rival to die? (4) Because Ridgeon loves Jennifer, should he try to save Dubedat, knowing that if he does, Dubedat will disillusion her and break her heart, or give up Dubedat to the boneheaded B.B., knowing that only Dubedat's death would preserve him as a hero in her eyes?

The last two ways of putting the question are most easily handled. Although Ridgeon is smugly convinced that Jennifer will marry him if Dubedat dies (3), Sir Patrick diagnoses that Ridgeon has been feeling vaguely unsettled because he is a bachelor at a susceptible age, and Sir Patrick warns him not to behave foolishly. Obviously, Ridgeon's self-assurance is absurd. Sensibly, Sir Patrick urges him to regard the dilemma differently and tells him to choose without regard to Jennifer. Apart from the fact that this manner of phrasing the dilemma (4) is blarney—refusing to acknowledge the real problem, Ridgeon gives himself high points for nobility[6]—Sir Patrick wryly comments on this type of reasoning: "It's a little hard on a lad to be killed because his wife has too high an opinion of him. Fortunately few of us are in any danger of that."

The first two questions have a similar basis. Ironically, it is the fool B.B. who recognizes the impossibility, and therefore folly, of accepting patients on the basis of whether their lives are socially

---

6. Despite this motive, Louis Crompton believes Ridgeon when he says he acted disinterestedly. According to Crompton, Ridgeon is an honorable doctor. See *Shaw the Dramatist*, p. 139. More accurate, I think, is Robert B. Heilman, who says that Ridgeon tries to turn a failure into "an inadvertent virtue." See *The Ways of the World*, p. 186. Between Crompton's view and that of myself and Heilman is the more cautious statement of J. L. Wisenthal, who calls Dubedat's honor "questionable." See *The Marriage of Contraries*, p. 114.

valuable. To apply any known scientific test to this problem would lead to the conclusion that most patients would be better dead. Although Dubedat is a "vicious and ignorant young man with a talent for drawing," many of his patients are "vicious and ignorant young men without a talent for anything." If he were to consider their merits before taking them on, he admits, "I should have to give up three-quarters of my practice." Sir Patrick, who regards the choice as between an honest man and a blackguard who paints pretty pictures, puts the question to Ridgeon as "either to go through life and find all the pictures bad but all the men and women good, or to go through life and find all the pictures good and all the men and women rotten." When Ridgeon replies that he is unconvinced the world would improve if people behaved like Dubedat rather than like Blenkinsop, Sir Patrick pins him down with the experimental test: "Then why dont you behave as Dubedat does?"

Although Ridgeon confesses himself beaten by his colleague's argument, the fact is that his behavior—past and present—has been like Dubedat's. His attitude toward science resembles Dubedat's toward art. Like the artist for his art, he sacrifices people for his experiments. So little do human beings mean to him, he even forgets their names—Jane Marsh, for example, his washerwoman's daughter on whom be once experimented. Instead of curing her, the tuberculin he used rotted her arm off. When Sir Patrick reminds him of her, he dismisses the consequences of his failure: she now earns a good living by showing her rotted arm at medical lectures, and: "it's always the patient who has to take the chance when an experiment is necessary. And we can find out nothing without experiment." What Jane Marsh is to the professional doctor-scientist, people with money are to the professional artist: means to the end of working at a profession.

Before Ridgeon faces the dilemma, he declares that "to inject a vaccine into a patient without first testing his opsonin is as near to murder as a respectable practitioner can get. If I wanted to kill a man I should kill him that way." Significantly, because it forecasts what will happen, the statement is followed by his housekeeper's request that he see Jennifer. After he learns that B.B. has done what he has just described, Ridgeon concludes that to put a tube of serum into B.B.'s hands is an act of murder. And this—which Sir Patrick hypocritically assures him is perfectly respectable—is what he does. Yet his action is to no avail.

His self-assured assessment of Jennifer is wrong. For her even to consider marriage with him, "an elderly man," is absurd, she tells him in the final act. Besides, she has already remarried.

"I killed him," he confesses in the last act. "No," says Jennifer, who adds, "I dont believe you made any difference at all." While Ridgeon did make a difference, for he put Dubedat in the care of the professionally irresponsible B.B., Jennifer is correct in her belief that doctors do not hold foolproof keys to life and death. Ridgeon thinks he is "a little god," as Jennifer says, but he did not kill Dubedat. What he did was to give him a fifty-fifty chance of survival. With the same blundering methods used on Dubedat, B.B. had saved the life of a prince. As Sir Patrick puts it, what happened to Dubedat was what happened to Jane Marsh's arm. "He has got through three months galloping consumption in three days." Although Ridgeon "fully expected this," he could just as fully have expected Dubedat to recover, as the prince did. Chance and tuberculosis, not Ridgeon, killed Dubedat. By the same chance (an injection during the positive phase), B.B. might have saved him. Even so, B.B. did not kill him. Tuberculosis did. As Ridgeon himself admits, when another doctor uses his medicine "it kills—sometimes."

This argument is not merely a quibble. Instead, it leads to the heart of the matter, the basic social themes of *The Doctor's Dilemma*. "We're not a profession," says Ridgeon in the first act, "we're a conspiracy." According to Sir Patrick, "All professions are conspiracies against the laity." As Shaw declares in his preface, "Of all the anti-social vested interests the worst is the vested interest in ill-health." Although he does not believe doctors are either more or less impartial, honorable, or conscientious than anyone else who has a pecuniary interest in one side of a question, he regards it as socially deplorable for a community to pay better for its sickness (because sickness requires more visits, medicines, and operations) than for its health. In the play itself, the doctors frequently discuss the financial side of their profession. Schutzmacher explains how he amassed a fortune, Sir Patrick tells of the hundreds of guineas Walpole makes with each operation, Blenkinsop discusses people with employment-related health plans and those without, B.B. estimates his financial loss through time spent away from work, and Ridgeon computes the monetary value of Jennifer's consultations with B.B., Walpole, and Blenkinsop.

Shaw's solution to the social problems dramatized in the play, his preface states, is to bring "the medical profession under responsible and effective public control. . . . " Until society is organized along socialist lines, and this profession "becomes a body of men trained and paid by the country to keep the country in health it will remain what it is at present: a conspiracy to exploit popular credulity and human suffering." In the play itself, Shaw is only on one brief occasion explicit. After Blenkinsop's cure, says Jennifer, he declared that "private practice in medicine ought to be put down by law. When I asked him why, he said that private doctors were ignorant licensed murderers." While the four acts that precede this passage demonstrate the validity of Blenkinsop's observations, the play gives no clear-cut details as to what would replace private practice. In his new position as Medical Officer of Health—a public medical position in existence in capitalist England in 1906, before the National Health—he successfully cures the chairman of the Borough Council. Inept in private practice, Blenkinsop, Shaw implies, becomes something of a public benefactor in a responsible public position. Except as a starting point, though, this position is insufficient to improve medical practice (Blenkinsop uses his old prescription, greengages). More is required.

With the rearrangement of society, a man of honor can retain and improve his professional skills, and his patients will not have to worry about the cost of a cure. Under such social rearrangement, medical facilities will be sufficient that doctors like Ridgeon will not have to face his dilemma. In a society dedicated to the public good, rather than to the financial good of its various professions, public officials would monitor medical practice so that it would become "an indictable offence" to do what Ridgeon, early in the play, laments is difficult or impossible to do under private medical conditions: recommend or employ an ignorant, licensed killer like B.B. Such a doctor resembles what Walpole calls the incompetent professional newspaperman present at Dubedat's death: illiterate, with neither adequate qualifications nor public accountability.

As for Dubedat, says B.B., "He had only two failings, money and women. Well, let us be honest. . . . Are these two matters so well arranged at present that a disregard of the usual arrangements indicates real depravity?" As Shaw says in a program note to Granville Barker's 1915 New York production, "if people wish to enjoy fine art they must create social conditions in which an artist can be honest and scrupulous, without privations which are, to his nature, intolerable."[7]

Under a more socially responsible form of government, an ineffective doctor in a poor neighborhood can become effective; a dedicated scientist, who—in a capitalist society where private medical practice prevails—considers himself a special person and his patients his "chosen" people, need not face a dilemma that pushes him into immoral alternatives and forces him to become a hypocrite to salvage his self-respect; and an artist, who considers himself special and above the common herd, need not be dishonest. Under socialist conditions, says Shaw, all professions can become socially responsible. But *The Doctor's Dilemma* only hints at these thematic statements. Apart from Blenkinsop's single remark, which is given only at second hand, it offers no explicit solution. In this play about professional classes and society, Shaw dramatizes what his title says he does: a dilemma.

* * * *

Even if one is unaware of the identity of the historical Galileo, who is certainly a special person, Brecht's *Life of Galileo*[8] clearly establishes his preeminence as a scientist. Apart from the superior reasoning ability he displays in various scenes, his peers recognize him to be special among themselves. In the dedication of a scientific book, he is called "the greatest living authority on physics."

7. Bernard Shaw, *The Bodley Head Bernard Shaw*, 3:444.
8. Brecht completed three versions of this play. In the first (1938), Galileo cleverly outsmarts the Inquisition. In the greatly revised second version (1945), translated by Charles Laughton as *Galileo*, the scientist is cowardly and contemptible, as he is in the third (1955), also a major revision, which treats him more harshly and renders Brecht's viewpoint more explicitly. Because the third version, translated by Wolfgang Sauerlander and Ralph Manheim as *Life of Galileo*, more explicitly conveys the author's viewpoint than the second (whether such explicitness improves the play is an open question) and because it represents his final version, I employ it. Apart from implicitness and explicitness (and with the latter, much more dialogue), the most important other difference, in my judgment, is the final scene. At the appropriate point in my analysis, I will compare it in the second and third versions of the play (the latter resembles the first). Both of these versions are in Bertolt Brecht, *Collected Plays*, ed. Ralph Manheim and John Willett, vol. 5.

At the outset, Brecht establishes his dominant themes. A dedicated professional man who subordinates everything to his work, Galileo, in the play's first speech, commands Andrea, his housekeeper's son, to put the milk on the table but to leave his books open. Not even food, which Galileo relishes as much as his work, may interrupt that work. Both work and food, however, require money, for which the scientist depends on the marketplace. In the play's second speech, Andrea reminds the master that if they do not pay the milkman, "he'll make a circle around our house. . . . " In the third speech, Galileo reveals the relative unimportance he places upon money, the supreme importance he attaches to his profession, and the social relationship between his profession and the common people. "You must say 'describe a circle,'" says Galileo, who then tests his housekeeper's son on the shortest distance between two points. Andrea passes. Soon, Galileo gives him a lesson in Copernican astronomy: he moves a chair (symbolic of the earth), on which the boy sits, around a washstand (symbolic of the sun). Vividly, and with dramatic economy, Brecht demonstrates the accessibility of science to the common people.

Both science and its accessibility herald a new age, which Galileo eulogizes in the first scene. A very special person, Galileo is concerned not only with the earth but with the heavens themselves. To Brecht, however, and to Galileo as well, this moment in history could make every human being special, for each has the same curiosity and intellectual capacity to question, test, and discover. At this moment, everyone is becoming aware of the implications of science. "For two thousand years," says Galileo, "men believed that the sun and all the stars of heaven were circling around them. The pope, the cardinals, princes and scholars, the captains, merchants, fishwives and schoolchildren"—in other words, every social class—"all thought they were sitting motionless inside this crystal sphere." Everything has changed. In what is a new age, one now says, "Since things are thus and so, they will not remain thus and so." That is, society is susceptible to alteration, and "where faith had ruled for a thousand years, doubt has now set in." As Galileo understands, the scientific profession is not the only class that employs reason to challenge established social practice and custom. As a youth, he observed masons, after employing scientific logic, discard a traditional method of moving granite blocks in favor of a new, more practical technique. In every social class, "Things that were never held in doubt are being doubted now." He foresees that in his lifetime "people will talk astronomy in the market place. Even the sons of fishwives will go to school." Galileo enunciates and accepts the social responsibility of his profession. He wishes to make everyone understand science, particularly his housekeeper's son.

Although Galileo is a recognized authority in his profession rather than an outsider trying to claw his way into it, as Solness once was, or a member of the younger generation knocking at the door, as Ragnar is, Galileo's heterodox views, which challenge the judgment of the authorities—represented in this play by the Church—make him an outsider who seeks entry in order to topple the old and orthodox. Despite his ode to the new era and his recognition of the importance of his work to the masses, Galileo resembles Dubedat and Ridgeon. Like these other special professional people, he has one point of honor, his work, to which he subordinates and sacrifices everything.

The first thing Galileo gives up in order to pursue his work is the person that he particularly wants to understand that work, Andrea. A young nobleman, Ludovico, arrives to take lessons from Galileo. Although Ludovico admits he has "no head for science," he has sense enough to understand how important science is becoming: "Everybody's eating and drinking science nowadays, you know." A new age may have dawned, but—to put the matter Ptolemaically—the sun has not yet risen. Because Galileo must pay his bills, he takes on the young man. "Naturally I'll have to drop you," he tells Andrea. "You understand, you don't pay." In order to pursue his profession, Galileo rejects its social responsibility, which he had insisted upon a few minutes earlier.

His next sacrifice for his profession is his honesty. When the procurator of the University of Padua arrives, Galileo rediscovers the relationship between business and science. Galileo's request for a raise in salary is denied. The university does not want pure science, but "another invention as clever as that splendid proportional compass of yours which a person ignorant of mathematics can use to . . . compute compound interest, reproduce a land survey in enlarged or reduced scale, and determine the weight of cannon balls." That invention, the procurator explains, enriched the leading citizens and the university. Galileo then does what Dubedat habitually does: he swindles people who have money. Having learned the nature of a telescope from Ludovico, who saw one in Holland, Galileo palms it off as his own invention. This "highly salable tube" for businessmen "to manufacture and market" assures his raise in salary.

To continue working, Galileo first sacrifices Andrea, then his integrity. Later, he sacrifices his daughter's happiness. Even though he knows that if he returns to his forbidden scientific pursuits Ludovico will break his engagement to her, Galileo unhesitatingly returns to them. He is ready to sacrifice himself as well. Despite the plague, he refuses to leave his home, since it contains all of his notes from the last three months, which would become useless unless he immediately follows through on his findings.

Returning to the telescope swindle, the episode has several results other than an increased salary for Galileo. As Brecht points out, the commercial article he makes for money proves useful for the research he must suspend in order to make it.[9] Also, as Frank K. Borchardt observes, there is significance in the fact that Galileo's tube is colored differently from the green one Ludovico described: Galileo's red tube "means revolution, here, more than just the revolution of the planets."[10] Furthermore, when Ludovico, who is unaware of Brecht's symbolism, points out that the difference between the telescopes is one of color, he suggests that while he has no head for science itself, he has a head for the business relationship between science and society— knowledge he will later reveal more clearly when he breaks his engagement to Galileo's daughter. Finally, Galileo's action with regard to the telescope foreshadows his action with regard to the Inquisition: in both instances, he hides the truth about his profession in order to survive and to practice it.

A major consequence of the series of events that result in Galileo's swindle is his decision to leave Padua for Florence. In Padua, the procurator reminds him, the scientist has freedom of inquiry. Galileo derides such freedom as merely "good business. . . . You get good teachers for low pay by pointing out that other towns are run by the Inquisition, which burns people." Moreover, the work he must do to earn money from Paduan

9. Bertolt Brecht, *Brecht on Theatre*, trans. John Willett, p. 200.
10. Frank K. Borchardt, "Marx, Engels, and Brecht's *Galileo*," in *Brecht Heute/Brecht Today*, ed. John Fuegi, 2:157.

Special, Chosen People   67

businessmen draws time from research he considers more important. "What good would it do you to have all the time you want for research," counters the procurator, "if any witless monk of the Inquisition could simply suppress your ideas?" "And what's the use of free investigation without free time to investigate?" Galileo retorts. In this exchange, Brecht inadvertently reveals that Galileo might ultimately have been better off serving the Paduan businessmen. Although it would have taken longer to complete the work, that work would not have shed its benefits to society as a whole. When Galileo decides to go to Florence, which the Church rules, he begins the road to his downfall, for he goes to a place where the authorities can prevent his work from having social consequences that benefit mankind.

These authorities—both churchmen and the nobility—are well aware of the revolutionary implications of this scientist's apparently specialized research. "Consider the cruelty of those who have their peasants whipped half-naked around their estates in the Campagna," Cardinal Bellarmine tells Galileo, "and the stupidity of the wretches who kiss their feet in return." According to the Church, class stratification is part of God's master plan. To accuse God of not knowing how the planets move would be socially unsettling. Similarly, the Little Monk argues that to his parents, poor peasants, the cyclic rhythms of nature embrace the care of olive trees and the payment of taxes. What would happen if the Bible, which demonstrates the necessity of their sweat, hunger, and submission, turns out to be filled with errors? But why, demands Galileo, must people like the monk's parents work themselves to death? Why must they be hungry amid overflowing wheat fields? Why must their taxes subsidize papal wars? The question of the planets, agrees Galileo, is really the question of the peasants, and he concludes that virtue is not linked to misery. It might upset the peasants, says Ludovico, who represents the nobility, if they heard that attacks on church doctrine went unpunished. He means that it might upset his own social class. As Galileo recognizes, Ludovico's aristocratic family is among those who, in order to keep discipline, have their peasants whipped (Ludovico calls the peasants "brutes"). Galileo also recognizes the basis of the aristocrat's demand that he refrain from questioning papal doctrine. He might stimulate Ludovico's peasants to think new thoughts. He might, he considers, "write in the vernacular for the many instead of in Latin for the few."

Brecht does not rely on discussion alone to reveal these ideas. In the carnival scene, he expands the social framework to show the dissemination of Galileo's doctrine among the common people. When God made the earth the center around which the sun revolves, sings a balladeer, he also made the pope the center around whom cardinals revolve, around them bishops, then in turn secretaries, aldermen, craftsmen, servants, dogs, chickens, and beggars. If Galileo's doctrine were correct, servant girls would refuse to make their masters' beds; carpenters would build homes for themselves, not pews for churchmen; cobblers would make shoes for themselves, not for their wealthy customers; tenants' wives would give milk to their children, not to fat churchmen. With the traditional planetary order destroyed, in other words, so would the traditional social order be destroyed. As the Inquisitor puts it, if the people begin by doubting that the sun stood still, as the Bible informs, they will soon question whether to contribute at church collections and whether the master-servant relationship is really immutable. Galileo's work has begun to have social repercussions throughout Italy, even among the lowest social classes.

On Galileo's side are the rising bourgeoisie, who would profit by many of these social repercussions. An iron founder relates Galileo's experiments to the invention of a mechanical cultivator, medical experiments, money markets, trade schools, regularly printed newspapers, and the expansion of industry. In Church-controlled Florence, however, such allies are dangerous, and Galileo takes another step toward the abnegation of his social responsibilities. All he has done, he tells the iron founder, is to have written a book on the mechanism of the universe. "What people make or don't make of it is no concern of mine."

When Barberini, a mathematician, is elected to the papacy, Galileo hopes for a reversal of the Vatican decree that the Copernican doctrine is heretical. Ludovico knows better: any new pope will have to consider the wishes of the Italian nobility. Once Barberini dons the clothes of his new office, he becomes his office, that is, a symbol and upholder of the traditional order. In Marxist terms, his social position determines his social actions.

With Galileo's recantation, he places himself in league with the forces of reaction. This too has social repercussions. In Italy, as Andrea tells him, no work with a new hypothesis has been published since his abjuration. Even in countries outside papal jurisdiction, Galileo's retraction has caused a scientific setback that the Church finds gratifying. Now, Galileo himself publicly supports reactionary principles, and he gives public support to dispensing soup to rebellious ropemakers in the name of Christian charity, rather than increasing their wages, since such a policy strengthens their faith and not their greed. Despite the fact that he is under house arrest, physically removed from society, Galileo's action does not alienate the scientist from social forces. When a major member of an important profession does not make himself responsive to progressive social forces, as Brecht demonstrates, he becomes responsive to regressive social forces.

Nevertheless, Galileo's abjuration permits him to write the *Discorsi*. Ironically, his decision to leave Padua for Florence, where the Inquisition keeps him prisoner, enables him to achieve his goal: time to conduct scientific investigation without worrying about money. Yet his science serves people other than those he claims he wants to serve. In the first scene, he tells Andrea he wants to make everyone understand science. In the penultimate scene, he tells Andrea that his recantation has prevented him from achieving this goal. Whereas Andrea declares that in science all that counts is contribution to knowledge, Galileo believes otherwise. Earlier, Galileo insisted that "to know the truth and call it a lie is criminal!" and that "truth prevails only when we make it prevail." With the *Discorsi* completed, Galileo reiterates these statements and condemns himself. The true aim of science, says he, "is to lighten the toil of human existence." If scientists grovel before reactionary rulers, as he has done, and acquire knowledge merely for the sake of knowledge, divorced from beneficial social functions, as he has done, then new inventions will mean new hardships for the people. As a renowned scientist, he had a special, unique opportunity, for at the time of his discoveries, science excited the lower and middle classes, who delighted in what Galileo calls the hallmark of science, "knowledge distilled from doubt." The members of these classes metaphorically turned his telescope from the skies to members of the higher classes—the nobility, the priests, and the landlords—who were responsible for the man-made miseries that human beings could remove by getting rid of the responsible parties. Because he turned his back on the people, not doubt but credulity prevailed, and with it those man-made miseries. If he had remained steadfast, his refusal to recant might have had widespread consequences for the social improvement of mankind, and scientists might have developed a Hippocratic-like oath "to use their knowledge only for the good of mankind." Instead, he laments, he has betrayed his calling. Although Andrea refuses to accept Galileo's analysis as the final word on the subject, Brecht states in a note on the play that he shares Galileo's view.[11] To Brecht, what matters most are the social consequences of an action.[12] The result of Galileo's action was social regression, not social progress.

But did Galileo really have a choice? Could he have held out, as he blames himself for having failed to do? Was not death the only real alternative to recantation? In 1600, Giordano Bruno was burned for professing what Galileo professes. In a note on the play, Brecht says that by the time Galileo faced the Inquisition, social circumstances had so altered, and the middle class, which could exploit scientific achievements, had become so much more powerful that it might have succeeded in changing the ideology that obstructed its further rise.[13]

What does the play say? Scenes 1 (1609) and 3 (1610) remind the audience of Bruno's burning and the reason for it. In scene 6 (1616), an old cardinal tells Galileo he resembles the man they burned a few years ago. In scene 7 (also 1616), Cardinal Bellarmine tells Galileo that while the Vatican declares Copernican doctrine to be heretical, Galileo is free to deal with it "as a mathematical hypothesis." Cardinal Barberini advises him, "We need you more than you need us." Although Barberini does not explain the statement, a later scene suggests that the need may relate to the Church's financial interests in shipbuilding and co-

---

11. Brecht, *Collected Plays*, 5:230. Yet as Esslin points out, though not in connection with *Galileo,* Brecht frequently praises unheroic heroes who accomplish their goals without seeming brave or virtuous, and Esslin cites Brecht's alter ego, Mr. Keuner, that the bearer of knowledge must not fight or fail to eat, and that his sole virtue consists of bearing the truth (Martin Esslin, *Brecht: The Man and his Work*, pp. xi–xii).

12. Compare Raymond Williams, *Modern Tragedy*, p. 200.

13. Brecht, *Collected Plays*, 5:250.

lonialism. In scene 9 (1622), Galileo fears he might be burned at the stake. In scene 12 (1633, eleven years later), the Inquisitor admits that the Church must yield to the material interests of Italian shipowners who need Galileo's star charts, but he suggests the Church can accept the star charts while it rejects the doctrine on which they are based. What if Galileo remains stubborn? Says the Pope, "At the very most the [torture] instruments may be shown to him." In scene 13 (also 1633), Galileo returns, after having recanted. Because he is not present when the Pope says that *at the very most* the Inquisitor may *show* him the torture instruments, then for all he knows, and probably believes, these instruments will be used on him.[14] Nevertheless, in the next scene, in which he condemns himself, he concludes that he was never in real danger, but was as strong as the authorities. What led him to this conclusion, he does not explain.

Without that explanation, and since Galileo does not know what the Pope told the Inquisitor, one might agree with Andrea's assessment rather than with Galileo's or Brecht's.[15] One could therefore absolve Galileo and blame society for presenting him with what looks like a choice between living as a coward and dying as a hero.[16] Even so, one could still agree with Brecht that motive notwithstanding, and also add that blame notwithstanding, the social result of Galileo's action is what Galileo describes, and that the result is what matters.

In the final, epiloguelike scene of the third version of the play, *Life of Galileo*, which is close to that of the first version, Brecht undermines Galileo's self-condemnation. At the Italian border, over which Andrea takes the *Discorsi*, several boys argue as to whether an old woman is a witch who flies through the air. Since the boys do not notice a coachman carry Andrea's box over the border, they are amazed at its disappearance. One boy claims

14. In Brecht's *Aufbau eine Rolle: Laughtons Galilei*, p. 56, a photograph of scene 12 in the 1947 production of the second version, *Galileo* (scene 13 in the third version), directed by Joseph Losey with Brecht's collaboration, shows Charles Laughton seated, facing the audience, while behind him, projected on a screen, are instruments of torture. In Galileo's mind, the picture implies, torture and perhaps death comprised the alternative to capitulation.

15. According to Eric Bentley, the play itself does not fully justify the virulence of Galileo's self-condemnation. See *Theatre of War*, p. 153.

16. Compare Borchardt, "Marx, Engels, and Brecht's *Galileo*," pp. 161–62.

the devil spirited it away. In the scene's last, upbeat speech, Andrea tells the boys that no devil took the box over the border and that no one can fly through the air. With twentieth-century hindsight, Brecht has him add that machines might enable people to fly. "Such machines don't exist yet. Maybe they never will because man is too heavy. But of course, we don't know. We don't know nearly enough, Giuseppe. We've barely begun." No matter what Galileo says in the previous scene, this scene—in which the *Discorsi* crosses the border—and especially this last speech, which forecasts social advances through science, suggests that Galileo did not abort the new era.

By contrast, the final scene of the second version of the play, Laughton's *Galileo*, supports Galileo's contention. In this scene, a boy insists that an old woman is a witch, and points to a shadow which he interprets as the witch stirring hell-broth with a broomstick. Andrea lifts him up to see what the boy admits is just an old lady stirring porridge with a soup ladle. After Andrea crosses the border, the boy ignores the evidence of his own eyes and cries, "She *is* a witch! She *is* a witch!" Although Andrea reminds the boy to consider what he just saw, the boy joins his friends in a concluding song, that this old woman is a witch who rides on a broomstick at night and spits on the church steeple. The second version of the play dramatizes the results of Galileo's having divorced science from the common people. Ignorance and superstition, not reason, prevail.

*   *   *   *

Regardless of the final scene, *Life of Galileo*, like *The Master Builder* and *The Doctor's Dilemma*, dramatizes the relationship between society and a prominent representative of the professional classes. Like *The Doctor's Dilemma*, though much more explicitly, it insists on the social responsibility of the professional classes to society at large, and it condemns those "special, chosen people" who abnegate such responsibility and turn their professions into what Shaw calls conspiracies against the public.

Furthermore, all three plays dramatize how these "special, chosen people" regard their own professions. While the view of a profession in *The Master Builder* is the most self-contained, in that it places less emphasis than the other two plays on the relationship between members and nonmembers of the profession (house building or architecture), it expresses the view of this professional class that the profession itself is part of competitive, capitalist society, in which the success of one person means the failure of another. To the members of the medical profession in *The Doctor's Dilemma*, the relationship of their profession to nonmembers is an aspect of paramount importance. How do they view their profession? In this play, their views partly reflect those of the chaotic, competitive, capitalist society of which it is a part. After receiving their professional licenses to cure or kill, they are free from further tests of competence. Competitive, each denigrates the medical theories and practices of rivals, and each considers himself a public benefactor. One doctor concludes that medical practice should be public, not private. If this comes about, society will establish standards for the evaluation of members of that profession. In this play, a work of dramatic art, the author comes down hard upon the artist, a socially reprehensible character who is not balanced by an artist who is an honest man. In one respect, this artist is a microcosm of capitalist society, for he employs its methods, honest or otherwise, to obtain money: sell, borrow, trade in futures commodities, and so forth. The value of his product, beautiful paintings, is negligible compared to the nonaesthetic social value of any decent human being. Does this view, by extension, apply to the play that dramatizes it? Possibly, for if the play is a challenge to society and to that part of it known as the medical profession, its social value is measurable by its ability to improve both. In depicting professional classes in capitalist society, Shaw does not spare his own. How members of a professional class should regard their profession in itself and in relationship to society is a vital question in Brecht's play, whose central figure is a major scientist. Indeed, he and his (dramatically) foremost disciple debate that very question in a crucial scene. Despite the Renaissance setting of the play, one may make inferences about the question of the comparative social values of the scientific profession in capitalist and communist societies, for the Church-controlled society into which Galileo moves has much in common with the latter. Brecht answers neither question. The first, he keeps open so that audiences should ponder it. As for the second, whatever he says outside the play, inside it he dramatizes the drawbacks of both societies. Ironically, of this trio of authors who criticize the societies of which their professional classes are members, the dramatist whom many would consider the most radical (Brecht) is the only one to suggest—consciously or not—the disadvantages of the society he would offer as an alternative.

4.

Society's Crumbling Foundations—Potential Destruction
Pillars of Society, Heartbreak House, Puntila and Matti, His Hired Man

This trio of plays rests on the premises that the foundations of capitalist society are unstable, that this society fails to benefit all of its members, and that its destruction might occur. In a society shaken by social unrest, the confrontation between exploited workers and businessmen or landowners who exploit them could dramatize the question of whether the owners or the workers are the true foundations of society. This issue is part of Ibsen's play. It is untouched by Shaw, however, who restricts himself to the demonstration that capitalist society's pillars, however beautiful they might appear, are incapable of supporting it. In Brecht's play, there is less direct confrontation than in Ibsen's, but—far more than in Ibsen's—it presents the two classes as hostile antagonists to each other; and, as in Shaw's, the play prophesies destruction of the foundations of capitalist society, which would crumble when the workers, who make its existence possible, refuse to give those who are its pillars the help they need to prop it.

Each dramatist portrays a different facet of the subject, a different attitude toward the pillars of capitalist society, and a different conclusion. Each of the more recent plays is more radical—though not necessarily dramatically better or worse—than the earlier play. To Ibsen, the capitalists are capable of reform, and of constructing a mutually beneficial alliance with their workers; but they are also capable of doing the opposite. To Shaw, the pillars of capitalist society are for the most part charming and delightful, but this factor is no reason to permit them to govern a country; unlike Ibsen, he does not regard them as capable of reforming or of preventing their own destruction. To Brecht, they are incapable of constructing a mutually beneficial alliance with their workers, and their relationship to these workers is exploitative; unlike Shaw, he portrays society's pillars as trying to prevent their own destruction, and he urges the working classes to destroy their exploiters.

* * * *

On the basis of the opening scene of *Pillars of Society*, a management-labor confrontation, one expects a drama that focuses on class antagonisms. Instead, Ibsen dramatizes class antagonisms as social background, plot device, and symbol. Nevertheless, *Pillars of Society* is a satiric denunciation of the capitalist ethos. Ibsen's targets are the businessmen who are regarded by themselves and others as society's foundations, but the foundations with which he would replace these morally rotten pillars are not proletarian.

Class antagonisms form part of Ibsen's picture. As the play begins, the shipyard foreman Aune receives a dressing down, not from Bernick, who owns the shipyards, but from Bernick's proxy, his head clerk Krap (like Aune, a worker), who tells Aune that he must stop stirring discord among the workers in the shipyards. The opening scene casts an ironic light on the title. As it reveals, the actions of one of society's pillars nourish discontent among society's members. Because this pillar has a deputy act in his behalf in dealing with a representative of the majority of society, the scene hints at his isolation from them. It also demonstrates that the convenient catchall term *society* may be a misnomer, for society comprises different social groups—that is, different societies—each with its own class interests. White-collar worker Krap demands that blue-collar worker Aune stop making speeches to the workers on Saturdays. When Aune, head of the workers' union as well as a foreman, protests that he can do as he likes with his free time, Krap forbids him to use such time "to make other people useless on the job," as he does when he tells the workers that the shipyards' new machines and new working methods are dangerous. "I did it for the betterment of society," protests Aune. To the shipyard owner, however, such talk will result in "the ruin of society." Though Aune concludes, "My society isn't Consul Bernick's society," Krap—reminding him of his job as foreman—insists that it is: "Above all else . . . you have your duties to that society called Bernick and Company, because *that's* what supports every one of us." This statement implies that while the society of the play's title apparently refers to the organization that binds every member of the community, it really consists of Bernick and Company, which is shorthand for capitalist society.

Soon after the start of the next act, paralleling the opening of the first, Ibsen further elucidates the class antagonisms that underlie society's shaky foundations. This time, Bernick confronts Aune directly. "Don't think this is just a matter of profit," says Bernick of the new laborsaving, job-destroying machines he has introduced to create bigger profits. His concern, he protests, is for both his community and his business. "Progress has to come from me, or it won't come at all." When Aune pleads that he too wants progress, Bernick—conveniently ignoring the number of people involved—argues that the progress Aune wants is only for Aune's "own narrow faction, for the working class." When real progress is at hand, "agitators" like Aune "get scared." Admitting he is scared that workers will lose their jobs because of the machines that represent progress to their owners, Aune tries to reason with his employer: "You're always talking about caring for society, Mr. Bernick, but I think society has a few obligations of its own. What right do technology and capitalism have to introduce all these new inventions before society's trained a generation in how to use them?" All that Bernick can do is pontificate that reading and thinking "too much" (he neglects to say how much is enough) are not good for Aune because they make him unhappy with his job, and to argue by analogy: "When printing was invented, a lot of scribes went hungry." Aune's reading and thinking permit him to respond in terms of the same analogy. "How'd you like it, Mr. Bernick, if you'd been a scribe at the time?" Having thus lost the argument, Bernick uses his more powerful social position to end it.

The schoolmaster Rørlund, who teaches social values—that is, those of Bernick's class—pompously dogmatizes about the false values of large, modern industrialized societies, whose glittering facades mask corruption. Lacking moral foundations, in contrast to such small communities as the one in which he lives, they are "whited sepulchers." What Rørlund fails to perceive is that the big industrialized societies are the small ones writ large, and that the values he condemns inhere in the smaller societies, which are in the very process of expansion. Coming as it does after the scene that concerns the progressive, laborsaving machines introduced by Bernick, Rørlund's sermon functions as an ironic denunciation of what he thinks he praises. Moreover, the values he stresses expose the distinction between moral ideal and immoral practice; in short, hypocrisy. Within a corrupt society are ideals that threaten to expose its practice and perhaps destroy its foundations.

The unethical practices of Bernick's society belie the ethics it preaches.[1] Before the play begins, Bernick was instrumental in preventing the building of a coastal railroad—which he called a symbol of the evils of modern industrialism—that would connect this small Norwegian shipping town with larger, morally corrupt cities. When the issue of the railroad revives, he reveals the real reason for his action: the coastal railroad would have competed with his shipping interests. Now, Bernick and his cohorts favor a railroad. A branch line, going inland rather than along the coast, will bring additional goods for their businesses to ship. To their greater profit, he and other tycoons have embarked on a speculative enterprise. By secretly purchasing, at low prices, apparently worthless land from owners who do not know the railroad intends to buy, they hope to reap windfall profits. Once information about the new railroad becomes public, land values will skyrocket. If the branch line develops as planned, Bernick expects to become a millionaire. If not, he will be ruined. Publicly, this pillar of society provides an altruistic reason for his actions. If he had not acted as he did, others would have done so, bungled the operation, and left it open to exploitation by foreigners who, unlike him, would not be responsive to community needs and not provide jobs for local citizens.

Rørlund calls Bernick's home fine and decent, a place "where family life shows itself in its highest form—where peace and harmony rule. . . . " Yet that home is a microcosm of the society of which Bernick is a pillar. Like that society, it rests on pretenses and lies, feeble foundations that can crumble. His son wants to run away from its oppressiveness. His ward, Dina Dorf, wastes under its confining, soul-destroying moralisms. Although Bernick once loved Lona Hessel, an emancipated spirit whose honesty and self-reliance contrast with his dishonesty and fear of the opinion of others, he married her half-sister, Betty, since Betty

---

1. As Hermann J. Weigand puts it, "Talk service and think profits" is the motto of the town's businessmen. See *The Modern Ibsen*, p. 6.

and not Lona would inherit the family fortune. Because Johan, his wife's brother, was leaving for America, he agreed to assume guilt for the crime of embezzlement, which society would otherwise attribute to Bernick; and Bernick permits people to think that Johan had an affair with Dina's mother (the culprit was Bernick himself). In private and public life, Bernick embraces money rather than honesty, and lies of private life parallel lies of public life.

Like his society, Bernick's personal public stance consists of virtue and morality. In private too, spokesmen of both actually believe both to be virtuous and moral. How else can one live with oneself? Such people do not make Miltonic statements like "Evil, be thou my good." They have persuaded themselves that profitmaking is good. Behind a facade of harmony, decency, and integrity, Bernick's home—like the society of which it is part—is disharmonious, corrupt, and unjust.

To what extent were Bernick's actions really reprehensible? By repudiating stories about his mother's fiscal irresponsibility, he succeeded in placating his creditors and gaining time to make the family firm solvent again. In fact, no one stole any money, and through Bernick's actions, no one lost any. Since Johan was thousands of miles away, he did not feel society's opprobrium. Yet in acting as he did, Bernick not only wasted several people's lives—including Betty's, Lona's, and Dina Dorf's—he lost his own identity and assumed that of his social role. In his words, "a businessman, under the pressure of immense responsibilities, grows to be part of the business he inherits." When Lona asks whether he told his wife any of this, Bernick replies that he would not give her pain "to no profitable end." The revealing adjective does not escape Lona. "Profitable, you say? Oh, yes, you're a businessman; you must be an authority on profit."

Still, Bernick considers himself and his community morally superior to the bigger capitalists and the larger industrialized communities outside. "Absolutely disgusting!" he exclaims when he reads a telegram sent by the American owners of a boat that has just docked and is being repaired in his shipyard: "'Do least possible repairs. Send *Indian Girl* over soon as seaworthy. Profitable season. Cargo will float her in emergency.'" Bernick is genuinely indignant: "Those men know very well, with that cargo she'd go down like a stone if anything happened.... No concern for human life when there's profit involved. . . . I'd like to see the shipowner among us who could stoop to anything like this! Not *one*, not a single *one*—."

Others recognize that the same greed exists inside the community, with local businessmen as well. Hilmar Tønneson perceives that to them everything revolves around material profit. Those who work at "defending their bankbooks" are the pillars of society. Indeed, bankbooks themselves are society's pillars.

Bernick's denunciation of capitalists who disregard human life when profit is involved resounds ironically when he reveals himself to be such a person. Because Johan threatens to expose him when he returns from a voyage on the *Indian Girl*, Bernick orders the unseaworthy ship to sail. But Bernick is shrewd. When Aune tells him that its hull is too rotted to be patched in the two days Bernick gives him, Bernick threatens to fire him unless he does the job. With Aune's reputation for opposing Bernick's new machines, people will consider this, rather than the large extent of the ship's damage and the short amount of time given him to repair it, to be the real reason for its subsequent sinking. Since Aune fears for his job, he capitulates. When Krap, who values human life, discovers that Aune's repairs are so shoddy that the ship will sink, he tells Bernick, who seizes upon the disclosure as an excuse to discredit a working-class troublemaker and simultaneously reap moral profit. Not only are human lives at stake, Bernick piously declares, but an "immense amount of capital . . . would be lost." However, Krap fails to get the "absolute proof" of Aune's negligence that Bernick demands. With Johan's threat in his mind, Bernick turns a deaf ear to what he knows are Krap's valid pleas that if the boat sails it will sink. Even with the announcement of an impending storm, Bernick orders the *Indian Girl* to sail. As his actions demonstrate, Bernick is no better than the greedy, inhumane capitalists he denounces.

The final act sees Bernick's gradual redemption. At first, he claims it is too late for him to stop deceiving the populace. Although he prepares "to go down in ruin, like this whole corrupt society," he excuses himself on the basis of the next generation. "It's my son that I'm working for. A time will come when truth is rooted in our social structure, and on that he'll build a happier life than his father's." Lona Hessel penetrates the speciousness of Bernick's justification. What kind of life can his son build, she demands, with a legacy based on lies?

Two courses of action are open to one who perceives the truth about this type of society.² One is to leave it for a better. This Dina Dorf does when she leaves for America with Johan. (In *Pillars of Society*, Ibsen distinguishes between America, which he makes a symbol of bloated capitalism, and Americans, who exemplify the freedom and honesty that contrast with local society. In leaving with Johan, Dina goes to join the free Americans.) The second alternative is to try to change society's foundations. This Bernick does. His method is to reveal the truth about them. But Ibsen is not simpleminded. He recognizes that a recitation of a catalogue of vices is insufficient.³ Preceding the revelation of truth must be action, which itself must derive from inner redemption. Before one can act to redeem others, one must undergo spiritual redemption. After Bernick recognizes the moral rot that is the basis of his life and his society, after he recognizes that to leave his son a legacy based on it is to ruin him, and after he acknowledges his own guilt, he learns that Johan and Dina have not sailed on the *Indian Girl*, but on another boat. Even so, he reverses himself by ordering the *Indian Girl* to remain in port. His action, therefore, derives not from a purely personal situation but from his recognition that human life (sailors he does not personally know) has greater value than profit. But he acts too late. Krap tells him that the boat has already sailed. Only after he receives this information does he learn that his son stowed away on it.

Although Bernick's inner redemption does not affect his son's life, Ibsen establishes through post hoc events a spiritual propter hoc significance. After Bernick's demand to stop the *Indian Girl* comes the news that the worker Aune, on his own initiative and at the eleventh hour, ordered the boat to stay in port. Just as the worker makes it possible for the owner's property to thrive, so does the worker make it possible for the owner's family to stay alive. Because of the temporal sequence of events (post hoc), Bernick's inner salvation links in a quasi-causal manner to his son's physical salvation (propter hoc). Logical fallacy acquires thematic validity.

Bernick's confession of guilt before the populace is not merely

---

2. Rolf Fjelde points this out in his Introduction to the play in Henrik Ibsen, *The Complete Major Prose Plays*, p. 11.
3. See Weigand, *The Modern Ibsen*, p. 13.

a pious recital but rather a public acknowledgment of private upheavals. And he atones in the most appropriate way. After telling the truth about his business activities with the railroad, he takes what was to have been personal profit and establishes the properties as a public corporation, available to the people at large. What he apologizes for, however, is duplicity for his own profit, which he renounces, not ambition for power, status, and influence, which he believes makes him worthy of a place among the ablest businessmen in town. He still judges that the properties he and his cohorts acquired could develop best under the management of one man, but he leaves it to the citizens to decide whether he should be that person.

Here too, Ibsen is not simplistic. Not only does businessman Bernick select what to apologize for and what not to apologize for, but the public response is far from an upbeat burst of applause for his candor. Instead, "*The onlookers melt away through the garden.*" Onstage are the Bernick family and Aune. Father and son reconcile. Bernick takes back his threat to fire Aune if the *Indian Girl* did not sail. For his part, Aune agrees to try to work with the new machines. The family reconciles, management and labor reconcile. Lona Hessel gives her approval to the genuineness of Bernick's spiritual and material change. As she says, and he agrees, "the spirit of truth and the spirit of freedom—*those* are the pillars of society." If family and the management-labor relationship in one firm can reconcile on the basis of these pillars, perhaps the society of which these are parts can also rest on them. Ibsen dramatizes individual regeneration, and its effect is restricted. He does not dramatize the effect of such regeneration on society as a whole. While Bernick forces his former partners in the railroad fraud to acquiesce to his new plan, they do so grudgingly. They are unregenerate. Will they launch new fraudulent schemes? In this regard, and in respect to the public's response to Bernick's admission and action, the end of the play is ambiguous. Seeds of salvation are present, but seeds of destruction remain.

*   *   *   *

Like *Pillars of Society*, *Heartbreak House* includes among its dramatis personae what one of them calls "rather a favorable specimen of what is best" in society. Both plays expose the social deficiencies of *what is best*. Ibsen's play dramatizes one social pillar who replaces the lies and hypocrisy that are the shaky foundations of his private and business lives with truth and freedom from the fear of what others may say; it presents capitalist society with the choice of retaining the similarly shaky foundations that may destroy the entire edifice, or of emulating his actions to replace them with sturdier foundations. Shaw's play, however, dramatizes capitalist society as incapable of saving itself. Completed forty years after *Pillars of Society* and written during a cataclysmic war that was in the process of destroying Europe's social foundations, *Heartbreak House* suggests that capitalist society no longer has the type of choice Ibsen gave it. Whereas Ibsen's businessman publicly tells the truth about capitalist practices and everyone believes him, Shaw's businessman complains that while he is telling the truth about his money for the first time in his life, it is the first time anyone has ever doubted him. The people who are the social pillars of Shaw's play are unable or unwilling to prevent the destruction of capitalist-aristocratic-liberal England.

Whereas Consul Bernick owns a shipyard, Shotover, a former naval captain, lives in a house that is built to resemble a ship. Explicitly symbolic of what one character refers to as "this soul's prison we call England," Heartbreak House is presided over by this captain who retains his title but not his function (like Britain, he no longer rules the waves). Have its foundations begun to crumble? According to another character, it is a "house without foundations." With no foundations, or with crumbling foundations, destruction—of the house and the society it symbolizes—is imminent.

Elsewhere, the latter character, Ellie Dunn, complains, "There seems to be nothing real in the world except my father and Shakespear." Shaw knows not seems. In "the world"—the society the play represents—nothing *is* real. As Shaw says in his preface to the play, while its "nice people" read about reality, they shrink from contact with the forces that shape it. They do "not wish to realize Utopia for the common people . . . [but] to realize their favorite fictions and poems in their own lives; and, when they could, they lived without scruple on incomes which they did nothing to earn." Appropriately, the play shows not what is real in the world but surrogates for what is real. Mangan is not a capitalist but a surrogate for capitalists. For expenses and commissions, he acts in behalf of capitalists who really own the businesses people think he owns. Is capitalist society cultured? Mangan is named for a poet but is not a poet (he is called Alfred, after Tennyson),[4] and Ellie copies paintings but does not create her own. Is she really a lover of Shakespeare, as she claims to be? At the start of the play, she falls asleep reading *Othello*, a play she insists she likes, with a hero who Hector says is her favorite. In first name only is Mazzini Dunn revolutionary; in reality, he is not. Randall and Ariadne do not govern England's colonies, but are surrogates for his brother, her husband, who does. Although Hector has committed heroic deeds, neither he nor anyone else provides any details about them. Since one hears only fictitious stories he has invented, surrogates for reality, he is a surrogate hero, not a real one. As Shotover himself admits, he is only an echo of his former self, a fading sound of it, not the real thing.[5] In this house, Shaw emphasizes, even the burglar is not a real burglar. Not only its foundations, but the people in it as well, lack substance. This particular society is crumbling, disintegrating.

Can any of these people, part of and representative of that society, prevent its destruction? The nature of that society makes such action unlikely. Under capitalism, an individual fends for himself, not for others. So in this house an individual is untended. Even though Ellie has been invited for the weekend, Shotover recognizes, no hostess is at hand to welcome her, and she is ignored and abandoned. As Ariadne observes, the same disorder that exists in the house exists in its ideas.

Suggestive of the characters' inability to remain alert to prob-

---

4. As A. M. Gibbs suggests, Mangan's surname may derive from that of James Clarence Mangan (*Shaw*, p. 76). This Irish poet adored the "Dark Rosaleen." As G. K. Chesterton puts it, he "dreamed" and was "heedless, irresponsible" (*Irish Impressions*, p. 13). Shaw's Mangan loves Hesione, who has "*magnificent black hair*"; Ellie puts him to sleep; and in relationship to society he is heedless and irresponsible. In 1919 (its London publication preceded the American by a year), Shaw reviewed Chesterton's book. Shaw's comments reveal his familiarity with James Clarence Mangan. See Bernard Shaw, *The Matter with Ireland*, ed. David H. Greene and Dan H. Laurence, pp. 209–10.

5. It is such self-perception that helps endow Shotover with what Frederick P. W. McDowell calls "unexpected depths below [his] surface peculiarities." See "Technique, Symbol, and Theme in *Heartbreak House*," *PMLA*, p. 340.

lems that may lead to the destruction of the edifice, sleep plays a prominent role in the play. Ellie falls asleep, later puts the businessman Mangan to sleep. The surname of the host and hostess is Hushabye. Also suggestive of their inability to deal effectively with problems that might destroy their society is their inability to cope effectively with a burglar who enters their home. Finally, it is revealed that this burglar, who is likewise ineffective as both burglar and blackmailer, is one of them—not only a thief like Mangan (Shaw recalls Proudhon's dictum that property is theft), and a potential businessman also like Mangan, but a former sailor under Shotover's command and the husband of Nurse Guinness.

Nor is there a new generation to salvage the house. Although the Hushabyes have children, Shotover says they "are not youthful." Equally important, Shaw does not bring them onstage.[6] Instead, he dramatizes adult childishness. Grown men behave like children, not responsible adults. Randall has a temper tantrum. Childlike as well, Hector mimics a duel and later plays a dress-up game. Shotover confesses he is in his second childhood. Unable to prevent society's destruction, childlike, irresponsible adults are part of its crumbling or unreal foundations.

Those who live in Heartbreak House are the futile, artistically cultivated, and politically aware members of society. Related to them are the inhabitants of Horseback Hall—reactionary, well-mannered barbarians. The two groups mix—"horsebreakers and heartbreakers," Shaw calls them in his preface. Also at home in Heartbreak House are such guests as businessmen, ineffectual liberals, and social climbers. None of the people who own or visit Heartbreak House can save what it represents.

As Shotover says, Hesione does nothing but upset the house. Hector is merely a domesticated lapdog. While he regards the capitalists who rule England as "human vermin" and fulminates about "the powers of destruction" they wield, which he compares to a badly raised child playing with a torpedo, he only talks. If he had the power to exterminate them, he would not do so but would spare them. As Arthur Nethercot notes, Hesione's

---

[6]. Joseph Frank notes the absence of children in *Heartbreak House* and observes, "The only eggs laid in the play drop from the intestines of a German bomber" (actually, it is a zeppelin). See "Internal vs. External Combustion: Dickens' *Bleak House* and Shaw's *Major Barbara* and *Heartbreak House*," *The Shaw Review*, p. 129.

name suggests the Trojan princess who became one of the causes of the Trojan War; her husband's name, one of its chief heroes.[7] But though the legendary Hector tried and failed to save his society, Shaw's Hector does not even try.

Partly because his clever talk seduces spectators into considering him admirable, Captain Shotover may be more pernicious than either Hesione or Hector. He cannot save the society of which he is a part. "I am half dead," he confesses, his "last shot was fired years ago." The very happiness he brings is cursed, he admits, for it is the type "that comes as life goes, the happiness of yielding and dreaming instead of resisting and doing, the sweetness of the fruit that is going rotten." Despite his awareness that capitalists are "hogs to whom the universe is nothing but a machine for greasing their bristles and filling their snouts" and that one's knowledge of their capacity "to render all our aspirations barren prevents us from having the aspirations," he works for them. The inventions he sells them—mainly death-dealing weapons—are very much like the torpedo of Hector's analogy. As the first act ends, he puts his abilities to work to invent an instrument that will destroy half of Europe with a single explosion. Since he engages in this type of activity, is it any wonder that Heartbreak House is on the verge of collapse? He helps create the seeds of its destruction.

Ariadne, a personification of Horseback Hall, represents the stupidity of the aristocracy. Sir Hastings Utterword, her husband, can save England, says she, by employing the same method he uses to keep order in the colonies he governs: "a good supply of bamboo to bring the British native to his senses." Her flirtatious methods parallel her husband's governing methods. Though she takes, she does not give. Keeping her male admirers at arm's length, she uses them to gratify her vanity, but in return offers no more than platonic relationships. What Hector says of her—"She makes you her servant; and when pay-day comes round, she bilks you"—applies as well to her colonialist husband.

Sir Hastings's social worthlessness is also stressed by the social worthlessness of his brother Randall, whom Ariadne describes as the incarnation of idleness and selfishness. Called "the Rot-

---

[7]. Arthur H. Nethercot, *Men and Supermen*, p. 299.

ter," Randall personifies the essential rot of a moribund social class whose foundations are crumbling.

Mazzini Dunn calls himself a "soldier of freedom," but his arms are at the service of businessmen like Mangan, for whom he works, whom he defends, and of whose real actions he is ignorant. An ineffectual liberal with no staying power, he once believed that joining societies, making speeches, and writing pamphlets would effect social progress. When nothing happened as a result of these activities, he stopped doing them. He marvels at how well everyone gets along, "all things considered," and he gives credit to a prevailing providence. But Shotover reminds him that providence has a way of sending drifting ships on the rocks.

Like father, like daughter: Ellie Dunn also drifts. From an aborted romantic involvement with Hector, she moves to a business alliance with Mangan, whom she tells, "a woman's business is marriage." If she cannot have love, she decides, she need not have poverty. She intends to marry Mangan for his money. Like her father, though, she has neither staying power nor a sense of business. She drops the wealthy Mangan. Instead, she "weds" the decrepit Shotover, who is more than old enough to be her grandfather. In the Heartbreak House that is England, the only young person in the play named for that house allies herself with a man on the brink of death and devoted to inventing instruments of death. Just as Shotover's last shot is over, as his surname suggests, Ellie's surname is a homonym of *done*, whose meanings include *finished* and *spent*.

"Not ablebodied" is Shotover's accurate assessment of Mangan, whom Hector calls "the bloated capitalist"—literally inaccurate, but symbolically apt. Nevertheless, Mangan is a welcome guest of the people who live in Heartbreak House. Its master works for people like him. As capitalism governs England, Mangan represents government as well as capitalism. His business actions in regard to Mazzini Dunn parallel his governmental activities. He uses Dunn's abilities, then for his own profit ruins him—or rather, helps Dunn ruin himself—so that he can step in to reap a profit. So does he ruin England—or help England ruin herself—also for his profit. At the prime minister's request, he boasts, he joined the government "without even going through the nonsense of an election, as the dictator of a great public department." His sole qualification was his standing as "a practical business man." As Shaw indicates in his preface, such people "had become rich by placing their personal interests before those of the country, and measuring the success of every activity by the pecuniary profit it brought to them and to those on whom they depended for their supplies of capital." Not only did they demonstrate their uselessness for public work, they also proved that "in a well-ordered nation they would never have been allowed to control private enterprise." In the play, Shaw reveals that Mangan knows nothing of the businesses he operates except how to get profit from them, and that his administrative ability in government—Mangan himself says this—consists of knowing how to stop other people from saving the country and depriving him of the credit and the chance to acquire a title. He saw to it that if they would not let him save the country, they would not do so either. "I may not know anything about my own machinery; but I know how to stick a ramrod into the other fellow's. . . . If that isnt a triumph of practical business, what is?" In government as well as business, Mangan operates entirely for his own profit and his competitors' loss. Both goals differ from the public good. To Mangan's question, Hector replies with another question: "Is this England, or is it a madhouse?" Clearly, Mangan is among the seeds of his own society's destruction.

Can no one save that society? In *Man and Superman*, Don Juan perceives that "to be in hell is to drift: to be in heaven is to steer." Often, a drifting ship goes "on the rocks or to the bottom." Under the command of skippers unable to steer, says Shotover, echoing Juan, ships "run . . . on the rocks." What is the solution to the problem of the drifting ship of England, which is apt to "strike and sink and split"? "Navigation. Learn it and live; or leave it and be damned." The people in Heartbreak House, and the society of which it is symbol, leave it. None learns navigation. Most leave the job to two types of person. One is exemplified by Sir Hastings, who keeps order in the colonies by means of brutality. Since keeping order differs from steering society in a specific direction, and since it unwittingly perpetuates or creates conditions that impel others to steer it in a direction different from what people like Sir Hastings want (no society is static), this method is not navigation but drift, ultimately toward rocks that will strike, sink, and split the foundations of Sir Hastings's ship. Mangan exemplifies the other type.[8] He does not navigate in government, but prevents others from navigating. His actions too constitute drift; their inevitable consequence, destruction. Because the futile heartbreakers are incapable of navigating and because they put such people as Sir Hastings and Mangan—representatives of the aristocracy and the plutocracy—in charge of government, they too are among the seeds of society's destruction. What is wrong with Heartbreak House? Hector understands: "We are wrong with it.... We are useless, dangerous, and ought to be abolished."

At the end of the first act, Shotover calls for inspiration to create instruments of death. At the end of the second, Hector invokes the heavens to "fall and crush." In the third act, destruction begins to fall from the skies and is welcomed. Small wonder, for destruction inheres in what is below. Apart from the characters themselves, the grounds of Heartbreak House contain a gravel pit with a cave where Shotover stores dynamite. "Isnt that rather risky?" asks Randall in what may be his only intelligent remark in the play. When zeppelins fly over the area, their bombs first hit the church. Their next target is another bastion of English society: business. The practical man of business and the burglar who used to be a pirate—both are thieves, says Shotover, and Hector calls them "two burglars"[9]—literally bring themselves to destruction. Not knowing what is in the cave in the gravel pit—a parallel to Mangan's failure to understand the workings of the businesses he administers—they run there for safety. A sensible action, believes Mazzini Dunn, the wishy-washy liberal who is Mangan's middle-class lackey and apologist, "and it is they who will survive." Wrong again. The next bomb hits the gravel pit, killing them. Mazzini considers going to the cellar, but as usual he does nothing. The helpless Randall tries to play the flute, a typically worthless gesture. Ariadne, who is the class-conscious Lady Utterword, refuses to go to the cellar because the servants are there. Hector, who had said that people like him should be abolished, turns on all the house lights

---

8. J. L. Wisenthal points out (*The Marriage of Contraries*, p. 155) that these two are the only characters either in the play or referred to in it who hold political power.

9. Wisenthal notes another link (*Marriage*, p. 159): Mazzini Dunn makes Mangan's wealth possible and it is he who suggests that the burglar might make a living as a locksmith.

so that the planes will have a clearer target, and his wife helps. Thrilled by the sound of the zeppelins and the explosions of the bombs, Hesione compares them to an orchestral rendition of Beethoven. Equally thrilled, Ellie agrees, hugs Hesione excitedly, and hopes that they will give a return engagement the next night. The supposedly sage old former sea captain merely declaims that Judgment Day has arrived. "Courage will not save you; but it will shew that your souls are still alive." Although the words may sound inspiring, they are not a guide to salvation and their sense is a call for what Shaw in his preface accurately calls an absurd attempt by people who do not know how to live, to make a merit of how to die.

In *Heartbreak House*, Shaw dramatizes the seeds of society's potential destruction that reside in the members of its middle and upper classes. Unlike Ibsen's pillars, not even one of Shaw's replaces the crumbling foundations of his house or of society with sturdy foundations that might save it. Aristocrat and inventor, burglar and businessman, middle class and managerial class, they act either irresponsibly, ineffectively, or not at all. Some rush to destruction while they try to save themselves, others court destruction, others do nothing to prevent it. The only people who behave sensibly are the servants, who take refuge in the cellar. But they are workers in Heartbreak House, not seen by the audience and not regarded as pillars of this society, whose foundations are crumbling or perhaps nonexistent.

*   *   *   *

Although it was written two-thirds of a century after *Pillars of Society* and a quarter of a century after *Heartbreak House*, during a war even more cataclysmic than the war that raged while Shaw wrote his play, Brecht's *Puntila and Matti, His Hired Man* demonstrates that the social pillars dramatized in Ibsen's and Shaw's works still stand. Whereas Ibsen presents his chief social pillar as capable of inner regeneration, and Shaw presents most of his as charming and delightful, Brecht presents his as brutal slavedrivers who not only exploit their workers but tread on their dignity as well. Unconnected to the sea, and to the potential freedom it represents, as Ibsen's and Shaw's chief male characters are, Brecht's Puntila, an immensely wealthy owner of a large estate, is landlocked. Like Shaw's Sir Hastings Utterword, Brecht's Puntila is unabashedly vicious to his social inferiors. When Shotover's nurse speaks on familiar terms to her social betters, she receives a mild reprimand or none at all. However, Puntila threatens to fire his hired man if he hears him talking to his daughter instead of removing his cap and standing silently at attention. "You're expected to look up to your employer's daughter as you would to a higher being who has descended to earth."[10]

While Ibsen's cast of characters embraces a wide spectrum of society, the most obvious meaning of his title is only its upper echelon; and Shaw's focus is on society's upper and middle classes. Brecht's title, reflective of his concern with both higher and lower classes, indicates their unequal relationship: *Herr Puntila und sein Knecht Matti*, which might more accurately be anglicized as *The Master Puntila and His Menial Matti*. In Ibsen's and Shaw's plays, class antagonism is a minor theme. In Brecht's, it is major. Perhaps for this reason, the worker of Brecht's title is a chauffeur. Chauffeurs usually have no respect for the upper classes, as Matti says, because they hear members of these classes talking in the back seat.

The play's title indicates class differences, and it suggests class antagonisms. In *Mother Courage and Her Children*, whose major theme revolves around business, every scene but one contains business transactions or references to them, and the exception displays a symbol of business. In *Puntila and Matti, His Hired Man*, whose major theme revolves around class antagonisms, every scene, with no exception, dramatizes or discusses such antagonisms.

In *Pillars of Society*, the businessman climaxes the play with the truth about himself, which is a secret, and his surprised listeners believe him. In *Heartbreak House*, the businessman tells the truth about himself, also a secret, and he complains that no one believes him. In *Puntila and Matti, His Hired Man*, the landowning master tells the truth about himself, and his statement does not matter. It is no secret. The workers already know it. While schoolbooks inform people that their native soil is both hard to till and rewarding, says one of the workers, the books fail to mention who does the tilling and who receives the reward.

---

10. Quotations from this play are from Ralph Manheim's translation, in Bertolt Brecht, *Collected Plays*, ed. Ralph Manheim and John Willett, vol. 6.

In a prologue, the Dairymaid makes it clear that the landowning class, exemplified by Puntila, should be extinct, which means that audiences should take measures to exterminate it. Like the people in *Heartbreak House*, the type of person Puntila represents is more than socially useless, he is socially harmful. As she says, a landowner's "food and drink consumption couldn't be higher/And uses it has none." Such a creature "is a plague." She does not have to state what is common knowledge, that plagues should be destroyed. This plague is harmful to those under its dominion—that is, its workers.

Although sober Puntila is obviously a plague with no remorse about the social harm he creates, drunken Puntila, friendly with and sympathetic toward the lower classes, is remorseful. In the first scene, drunken Puntila pleads that he fights "attacks of raving sobriety," but "They're always getting the better of me." Note the accuracy of his statement. Sober Puntila *always* gets the better of drunken Puntila, who despite his amiability is merely an ineffectual, drunken slob. Although he buys drinks and embraces people of all classes, he does no more. "If I had my way," says drunken Puntila, "my help would live on roast beef." What is to prevent landowner Puntila from having his way? The fact that he is a landowner suffices. Even though he is drunk, moreover, he calls the people who work on his estate *his* help, an adjective that is possessive in a sense other than grammatical. Later in the play, drunken Puntila says he is "practically a communist, and if I were a hired hand, I'd make life hell for Puntila." *Practically* is as good as *not*, and *if* is so speculative that it fails to represent even wishful thinking.

Through the worker Matti, Brecht also stresses that drunkenness does not alter class antagonisms. The only distinction Matti makes between sober and drunken Puntila is that he permits himself no more than irony with the sober master but can be frank with the drunk. When drunken Puntila asks Matti if he is his friend, the menial answers honestly: "No."

In *The Good Person of Szechwan*, the exploiting Shui Ta, submerged in the exploited Shen Teh, is a part of Shen Teh that emerges on various occasions. In *Puntila and Matti, His Hired Man*, the drunken Puntila is a latent part of the sober Puntila, who is addicted to drink (and the humanity it releases). More important, however, the sober Puntila is a submerged part of the drunken Puntila that emerges *even when Puntila is drunk*. At his most apparently convivial, the boozing Puntila is socially harmful. Because he is a wealthy landowner, he can (and does) intimidate and bully the waiter, whom he forces to work beyond regular hours to serve him liquor and browbeats into saying that Saturday is Friday. When Puntila seems most humane, he still lives prodigally at the expense of others. Tired of waiting in the car for two days while Puntila swills liquor, Matti complains: "I'm your chauffeur, Mr. Puntila. . . . I'm not going to wait out there another minute. . . . You can't treat a man like that." Inadvertently revealing his actual attitude, Puntila turns Matti's complaint into an occasion for self-amusement. "Are you a man? A minute ago you said you were a chauffeur." To Puntila, drunk or sober, Brecht emphasizes, a chauffeur is as much an object, and a possession, as a car. As with Shen Teh and Shui Ta, the two Puntilas are the same person.

While the drunken Puntila talks of social equality, even this drunken talk rests on class differences. Thus, the inebriated Puntila's humane dialogue amounts to a paternalistic arrangement with him on top, as he is when sober, and he regards his social inferiors as yes-men. Inadvertently, drunken Puntila reveals his paternalistic attitude (*he* will decide to raise wages), his refusal to share his possessions (*he* will keep *his* forests), and his class-stratified view of his relationship to his workers (there is enough for them and for himself, the *master*). Matti understands all of these implications. When Puntila pleads for elimination of the social gulf between them, Matti recognizes his employer's fundamental insincerity, which Puntila shows as he corrects the worker and then, ignoring what Matti says, gives him orders:

> PUNTILA. I only want to be sure there's no gulf between us. Say there's no gulf.
> MATTI. I take it as an order, Mr. Puntila. No gulf.
> PUNTILA. Brother, we have to talk about money.
> MATTI. Definitely.
> PUNTILA. But it's sordid to talk about money.
> MATTI. Then we won't talk about money.
> PUNTILA. Wrong again. Why shouldn't we be sordid. Aren't we free men?
> MATTI. No.
> PUNTILA. See? And being free men, we do what we please. And right now we please to be sordid.

Puntila's *brother* is no brother at all, and *we* is the royal *we*, which means *I*.

When Puntila daydreams about their comradely activities, his vision is of the hired man doing the work while he, the master, does none: "when we're tired, we'll drop into a little bar like this and have a drink or two in exchange for chopping wood, you could do it with one hand behind your back, brother." Such brotherhood is convenient for only one of the brothers. Visually emphasizing the disparity between Puntila's speech and social reality, a stage direction has him depart, with Matti—not him—"*carrying the judge*," a member of a higher social class than Matti, whom Puntila plied with liquor until he passed out.

Not only is Matti class conscious, he recognizes the class consciousness of the pillars of the society for whom he labors. When he worked for a brewer's wife, he reports, her daughter—who regarded him as a manipulable object rather than a male human being—stood naked in the bath hut and ordered him to bring her a robe because "'the men always look when I go for a swim.'" Although Matti stayed in the car for two days while Puntila got drunk, Puntila's daughter orders him, after he brings his master home, to stay up with her to make sure Puntila does not drink and hobnob with "the help." Matti's ironic dialogue is a veiled manifestation of class antagonism. When he talks to his employers, he tells her with mock naiveté, he does not have opinions, since they do not like "the help" to have them. Knowing he might be fired if he does not stay up with her, he explains, also ironically, that he concentrates better with his eyes closed.

Matti recognizes that when the upper classes express sympathy or offer to do something themselves, their words are empty. At one point, the judge and lawyer enter while the maid Fina sits on Matti's lap. Ignoring the situation, which is to dehumanize it, the judge asks for buttermilk. Matti politely inquires whether they would like it brought to them. Although the judge responds negatively, the hired help know better: "*Matti ladles some out for them. Fina goes out.*" Soon, a bell rings. "You'd better go see what they want," says the judge, more candidly than before. "Or would you like us to tell them that you believe in the eight-hour day?"

Class antagonisms pervade the entire play. Drunken Puntila—who is still Puntila the wealthy landowner—reprimands a telegraph pole, into which he has crashed his car, for not knowing its place: "Who do you think you are? Do you own a forest, do you own any cows?... When I call the constable and he pulls you in for a Red, you'll be sorry. . . ." In the same scene, workers complain of their lot. Although the pharmacist's helper spent four years at a university, he pays her less than he does his cook. The medicines she handles continually burn her dresses, and laundry is expensive. The dairymaid rises at 3:30 A.M., cleans the manure in the barn, brushes the cows, milks them, washes the pails with lye that burns her hands, and only afterward has a cup of coffee with a slice of bread and butter. Her lunch consists of potatoes and gravy, but no meat, though occasionally the housekeeper gives her an egg or she finds one. She milks as many as thirty gallons a day from the cows, but receives only two quarts per day. Her other food she must purchase from the farmer. Except for a free Sunday every fifth week, she works seven days a week.

At the Hiring Market, Puntila buys people as he would buy merchandise. There, more explicitly than elsewhere, human beings are commodities for hire by the wealthy classes who are their society's pillars. Sober Puntila treats men as commodities. If a laborer's pants are too good, he thinks he is too good to work; if too ragged, his character is bad. Nor does he want a smart worker, for he would spend all day calculating how many hours he has worked. Yet like the drunken Puntila, the sober Puntila says, "I like to be on friendly terms with my help." In both cases, friendliness is a means of exploitation. Between master and worker, Brecht thereby implies, there can be no friendliness.

Although the drunken Puntila professes to believe that human beings should not be marketed, he nevertheless hires workers at the Hiring Market. He is more socially harmful than sober Puntila, who acts more straightforwardly. To gullible workers, drunken Puntila usually gives friendliness and false expectations, rather than binding contracts. Caught in the middle, Matti tries to assist both the workers and his master. When drunken Puntila says he wants to hire a sickly looking worker because he likes his eyes, Matti—who recognizes the market will soon close and after that the worker will be unable to find a job—diplomatically advises Puntila that the man would collapse after working eleven and a half hours each day in the summer and that Puntila will fire him when he discovers the man cannot do the work or when he sees him in the sober light of the next morning. Since drunken Puntila will not permit Matti to turn him into the sordid landowner who is sober Puntila, Matti urges him to give the workers he hires contracts and earnest money to validate them. His entreaties are usually in vain. Drunken Puntila pledges his word, which he claims is as firm as a contract. Ironically, Puntila—in a properly businesslike manner—gives ten marks earnest money to Surkkala, a man the parson made Puntila promise to fire because he is a communist. When Puntila sobers up, he destroys the intentions of drunken Puntila. As Matti predicted, he fires the sickly looking worker, because he recognizes the work would be too difficult for him. When the man protests that the Hiring Market is closed, the sober Puntila—whose word, according to the drunken Puntila, stood firm—callously tells him he should have thought of that earlier and not taken advantage of his friendliness. And this man, whom drunken Puntila drove to his estate, must walk back five miles. The lesson of class antagonism is not lost on him: "That's what happens when you fall for their friendly act."

According to Brecht, workers should not accept promises of gifts from the upper classes, who—good intentions notwithstanding—would cheat them once they get what they want. A telephone operator tells a story about a landowner who once had to cross a six-mile frozen lake at night. While he knew the ice was cracked, he did not know where. Therefore, he promised one of his tenants a horse if he led the way. In the middle of the icy lake, he promised a calf. When they saw the village lights on the other side, he promised a watch; fifty yards from land, a sack of potatoes. Once they arrived safely on shore, the landowner gave the tenant a mark and complained how long it took to bring him there.

Brecht goes further. To accept gifts from landowners is implicitly to agree that they have the right to wealth that enables them to give gifts. To the contrary, says Brecht, they have no such right, for their wealth belongs to the workers. And friendship, symbolized by a gift, must be mutual. A character tells a story about an imprisoned communist who refuses to accept a gift of food that a landowner gave his mother for him. He rejects that right and that friendship. The characters who hear the story praise the communist.

As the first story reflects the scenes between Puntila and the sickly looking worker, the second story foreshadows the scene between Puntila and the communist Surkkala. When the parson tells sober Puntila that instead of firing Surkkala, drunken Puntila rehired him, Puntila is furious both at Surkkala for having accepted the earnest money and at himself for having given it, especially since he must now pay him three months wages as compensation for firing him. He sends for Surkkala, who brings his children so that they may learn at first hand what landowners are like. In the meantime, Puntila has got drunk again. What is especially significant is that even when drunk, Puntila refuses to keep Surkkala on. Although his reason is different, drunken Puntila's action, like that of sober Puntila, is to the advantage of Puntila the landowner. Because Surkkala is unhappy at Puntila Farms, the drunken Puntila respects him. He advises Surkkala's children to become communists, and he castigates himself as a parasite, just like any other capitalist. Nevertheless, Surkkala must leave. Puntila then gives the money to Surkkala: "minus ten." Even while drunk, Puntila does not neglect to deduct the ten marks he paid in advance. When he offers to shake hands with Surkkala before the worker goes, Surkkala refuses. The money, payment in lieu of wages for which he contracted, Surkkala accepts, for it is due him. The handshake, a gift of friendship, he rejects. Like the imprisoned communist, he recognizes there can be no friendship between master and worker.

In the climactic scene, the drunken Puntila indulges in a flight of fancy that represents poetry for him, but work for his menial, Matti. Both, says the master, should climb Mount Hatelma one day and see its famous view. "We can do it in spirit," he decides, inspired. *We* means that Matti will do the actual work—and after his regular working day is over, to boot. Coming after the firing of Surkkala, this exploitation is the last Matti intends to accept. Puntila commands Matti to build a mountain—not for "us," but for "me." Wrecking some of Puntila's costly furniture, Matti uses the wreckage and a few chairs to create an imaginary Mount Hatelma on a billiard table. As always, drunken Puntila regards his supposedly friendly relationship with Matti in terms of superior master and inferior servant. To have a superior Mount Hatelma, he demands that his subordinate "follow my instructions, because I know what is needed and what isn't, and I'm responsible. If I left you to your own resources, you'd build a mountain that wouldn't pay off—no view, no pleasure for me...." Like sober Puntila, drunken Puntila wants something that will *pay off*, and though he said *they* could climb the mountain and see its view, the pleasure he wants is for *himself*. Matti recognizes Puntila's values for exactly what they are. Starting to climb, Puntila worries that he might break his neck. Holding him up, Matti observes, "You can do that on level ground if you haven't got me to hold you up." As Matti knows, the master's existence depends on the menial's work. Puntila, but not his menial, stands atop the makeshift mountain to enjoy the imaginary view. The scene ends on a class-conscious note. Puntila eulogizes the land, lakes, and forests. Then: "Admit that your heart swells when you see all that." Says Matti, obediently but wryly, "My heart swells when I see your forests, Mr. Puntila."

Finally, Matti leaves Puntila. In a monologue, he concludes that master and worker cannot mix. "It's time your hired hands showed you their rears," says Matti, implying that the latter are more appropriate portions of the human anatomy to present to the upper classes. Wanted, he adds, is a reversal of the present social order, one wherein the working men will be the masters.

Although the society represented by landowner Puntila is potentially self-destructive, as symbolized by his drunkenness, that potential, Brecht demonstrates, is unrealizable. The drunken Puntila exploits and almost invariably acts to the benefit of the sober Puntila, who undoes whatever humane and socially beneficial actions the drunken Puntila commits. For the pillars of this society to collapse, the workers must refuse to prop them. Exit Surkkala, exit Matti. By the end of the play, neither works for Puntila. Without menials to do its work, can this society survive? Although Brecht does not dramatize the collapse of Puntila's society, he dramatizes the absurdity of expecting it to crumble through its submerged humanitarian impulses, and he indicates that only the workers can cause its destruction.

* * * *

In *Pillars of Society*, Ibsen presents a possibility of averting society's destruction: replace shaky foundations with sturdy pillars. In *Heartbreak House*, Shaw dramatizes the seeds of society's self-destruction, which its pillars are either unable or unwilling to avert and which likewise render them incapable of preventing imminent destruction from without. In *Puntila and Matti, His Hired Man*, the potential destruction of society derives from exploitation of the working classes, who might destroy their exploiters. Like Hector Hushabye, the drunken Puntila, who is one of society's pillars, recognizes the immorality of an unequal distribution of wealth and the need to abolish that society in order to create better social conditions for workers. Like Hector, he does nothing to change the situation but just talks about it. If this society is to be destroyed, according to the Marxist Brecht, only the workers can do the job. More strongly and clearly than *Pillars of Society* and *Heartbreak House*, *Puntila and Matti, His Hired Man* dramatizes the need for the destruction of capitalist society, and Brecht brings to the foreground the class that might accomplish the job. What is avoidable in Ibsen's play is imminent in Shaw's and necessary in Brecht's. Do these plays increasingly approach the truth of the matter? Rather, each dramatizes a different view of the matter.

5.

"Scrap It"—Money and Morality
An Enemy of the People, Major Barbara, Saint Joan of the Stockyards

"What do we do here when we spend years of work and thought and thousands of pounds of solid cash on a new gun or an aerial battleship that turns out just a hairsbreadth wrong after all?" asks the capitalist Andrew Undershaft in *Major Barbara*. First, he answers his own question: "Scrap it without wasting another hour or another pound on it." Next, he advises his religious daughter Barbara that because her "morality or . . . religion or what not . . . doesnt fit the facts," she should "scrap it and get one that does fit."

In *An Enemy of the People*, written almost a quarter of a century before *Major Barbara*, religion does not enter the picture except as a minor theme. However, morality and solid cash do, and they are major themes. In Ibsen's play, it is the moralist who demands that the capitalists face the facts and scrap what has turned out to be far more than a hairsbreadth wrong. By their refusal to do so, they not only divorce money from morality, they also divorce it from reality. As the quotation might lead one to expect, *Major Barbara* demonstrates more than one type of morality. In Shaw's play, the force that represents money proposes a union with an effective force of morality. By contrast, the forces of money in *Saint Joan of the Stockyards*, written a quarter of a century after *Major Barbara*, propose a union with ineffective forces of what are commonly—though, in Brecht's view, inaccurately—called morality. His play reveals irreconcilable differences between the forces of money and those of true morality. Ibsen's, Shaw's, and Brecht's different views of the conflicting or harmonious forces of money and morality shape this trio of plays.

* * * *

The opening scene of *An Enemy of the People* contrasts how

two brothers, who personify the conflicting forces of morality and money, use money. To Dr. Thomas Stockmann, who becomes an exemplar of morality, money is a source of sustenance: health for himself and others, and strength for the future. Whenever anyone enters their home, the doctor or his wife offers food. Underscoring the symbolic aspect of food, he tells his brother Peter that young people must have food "for strength! They're the ones who'll put a kick in the future, Peter." Mayor Peter Stockmann, who has poor digestion, refuses roast beef. In place of the sustenance offered in Thomas's house, and his own too, he emphasizes the value of money; he considers bread, butter, and tea to be healthier "and a bit more economical too." A poor judge of nutrition, the mayor turns out to be a poor judge of other aspects of health. Later, he refuses different health-related advice from his doctor-brother, who is better qualified to judge. Linking the mayor's excessive concern with money to his poor diet, the doctor laments that the only thing his brother has is "business, business. And all that damn weak tea he's always sloshing down." By contrast, Thomas pays no attention to business matters, eats roast beef, and shares his food with others. Whereas Peter saves money, Thomas spends it to nourish himself and others.

In the play's early scenes, Ibsen reveals other contrasting values between them. "On the whole," says the mayor, "there's a fine spirit of tolerance in this town of ours—a remarkable public spirit." According to Petra, the doctor's daughter, whose thoughts resemble her father's and who increasingly becomes identified with his viewpoints, the town is hypocritical rather than tolerant. "At home we have to keep quiet, and in school we have to stand there and lie to the children." Thomas, complains Peter, tends inveterately to go his own way, which the mayor regards as "nearly . . . inexcusable. The individual has to learn to subordinate himself to the whole—or, I should say, to those authorities charged with the common good." As mayor, Peter is of course one of those authorities to whom he demands individuals subjugate themselves. To him, unlike Thomas, it is such authorities, not the individual, who decide what is the common good.

From different characters, the subject of the spa reveals different values and attitudes. According to the mayor, these baths, which are a major industry, "will become the very life-principle of our town." Of what does this life-principle consist? To the mayor, money, but though he is the mayor—supposedly a servant of all the townspeople—he regards the monetary life-principle in terms of only certain social classes. "Land and property values are rising every day," he proudly declares. When Hovstad, editor of the *People's Courier*, points out that unemployment is down because of the spa, the mayor interprets this benefit in terms of its advantage to the classes he really serves: public welfare taxes, which the propertied classes pay, have been cut substantially.

Unlike his brother, the doctor's concern is not limited to certain classes, but extends to all citizens. Ibsen takes pains to establish Dr. Stockmann's honesty and professional integrity. Although the doctor, whom the spa employs, first assumed, as did everyone else, that the previous summer's visitors brought their diseases with them rather than contracted them at the baths, he decided, as a scientist should, to test that assumption. He sent samples of both drinking water and sea water to the university, which has proper equipment for a strict laboratory analysis. The result of the university's impartial analysis shows that the baths are polluted and, whether they are used internally or externally, they are injurious to health. To Dr. Stockmann, the moral issue is immediately clear-cut. One simply does not perpetuate a system that ruins people's health. Delighted that he will save lives by locating the problem in advance of the summer tourist season, he is equally delighted with what he conceives to be a simple solution to the problem. Because the source of this health hazard—which becomes a moral issue—is a money-making industry, a mill that pours poisonous wastes into the water that flows to the baths, the obvious remedy is to relay the water system so as to divert the course of the polluted water from the baths.

Although Thomas Stockmann, as doctor and scientist, regards the water system and the moral issue in isolation (locate the problem, find the solution, put it into effect), editor Hovstad, who considers himself a radical, recognizes that both are inextricably interrelated with money, for the owners of the baths are the wealthy classes, who influence or are members of the town's government. Money—and with it, politics—links to the moral issue. To Hovstad, the doctor's exposure of the situation is a means of effecting revolutionary social changes, one of which will be to replace the present ruling class with himself and people who share his views, which he calls liberal. Using the terms *liberal* and *radical* interchangeably, Hovstad regards anything that will oust the wealthy ruling clique as revolutionary. To Aslaksen too, the doctor's exposure links to money. Representative of the middle class—small businessmen and homeowners—he believes that the doctor's discovery will make the town a more prosperous tourist center by improving the spa, it will therefore enrich the small businessmen whose shops the tourists will patronize and benefit homeowners by increasing property values. Both Hovstad and Aslaksen believe Dr. Stockmann's discovery will benefit them.

Mayor Stockmann, who represents the wealthy classes that own the baths, thinks differently. His confrontation with his brother on this issue is the confrontation of money with morality. At present, the doctor insists, the baths are poison that is "foisted on poor, suffering creatures who . . . pay us exorbitant fees to gain their health back again." Ignoring the question of exorbitance, the mayor refers to the baths as "our major source of revenue." To make the changes Dr. Stockmann demands would cost several hundred thousand crowns, he claims, take at least two years, and in the meantime force the owners to close the baths. Besides, adds the mayor, if people hear the rumor that the town's waters are contaminated, they are unlikely to travel there to patronize the baths. What of the health hazard, which the doctor calls "guaranteed poison"? When money is involved, self-deception is easy, for few people want to regard themselves as killers of innocent victims for profit. "From your report," says the mayor, "I'm unable to persuade myself that the condition of the baths is as critical as you claim." As a sop to the doctor's conscience, he proposes that "in time the directors will more than likely agree to take under consideration to what extent—depending on the funds available—they can institute certain improvements." Seeing through such phrases as *in time, more than likely*, and *depending on*, Dr. Stockmann denounces Mayor Stockmann's proposal as "a deception, a lie, an out-and-out crime against the public and society at large!"

Not only is the source of the community's affluence poisoned, with roots in a lie, the monied people who own the baths are directly responsible for the social infection. As the doctor accuses his brother, who represents these people, he is the person responsible for having the water system for the baths laid out where it is now. Unwilling to remedy the situation, the monied people and their representative are equally unwilling to admit they caused it.

As a result of this confrontation, in which neither party capitulates, the mayor uses the power of money to persuade the doctor's supporters to abandon him. He, but not his brother, understands the qualities of these supporters. Before he visits them, the liberal Aslaksen reveals that although he fearlessly attacks national politicians, since he is confident that these attacks enhance his reputation as a fighting liberal but do no real damage, he is cautious about hurting local authorities, who if ousted might be replaced by people who could harm property owners. Not only is editor Hovstad afraid to offend Aslaksen, because no one else would extend him credit to print his paper, he fears to alienate religious readers from his politically liberal paper, and—though he himself is irreligious—he prints fiction that has conventionally religious or moral uplift in the same issue with articles that contain social denunciations. His assistant, Billing, who also calls himself liberal, has a vested interest in the conservative authorities. He has applied for a position in the town clerk's office. When the mayor visits this trio of his brother's supposedly staunch supporters, he tells them what he told him, and adds his opinion that the doctor's findings are suppositions rather than facts. He also mentions that the money to repair the water system will come not from the owners of the baths but from municipal loans, which will mean an increase in property taxes. With barely a murmur, all three capitulate.

An unanticipated result of the fraternal confrontation is the radicalization of the doctor, who perceives that the problem concerns more than sewers and water mains. All society must be "purged and disinfected." He aims to launch an "entire revolution." He then learns that the "solid majority" no longer stands behind him. Hovstad refuses to print Dr. Stockmann's exposé in the *People's Courier*, and Aslaksen will not print it separately even if the doctor pays for it himself. Undaunted, he determines to hold a mass meeting where he will read his article aloud.

In act 2, a representative of the reactionary politicians and wealthy classes turns against the doctor. In act 3, representatives of the middle class and liberals turn against him. In act 4, at the mass meeting, everyone turns against him. Ibsen is explicit: the assembled townspeople are *"from all levels of society"* and several speaking characters are workers. Manipulating the people, the mayor prevents the doctor from reading his exposé of the baths, and he accurately points out that the doctor's proposal would mean increased taxes for everyone. With equal accuracy, the middle-class Aslaksen declares that the doctor really wants a revolution. The people turn against him.

Dr. Stockmann then launches a jeremiad against reactionary and liberal leaders: "relics of a dying world of thought" whom free men should exterminate just as they would exterminate any predatory animal. As for the people they dupe, "The majority is never right. . . . The minority is always right. . . . The truths accepted by the masses now are the ones proclaimed basic by the advance guard in our grandfathers' time. We fighters on the frontiers today"—the advanced minority, that is—"we no longer recognize them."[1] The masses are "inert, unformed," and "no more than the raw material out of which a people is shaped." Therefore they have no right "to admonish and approve, to prescribe and to govern," whereas "the few spiritually accomplished personalities" have the right. When he compares common mongrels with thoroughbreds, he does not refer to social classes. "The kind of commonness I'm talking of isn't only found in the depths: it teems and swarms around us in society—right up to the top." Presumably, too, and the final act bears out this inference, the kind of thoroughbred to which he alludes is also found in every level of society. As one might expect, statements that the majority is always wrong and that only people as advanced as he is are right are not apt to win the support of the majority, whom liberal and reactionary politicians tell are always right. In this scene, they denounce Dr. Stockmann as the titular enemy of the people.

The first act shows many persons flocking around Dr. Stock-

1. Today, a statement like this, on the relativity of truth, is commonplace. In 1882, it was a daring, even shocking repudiation of what James McFarlane calls one of "the most cherished beliefs of the nineteenth-century liberal mind. . . . Stockmann's outburst marked the start of a complex and protracted change in the European mind, in which a growing instability was to be its most conspicuous feature." See "The Mind of Modernism," in *Modernism*, ed. Malcolm Bradbury and James McFarlane, p. 80.

mann's family; the final act shows its isolation. Thomas is fired from his position at the baths, and his enemies will try to ensure that he will fail in private medical practice. His daughter Petra loses her teaching job and his two sons are expelled from school. The landlord gives them notice to leave. For having permitted the doctor to use his house as a meeting place, the individualistic sea captain Horster is fired by the shipowner who employs him. In the last act, the only person other than the doctor's wife and children who stands by him is Horster, who in the first act says that at sea, as the doctor comes to believe about land, *all* hands should not stand to the wheel. When Dr. Stockmann decides not to leave town, as planned, because "this is the battleground; here's where the fighting will be," Horster offers to share his house with the doctor's family.

What of Thomas's father-in-law, the wealthy capitalist Morten Kiil, who owns the mill that pollutes the water that runs into the baths and poisons the visitors (ultimately, the source of the town's physical and moral pollution is a capitalist enterprise)? Despite the fact that the people brand the doctor a public enemy, and despite the mayor's statement that the doctor's findings do not convince him, the owners of the spa evidently believe what he says, for Kiil is able to buy their shares at a low price. Shares in hand, he tries to make more money by a different immoral means, blackmail. He bought the shares with the money he was to leave Thomas's wife and children. If the doctor recants and proclaims the waters to be unpolluted, she and her children, his heirs, will be millionaires. Otherwise, the shares will be worthless and Kiil will leave everything else he owns to charity. Dr. Stockmann refuses to recant.

It is no accident that Ibsen makes the play's chief capitalist the doctor's relative by marriage, and the play's chief politician, who also represents monied interests, the doctor's brother. Initially related to money and the political status quo, morality at the end of the play severs all connections with both, because both demand the repudiation of ethical conduct. Since the characters who exemplify these forces are relatives, Ibsen is able to stress forcefully the symbolic renunciation of these forces from each other.

In the first act, the audience learns, the doctor is a "contributor to the *People's Courier*." In the last act, he aims to become more than a courier. He aspires to be the people's leader and guide. Although Thomas believes in rule by an elite minority, this elite transcends social classes. Like Jesus, he calls for twelve disciples. With his daughter, he will teach them. His sons will account for two of these disciples. The others will come from the lowest class of society, the same class for whom he plans to continue to practice medicine (those who cannot afford to pay him, he says, are those who need him most): "boys off the street—regular little punks . . . I want to experiment with mongrels for a change. There might be some fantastic minds out there." Previously, he had called the masses unformed raw material. If present politicians shape such raw material, the masses will remain ignorant. If he, one of the advanced intellectual minority, tries to shape them, he might enable them to turn into "free-spirited and accomplished men." By contrast, the mayor believes that commoners are unteachable. Those "of peasant stock," he says in the first act, "never can learn any tact."

As the play concludes, the doctor recognizes that "the strongest man in the world is the one who stands most alone." Although the representative of morality loses the battle, he does not leave the field. Instead, he gathers his forces for future battle. While the spectacle of the doctor's family of four surrounding him when he says he stands alone lends some irony to what he says, it does not vitiate the statement, which is essentially straightforward, since the small group constitutes a single unit that stands in opposition to the vast majority. Whatever may happen, Ibsen suggests, it takes strength and courage to buck the multitude.

Before leaving the play, however, one must face three questions. To what extent is the doctor blameworthy? If to a large extent, the play's meaning changes. To what extent is he Ibsen's spokesman? If to a small extent, his position is questionable. What might be the logical consequences of the actions Ibsen dramatizes? This relates to the second question.

The worst one might say of Dr. Stockmann is that he is naive, pompous, and impetuous. He is naive in that he believes the problem of the polluted baths can be solved easily. Since he is a doctor and scientist rather than a businessman or engineer, such a failing does not constitute a serious character deficiency. He is occasionally comic (as when he offers a glass of sherry to someone who has just told him he belongs to the Temperance Union), and both naive and foolish, in that he believes people will back him on moral principles despite the fact that such a stand will hurt their income.[2] Again, he is a moral man rather than a businessman. Does such naiveté or folly necessarily constitute a major character flaw? Rather, it seems, Ibsen intends it to contrast with the reprehensible attitudes and actions of the mayor and Morten Kiil. Pompous, Dr. Stockmann has an inflated sense of his influence. But such an attribute has no bearing on the validity of his claims, and he is disabused of this notion. When he restricts his area of potential influence to twelve disciples, there is pompousness in the apparent humility, for he implicitly compares himself to Jesus. Even so, an aspirant to the role of savior could easily find a worse model to imitate. Although the doctor is impetuous, he confines his impetuousness to personal dealings and matters of principle—as does the sea captain, for that matter. What this amounts to is that neither man is a politician (Horster does not even vote). Considering the immorality of the politicians Ibsen portrays, such impetuousness, foolish as it might be, suggests openness, in contrast to deviousness. Moreover, in his own profession, the doctor is anything but impetuous. Before he announces the results of his findings, he subjects the facts to impartial scientific scrutiny.

In contrast to Ibsen's usual dramatic practice, Dr. Stockmann is pretty much the author's mouthpiece.[3] Because Ibsen's statements in his own person are virtually identical to the doctor's conclusions, these represent the play's thematic statements—in practice, as I have tried to demonstrate, and in intent as well. In letters written in 1872, ten years before he wrote *An Enemy of the People*, Ibsen asserted, "my fundamental principle in every field and domain [is] that the minority is always in the right" and "the man who stands alone is the strongest."[4] In letters written the same year as the play, he denounced "the so-called liberal press" and declared it would be impossible for him "to join a party that has the majority on its side." Reasserting that "The minority is always right," he explains, "I mean that minority which leads the van and pushes on to points the majority has

---

2. Maurice Valency makes this point in *The Flower and the Castle*, pp. 164–65.

3. Robert Brustein (*The Theatre of Revolt*, p. 71) calls Stockmann "very much like an author's sounding board" and *An Enemy of the People* itself Ibsen's most straightforwardly polemical play.

4. Evert Sprinchorn, ed., *Ibsen: Letters and Speeches*, pp. 118, 123.

not yet reached." And he laments the decay of the "aristocracy of mind and spirit."[5] By *aristocracy*, he makes clear in an 1885 speech, he—like Dr. Stockmann—means "not . . . a nobility of *birth*, nor of that of *wealth*, nor of that of *knowledge*, neither of that of an *ability* or talent. I am thinking of a nobility of character, of a nobility of will and spirit. Nothing else can make us free." As to the source of such nobility or aristocracy, Ibsen is more explicit than the doctor, who regards the masses as raw material and asks his son to bring him lower-class boys from the street, that he may teach them. Says Ibsen: "This nobility . . . will come to us from two groups that have not as yet been irreparably harmed by party pressure. It will come to us from our women and from our workingmen."[6] Clearly, Dr. Stockmann's interpretation of events is Ibsen's.

What might be the logical consequences of the actions Ibsen dramatizes? Because he takes such care to stress the doctor's integrity and his ability as a scientist, the failings of the water system, as Dr. Stockmann predicts, "will come to light sooner or later anyway." When Horster says in the last act, "People will come around in their thinking, Doctor," the doctor replies, "Yes, maybe after it's too late." The only way people will come to agree with him is the only way the baths' deficiencies will come to light, when more visitors contract disease and perhaps die. If they die, agreement by the majority will indeed be too late. In either case, the divorce between the town's financial prosperity and the doctor's morality is absolute. If the owners of the baths had heeded the doctor's advice, morality would have won and they themselves might eventually have prospered. After all, one has only the mayor's word that repairs would be too expensive, take too long, and scare away future visitors. As matters stand, the owners' recently burgeoning business fails—as, indeed, they themselves realize when they sell their shares to Morten Kiil. Denying the demands of morality, they ironically create the conditions of their financial ruin.

* * * *

Like *An Enemy of the People*, a key question of *Major Barbara* is whether money will make morality its servant or whether

5. Ibid., pp. 198–99.
6. Ibid., p. 249.

moral forces will put money to their own use. In direct contrast to *An Enemy of the People*, *Major Barbara* culminates with the union of the forces of money and morality. Whereas Ibsen calls for a cultivated aristocracy of the spirit, Shaw calls for jobs with good salaries, since only they can enable people to become cultivated and spiritually ennobled.

The relationship between money and morality is the subject of the play's opening scene: Is it moral to take money from a man who earns it in an immoral profession? "What's the matter?" Stephen's and the play's first line is not only the signal for exposition, it is also a key question of the play, though not in the sense that Stephen intends. The matter is larger than a single family, which Stephen and his mother, Lady Britomart, discuss. Traditionally and in this instance, the family stands for the human family. Later, when Undershaft's estranged wife introduces his family, which includes their daughters' fiancés, Shaw suggestively has him express surprise that it is so large. As the play unfolds, it turns out to be larger than the number to which they refer. What is the matter with society? Although Undershaft, in his advice that Barbara scrap her useless ideas, partly answers the question, Shaw raises it at the play's outset.

Lady Britomart's response to Stephen's question, the play's second line, suggests that whatever may be the matter, she will get to it in her own good time. A liberal (her family, she soon boasts, is Whig, a party from which the liberals derive), she does not share the sense of urgency her son displays and tells him she will attend to him presently.

The matter she discusses is fundamental both to the family and society: money, which the play demonstrates is the basis of all aspects of society. In particular, this family needs more money because the three children will marry. The matter explained, Lady Britomart next proposes the solution: her estranged capitalist husband Undershaft will provide the money. Later, he provides the same solution to the larger matter. The power of Undershaft's money is pervasive. According to his wife, he has all Europe under his thumb, and she adds—in increasing order of importance—that neither the prime minister, *The Times*, nor the lord chamberlain (whose duties at the time included theatre censorship) would dare touch him. As the first act reveals, the aristocracy (represented by Lady Britomart) depends on his money, which he can give or withhold. Later acts demonstrate that his money, because he can give or withhold it, also controls religious institutions and, as Lady Britomart suggests here, the government and press as well.

In more ways than one, money is the inescapable matter of *Major Barbara*. So inescapable is it, that Lady Britomart explicitly declares, "it is not a question of taking money from him or not: it is simply a question of how much." As the play develops, the implication of the question of how much extends from the amount necessary to live well to the amount necessary to live morally and to achieve salvation.

In addition, the opening scene embodies a lesson in reality and power, which is another significant aspect of *Major Barbara*. In his refusal to associate himself with his father's money, which he regards as tainted because it was earned through the manufacture of weapons of war, the conventionally moralistic Stephen unrealistically dissociates himself from the power that money can give. In her acceptance of that money on her own terms, Lady Britomart, though she too is conventionally moralistic, demonstrates a realistic attitude, for she recognizes that no other source of money exists. Trace the source of any money, according to Shaw, and it leads to Undershaft or others like him. Lady Britomart aims to use Undershaft's money for specific ends, which do not conflict with any of his. Later, Barbara and Cusins learn what reality and power really are. When they accept Undershaft's offer, they aim to use it for their own ends, which may not fall so easily in line with Undershaft's goals as he hopes.[7]

In the first act, morality links with money. While Lady Britomart explains to Stephen what the matter is, she ties it to Undershaft's insistence that he follow his family's tradition to adopt its successors and leave the business to them—a moral principle according to Undershaft, who would consider himself dishonest were he to do otherwise, an immoral principle according to Lady Britomart, who considers the tradition improper and unnatural. Morality links with money, but beginning with the first scene, the play questions conventional notions about both. Representative of money (capitalism), Undershaft reveals his connection with religion, which his daughter (a major in the Salvation Army) represents. Not only does he assert that religion is

---

7. For an analysis of the play's structure, including these aspects, see my *Bernard Shaw, Playwright*, pp. 78–90.

the only subject that capable people like himself care for, this munitions maker also expresses interest in the Salvation Army, whose motto, Blood and Fire, he says might be his own—a statement that foreshadows his purchase of the Army. Unconventionally, he dissociates himself from capitalists who keep their financial interests and their morality in separate compartments. A Christianity that would enjoin him not to resist evil would bankrupt him. His morality must therefore accommodate his munitions business.

Whereas act 1 presents a view from the top of the social scale, act 2 presents a view from the bottom. The setting of act 1 shows the expensive home that is the result of a great deal of money; the setting of act 2 shows the workshop of the financially impoverished force of a religion that embraces traditional morality. However, the subject of the expository first scenes of both acts is the same: the acquisition of money by people who do not have it from those who do. In the first act, a capitalist's family obtains it from him; in the second act, unemployed workers obtain it from a capitalist-supported institution.

Snobby Price has no difficulty in morally reconciling his acceptance of food from the Army. Because capitalist thieves have stolen many meals from him, he advises Peter Shirley, "Get a bit of your own back." To Snobby, the exchange is a fair trade. Shirley, however, can reconcile his morality with the Army's charity only when Jenny Hill tells him that once he finds a job, he can repay the Army if he wishes. Like Price and Shirley, Bill Walker regards morality in terms of fair monetary exchange. Because he hit Jenny Hill, their accounts will be even if Todger Fairmile hits him. When he returns from his encounter, Barbara—as if in recognition of Bill's viewpoint—asks whether Fairmile has paid him back. Since he has not, Bill tries to pay Jenny back with a pound. As the three workers tacitly recognize, money is the basis of morality.

Money and morality interconnect. The millionaire Undershaft calls himself a mystic. What is his religion? "I am a Millionaire. That is my religion." What one needs for salvation, he says, is "money and gunpowder," that is, money, freedom, and power. Only with them can one afford honor, justice, truth, love, and mercy. Explicitly, Undershaft brings together religion and money. "Religion is our business at present," he tells Cusins, because only through religion can they win Barbara. He says that his gospel includes money, then announces that to win Barbara he will buy the Salvation Army.

Just as the business of the capitalist Undershaft is at present religion, which the play dramatizes, the major activity of the religionist Barbara is at present money, which it also dramatizes. Even before Undershaft buys the Army, Shaw thereby hints, Barbara has already gone part of the way to him. When she returns from a religious meeting, her first speech concerns not religion but money, and she soon admits she has begun to worry more about the collection than about people's souls. Upon her revelation that contributions were only two pence shy of five shillings, Undershaft offers to contribute the remainder, calling it "The millionaire's mite"—a pun on the widow's mite,[8] and a homonym of *might*, which he demonstrates later in the act. When Bill Walker—having failed to square accounts by making Todger Fairmile hit him—offers the Army a pound, Barbara's proud declaration that the Army will not be bought prompts his sarcastic comment that since she is an earl's granddaughter she (representing the Army) would consider nothing less than a hundred pounds. Promptly, Undershaft offers the other ninety-nine if she will take Bill's one. She chides her father for his extravagance: "Bill offers twenty pieces of silver," she says, referring to the fact that a (predecimalized) pound is the equivalent of twenty shillings. "All you need offer is the other ten." Later, the Army accepts Undershaft's offer of five thousand pounds, but here as later, Barbara refuses any money from him. Bill Walker, whose essential understanding is correct (he errs only in the amount), underscores the relationship between money and religious institutions when he throws his pound on the Salvation Army drum and demands Barbara take it or leave it.[9] After Undershaft buys the Salvation Army, Bill recognizes that he, not Barbara, was correct. "Wot prawce selvytion nah?" he asks her, explicitly identifying the monetary basis of religious salvation.

In an exceptionally penetrating article on the play, to which

8. Mark 12:42.
9. The Berkeley Repertory Theatre's 1977 production of *Major Barbara* vivified the point when Bill threw not a pound note but two ten-shilling coins, which resounded as they hit the drum. This conforms to the intent of Shaw, who specifies that Bill throws a sovereign, which the paper money superseded. In recent productions, including the 1940 film, the pound note has become traditional.

much of the foregoing is indebted, Sidney P. Albert—who takes his title ("The Price of Salvation") from Bill Walker's question—observes that the "key moral relationships among the characters are dramatized in economic terms." Religious conceptions, he demonstrates, receive monetary metaphors. Confident that she will succeed in converting Bill, for instance, Barbara challenges him to resist as much as possible so that the Army will not get him cheap. Barbara learns that the Army has its price. After Undershaft buys "the Army's integrity and independence," Albert points out, "Barbara performs the ritual of pinning her silver S brooch on her father's collar. . . . She has actually completed the act of purchase, turning over to him the goods he has bought."[10]

On the one hand, Mrs. Baines is right to take the money offered by Bodger and Undershaft, for she, like Lady Britomart (and Shaw), recognizes the impossibility of distinguishing between tainted and untainted money. Also, as Shaw says in his preface, the Army admits it "would take money from the devil himself and be only too glad to get it out of his hands and into God's." In this connection, Shaw's dramatic point is not whether Mrs. Baines is justified, but that in the society of which she and the Salvation Army are part, it is impossible for the Army to do the work it wants to do. At its source, the work is compromised. One of the play's better-known exchanges comes after Undershaft gives her the money the Army needs. "Thank God!" exclaims Mrs. Baines. Asks Undershaft: "You dont thank me?" As his quip suggests, the Army depends on him rather than on God for support, and it does his work rather than God's. Ironically, when the Army accepts his money, it simultaneously becomes financially solvent and morally bankrupt.

As Shaw says in his preface to the play, "Churches are suffered to exist only on condition that they preach submission to the State as at present capitalistically organized." The Salvation Army "is even more dependent than the Church on rich people who would cut off supplies at once if it began to preach that indispensable revolt against poverty which must also be a revolt against riches."

The play dramatizes these statements. When Cusins asserts that the Salvation Army is the church of the poor and therefore

---

10. Sidney P. Albert, "The Price of Salvation: Moral Economics in *Major Barbara*," *Modern Drama*, pp. 307, 314.

not for sale, Undershaft tells him that all religious organizations sell themselves to the rich in order to exist. Like the others, he forcefully argues, the Army draws the teeth of the poor. Does the Army preach sobriety? Sober workmen are good for business because they ensure larger profits. For a similar reason, he prefers honest workers. Since the Army preaches the virtues of attachment to home and family, workers will put up with anything sooner than change their jobs. Similarly better that the Army makes workers happy: it thereby provides a safeguard against revolution. Does the Army make them unselfish? By doing so, it makes them indifferent to their interests, which suits him. If it puts workers' thoughts on heavenly things, it thus turns their minds from trade unionism and socialism.

The workers understand these effects. In Snobby Price's words, the Army "combs our air and makes us good little blokes to be robbed and put upon." To prove the validity of this view, Mrs. Baines—attempting to persuade Undershaft to contribute money to the Army—reminds him that in 1886 the poor broke the windows of the rich men's clubs in Pall Mall and that were it not for the Army, similar rioting would have erupted this winter. When she calls upon Snobby Price to confirm her statement, he obliges. Ironically, Undershaft agrees that her methods are "convenient and gratifying to all large employers of labor."

In Shaw's dramatization of the relationship between religious institutions and money, the Fabian reveals himself to be more Marxist than his Marxist critics, who accuse him of selling out to capitalism in this play. In a well-known aphorism, Karl Marx calls religion "the opium of the people." In context, the statement demonstrates a more complex view than the short excerpt might indicate:

> The wretchedness of religion is at once an expression of and a protest against real wretchedness. Religion is the sigh of the oppressed creature, the heart of a heartless world and the soul of soulless conditions. It is the opium of the people.
> The abolition of religion as the illusory happiness of the people is a demand for their true happiness. The call to abandon illusions about their condition is the call to abandon a condition which requires illusions. Thus, the critique of religion is the critique in embryo of the vale of tears of which religion is the halo.[11]

11. Karl Marx, *Critique of Hegel's "Philosophy of Right,"* trans. Annette Jolin and Joseph O'Malley, p. 131.

To provide opium to sufferers whose pain it relieves is a compassionate act. By doing so, however, religion fails to alleviate the social conditions that create the suffering. Better than compassionate opium, says Marx, one should remove these conditions. Though not identical with Marx's view—since unlike Marx, Shaw is religious—*Major Barbara* dramatizes a view that is remarkably close to it. When General William Booth, founder of the Salvation Army, chose Blood and Fire as his motto rather than the cross, says Shaw in his preface, he was particularly inspired, and the motto, together with the militant form of organization, suggests the Salvationists' recognition that "they must actually fight the devil instead of merely praying at him." What Shaw objects to, he says in a quip that recalls Marx's admonition to abandon illusions and conditions that require illusions, is that the Salvationists "have not quite ascertained his correct address."

To Shaw, society's first order of business is the elimination of poverty.[12] This need precedes the desirability of spiritual regeneration, as Ibsen would have it, and precedes the desirability of completely reconstituting society along socialist lines, as Brecht would have it. Under present social conditions, according to Shaw, one can—and therefore should—destroy poverty. To impress upon readers and audiences the need to eradicate poverty, Shaw does more than call it undesirable or immoral, for even though both terms are accurate they are insufficiently shocking or novel to attract attention. In his preface to the play, he calls it criminal, and in the play he has Undershaft call it "The worst of crimes," for it blights entire cities, spreads pestilence, and pulverizes the souls of everyone who sees, hears, or smells it. Through Undershaft, Shaw appeals to selfishness as one reason to eliminate poverty. Poor people "force us to do away with our own liberties and to organize unnatural cruelties for fear they should rise against us and drag us down into their abyss." Not everyone fears crime, Undershaft adds, but everyone fears poverty. In his preface, Shaw in his own person emphasizes that Let Him Be Poor really means "Let him be ignorant. Let him become a nucleus of disease. Let him . . . drag his fellows down to his own price by selling himself to do their work. Let his habi-

---

12. See, for example, his explanation to Beatrice Webb, partly paraphrased and partly quoted, in her *Our Partnership*, p. 315.

tations turn our cities into poisonous congeries of slums. Let his daughters infect our young men with the diseases of the streets. . . ." And he concludes rhetorically, "This being so, is it really wise to let him be poor?"

Since one can destroy so monstrous a crime under capitalism, Shaw sees no reason to delay. Partly because of this, he makes Undershaft, who rids his factory town of poverty, not just any capitalist, but one whose particular business many people find reprehensible: the manufacture of armaments, instruments of slaughter. If even such a capitalist can do the job, according to Shaw, then let the job be done.

For another reason too, Shaw makes Undershaft a munitions manufacturer. Although the play is a parable, with the production of munitions a metaphor of making war on war, Shaw is earnest and straightforward when he has Undershaft insist that one should wage it and when he has him call the willingness to kill the only test of conviction. "I, who have preached and pamphleteered like any Encyclopedist," states Shaw in his preface, "have to confess that my methods are of no use," and he urges that "it is for the poor to repudiate poverty when they have had enough of it."

Readers, audiences, and critics often tend to regard the capitalist Undershaft as spokesman for the socialist Shaw. To a certain extent he is. Like Shaw, he perceives poverty to be a crime that must be destroyed. Unlike Ibsen's capitalists in *An Enemy of the People*, and unlike the Salvation Army in *Major Barbara*, Shaw's capitalist in this play is a true vehicle of morality, for he creates social conditions under which people may make themselves moral. He saves his workers' souls just as he saved Barbara's soul, by providing money enough for decent food, clothing, and housing.

Yet socialist Shaw takes pains to remind readers and audiences that Undershaft is a capitalist. Despite his perception that poverty is a crime and his elimination of this crime from his factory town, he is himself a blight on a society that should work primarily for the benefit of all the people rather than for the enrichment of his class. In what is still one of the most shocking speeches in this 1905 play, Shaw has Undershaft boast that it is he and the class he represents who create wars, raise prices, and mold public opinion, not elected officials or supposedly independent journalists. When Stephen refers to the government of his country, Undershaft sets him straight: "*I am the government of your country: I, and Lazarus.*" Amateurs like Stephen, sitting in Parliament, which Undershaft calls a "foolish gabble shop," cannot possibly govern the firm of Undershaft and Lazarus. Instead,

> You will do what pays u s. You will make war when it suits us, and keep peace when it doesnt. You will find out that trade requires certain measures when we have decided on those measures. When I want anything to keep my dividends up, you will discover that my want is a national need. When other people want something to keep my dividends down, you will call out the police and the military.

In return, Undershaft's newspapers will support, applaud, and make him imagine he is a great statesman. Emphatically, Undershaft concludes that it is he who pays the piper and calls the tune. His chief concern, like that of any other capitalist, is to make profits. Unlike the nineteenth-century robber barons, Undershaft perceives that the the elimination of the crime of poverty is not inimical to profits. Notwithstanding the substitution of well-paying jobs for poor-paying or no jobs, the result of his social improvement is not the elimination of class stratification, but rather an immense profit, which accrues to him. Representative of money, with morality a byproduct, Undershaft subscribes to the Armorer's Faith, which is to sell arms to anyone who pays well for them, no matter what his principles may be. No "morality mongering" for Undershaft, who—befitting his motto—is "unashamed" in his efforts to acquire greater profits through munitions-making. When he announces that good news has arrived from Manchuria, the goodness has to do with money, not morality. The victor does not concern him. The good news is that the product his firm manufactured is successful. The play provides no indication that socialist Shaw regards the accomplishment of capitalist Undershaft as the final word in social evolution, but a great deal to indicate otherwise. To Shaw, here as elsewhere, no word is final. Another achievement is always possible.

When Cusins and Barbara agree to join Undershaft, their acquiescence does not constitute capitulation. What he offers is power. To Cusins, the otherwise powerless intellectual, he provides the opportunity to turn ideas into deeds. Failure to accept Undershaft's offer to run the factory would be to choose what

Shaw calls "the Impossibilist position,"[13] which would leave Cusins as he is, unable to actualize any ideas he might have. What finally nails the Greek professor is Undershaft's wily paraphrase of the platonic ideal, that society can be saved either when Greek professors become makers of gunpowder or when makers of gunpowder become Greek professors. The man of thought agrees to become a man with the power to translate thought into action.

What does Cusins plan to do that differs from what Undershaft does? In act 2, he tells Undershaft that Barbara and he love the common people. Although Undershaft mocks such love, neither Cusins nor Barbara recants this sentiment. To the contrary, Cusins reaffirms it to Barbara at the end of act 3, after his debate with Undershaft, and he enunciates his goal of arming the common people "against the lawyers, the doctors, the priests, the literary men, the professors, the artists, and the politicians, who, once in authority, are more disastrous and tyrannical than all the fools, rascals, and imposters." He wants to give the common people a power "strong enough to force the intellectual oligarchy to use its genius for the general good." Work for the general good differs significantly from work for the immense profit of factory owners. In a Fabian fashion, Cusins hopes to build upon Undershaft's social advance, to turn the capitalism of Perivale St. Andrews—and by extension England—into a socialist democracy.[14]

What of the Armorer's Faith? Explicitly, Cusins repudiates it. He plans to sell cannons to whomever he pleases. Although Undershaft replies that from the moment Cusins succeeds to the inheritance he will never again do as he pleases, one need not accept Undershaft's word in the matter. While it is true that a social position may shape an individual, it is also true that an

---

13. Letter to Gilbert Murray, 7 October 1905, in *Collected Letters 1898–1910*, ed. Dan H. Laurence, p. 566.

14. Emma Goldman calls *Major Barbara* "one of the most revolutionary plays. In any other but dramatic form the sentiments uttered therein would have condemned the author to long imprisonment for inciting to sedition and violence." See *The Social Significance of Modern Drama*, p. 195. For a discussion of this scene written sixty years after Goldman's fine appreciation, see my *Bernard Shaw, Playwright*, pp. 283–84.

individual may shape that position. In act 2, Cusins tenaciously tells Undershaft that whenever he feels he must have anything, he gets it; since he feels he must have Barbara, Undershaft must regard the issue as settled. The future father-in-law capitulates. In the third act, Cusins defeats Undershaft in Undershaft's own area, business, when he persuades his prospective father-in-law to raise his salary. On the question of Cusins's hours of work, Shaw is ambiguous. When Undershaft tells him to report at six in the morning, Cusins firmly replies that he will not do so on any account; eleven to five will be his hours. Apparently, Undershaft capitulates again. He tells Cusins to come when he pleases, but he adds that within a week he will come at six and stay until Undershaft makes him leave for the sake of the younger man's health. While the play's final line is Undershaft's reminder that Cusins be in his office the next morning at six, Shaw specifies no response from Cusins. Because the outcome remains ambiguous, Shaw—who depicts what is (a character's intention) rather than what will be—keeps open the possibility that Cusins will have his way in this matter as in others.

Several matters, however, are unambiguous. First, Undershaft gets what he wants. What he wants, though, is not simply someone to replace him. Cusins will *succeed* him. As successor, Cusins agrees to write his own motto upon the wall beside those of his predecessors, and he clearly enunciates his social goal, perhaps the basis of that motto, which differs significantly from the Armorer's Faith of Undershaft.[15] Apropos, the discovery of vocation is an important related theme in the play. In the third act, Undershaft discovers one for Stephen. Before the play begins, Barbara discovers her own, though, as we shall soon see, she changes her place of employment, or in Shaw's terms, fights the devil at a different address. In the final act, Cusins discovers his vocation, which involves more than the acceptance of an administrative position. His enunciation of what he wants to attain vis-à-vis the common people is his discovery of a purpose in life, and his acceptance of the position Undershaft offers is an acceptance of the means by which he might achieve it.

When Undershaft forces Barbara to admit that her morality or religion does not fit the facts of life and challenges her to scrap it in favor of one that does, she rises to the challenge.

15. See my "Undershaft Maxims," *Modern Drama*, p. 99.

Using her father's social improvements at Perivale St. Andrews as a stepping stone, she aims to inspire individual regeneration while her husband tries to create further social advances. To refuse to do so would be to become as ineffective as the Salvation Army is. Like the Army, she accepts Undershaft's money; unlike the Army, she accepts what the Army is not offered, power. In Perivale St. Andrews, she will work not with starving people, who like Snobby Price and Rummy Mitchens would pretend to anything in order to eat, but with fullfed and quarrelsome people with a sense of their own dignity, whose acceptance of the salvation she offers would be based on free choice and therefore sincere. Paralleling Cusins's statement of principle about the workers, she declares that they think her father should be obliged to them because it is they who make so much money for him, and she adds what her father would not add, that she agrees with them. As Undershaft's workers are to him, so is she to God, his worker: "When I die, let him be in my debt, not I in his; and let me forgive him as becomes a woman of my rank."

Partly for this reason, perhaps, Shaw makes Undershaft a foundling, which gives Barbara what she calls the rank of a daughter of a foundling. She is not tied to the values or prejudices of any specific social class. Shaw stresses that Undershaft, though himself a foundling, is primarily a capitalist; Stephen, the son of a foundling, is a liberal; Sarah, a foundling's daughter, has the attitudes of high society; and Cusins, technically a foundling, is primarily an intellectual. Yet he emphasizes that because of Barbara's unorthodox religious views, she—in contrast to her siblings—has "no class . . . I come straight out of the heart of the whole people." She is neither proletarian nor nonproletarian.

With what kind of workers will she contend? Shaw does not leave the answer to the audience's imagination. Instead, he provides two examples. One is Bilton, the factory worker who is uppish with Lomax and unintimidated by either Lady Britomart or Undershaft. The other is Peter Shirley. Although he was fired from one job because he was too old, Shaw ironically has Undershaft give him a job as timekeeper. While his new job is appropriate to his saintly name—he keeps time at the gates of what one character calls a heavenly city—this aspect is ironic too, for Shirley is an atheist. In a different way from Bilton, he represents a challenge to Barbara.

In the first act, when Barbara and Undershaft agree to visit each other's place of business, she warns that his visit might result in his giving up his cannons for the Salvation Army, and he warns that her visit might end in her giving up the Army for his cannons. In different senses, each warning is prescient.[16] Although Undershaft does not give up his cannons for the sake of the Salvation Army, he plans to surrender them to a successor who will marry his Salvationist daughter. Although she gives up the Salvation Army, she does not give up salvationism for cannons, but instead plans to use what the cannons represent, money and power, for salvationism. Money and morality, major themes of the play, interconnect, interinfluence, and finally fuse. With the ascension of Cusins and Barbara to the seat of power, represented by Undershaft's factory, money and morality join, each the servant of the other. Dramatizing and discussing what Bill Walker refers to as the price of salvation, *Major Barbara* demands social improvement as the cost of spiritual regeneration.

* * * *

In *An Enemy of the People*, capitalists, refusing to face facts about their business, scrap morality, which they perceive to threaten profits. In *Major Barbara*, a capitalist faces business facts; he persuades a religionist to scrap a morality that does not conform to reality and to adopt one that does. In *Saint Joan of the Stockyards*, the most prominent capitalist knows the facts before any of his competitors, scraps his stocks when the new facts indicate the stocks will become unprofitable, and manipulates his competitors into scrapping theirs, which he buys when he, but not they, know they are about to become profitable. In this play, the most prominent moralist scraps one view after another when she learns it fails to fit the facts, and finally she scraps religion entirely. Like *An Enemy of the People* and unlike *Major Barbara*, *Saint Joan of the Stockyards* concludes with a divorce between money and morality.[17]

Unlike both plays, Brecht's is set in the United States (Chi-

---

16. See Alfred Turco, Jr., *Shaw's Moral Vision: The Self and Salvation*, p. 213.
17. From a different viewpoint, Eric Bentley compares Shaw's and Brecht's plays. See *Theatre of War*, pp. 201–5.

cago) rather than Europe, but—also unlike both plays—the setting is abstract: a large, major industrial city in a capitalist country. Unlike both plays, Brecht's includes representatives of a political organization that in his view might ultimately make morality prevail over capitalism: the Communist party. Whereas Ibsen's play dramatizes a stillborn revolution and Shaw's discusses but does not dramatize revolution, Brecht's dramatizes a revolution that begins, but fails.

The first two scenes of *Saint Joan of the Stockyards* establish the play's central themes and motifs. These revolve around the stock market that controls what happens in the stockyards; the moral, religious Joan; and the relationships among morality, religion, capitalists, and workers.

The first scene begins with a demonstration of the workings of large-scale capitalism: Mauler reads a letter from his Wall Street associates about an impending drop in prices on the stock exchange, partly because of a shrinking world market, and the desirability to sell his stocks before others learn the news. With this letter, Brecht not only extends the scope of the play's action beyond the immediate locale, he also establishes the international nature of capitalism.

In addition, the scene contrasts monetary and moral concerns. A ruthless businessman, Mauler deludes himself, while he defrauds a competitor, that his motives are entirely compassionate. Because his heart swelled at the sight of a dying ox who dumbly gazed toward heaven as it expired, he says, and not because of the Wall Street letter, he has decided to sell his stocks. Despite Mauler's successful self-delusion, he never permits his compassion to interfere with his profits. Rather than present a capitalist with humane impulses that might make audiences or readers sympathize with him, Brecht presents one whose self-delusions about such impulses are only self-indulgence. Sympathetic toward suffering animals, or so he claims, he is callous toward human beings. Although he professes to be upset by the death of an animal, the destruction of business rivals or the starvation of workers does not upset him at all. As his broker remarks, Mauler slaughters people rather than steers.

To the capitalist Mauler, who sells and buys cattle, people too are commodities for sale and purchase. He sees everything in such terms. According to a meat-packer, Mauler regards nature itself as merchandise and the very air as for sale.

In scene 2, set in the stockyards, the workers underscore Mauler's view of human beings. Do the capitalists believe workers will "stand around like steers" without doing anything about their wage cut? they ask.[18] Regarded as beasts, they are also regarded as commodities, and they stand, as they say, "ready to sell" themselves in the labor market. Like cattle, however, they have glutted the market, and no one wants to buy. The conception of man as both cattle and commodity is exemplified in another scene, which discloses that a worker, Luckerniddle, fell into a boiler, was caught in the bacon maker, and emerged from the machine as part of the bacon that will be packaged and offered for sale. As an apprentice puts it, with resonances far wider than the particular situation, Luckerniddle is going into the world "as bacon."

With such a view of mankind, the result is what the title character calls "dehumanized humanity." Into "a world like a slaughterhouse," Joan comes in the second scene to reestablish God. But in a world where human beings are treated in the image of commodities rather than of God, the morality she would bring has no place. By the end of the day, Brecht's legend informs the audience, Joan and the other Black Straw Hats have "ACCOMPLISHED JUST ABOUT NOTHING."

As Shaw does in acts 1 and 2 of *Major Barbara*, Brecht in scenes 1 and 2 of *Saint Joan of the Stockyards* presents views of society first from the top, then from the bottom. Throughout *Saint Joan of the Stockyards* are images of high and low. Brecht calls Joan's entry in the second scene her "FIRST DESCENT INTO THE DEPTHS." Not only do such images suggest class hierarchies under capitalism, they also suggest celestial and diabalonian spheres appropriate to the conception of morality implied by the title. However, Brecht does more than suggest. In scene 2, the workers more than once call the factory their hell, references that directly relate their suffering to capitalism. Ironically, their hell is simultaneously cold (because of the freezing weather) and hot (because of their smoldering grievances, which create what a stockbroker elsewhere in the play refers to as "cities that are burning from below"). Above is the comfortably

---

18. Quotations from *Saint Joan of the Stockyards* are from Frank Jones's most recent translation.

heated stock exchange, where capitalists are cool toward the workers' plight. In the world of capitalism, the area inhabited by the capitalists may be topmost in the earthly regions, but it is not heaven. "Unshakable above us," declaim the Packers, "stands economic law, the not-to-be-known." But the Marxist Brecht exposes this view as capitalism's justification of its actions.

From a Marxist viewpoint, Brecht's play dramatizes a system of exploitation, riven by class conflict. The confronting "givers and takers of work," says Paulus Snyder, head of the Black Straw Hats, are "warring fronts, irreconcilable." In war, he who does not win, must lose. Unless Mauler is "the best man in [his] class," he recognizes, he must "take the dark road down to the yards [himself]." Unless he exploits better than the other exploiters, exploits the exploiters as well as those whom they exploit, he will become one of the exploited. Though they are foils to each other, exploiters and exploited do not usually confront each other directly. To deal with the workers, the capitalists use surrogates, such as religious institutions (purveyors of morality), to draw the workers' teeth, and—should these fail—the police and army (purveyors of force).

To two social questions, Brecht provides Marxist answers as Joan learns the economic bases of capitalist society and the relationship between money and morality. What causes the sufferings of the workers? Forces of money, Joan learns, not those of morality. How can one create a better world? Not through prayer, pious phrases, or watery soup, she discovers, for these are mere palliatives, offered by the Black Straw Hats, who serve the capitalists. Neither is Mauler's belief true, she comes to understand, that before one can change the world, human nature must change. Nor is nonviolence effective, she also learns. Instead, she concludes, one must reject palliatives, reject the notion that humanity has an unchanging essence, reject God, and employ violence.

Brecht demonstrates how and why the stock market operates, together with its effects upon capitalists and workers. To the foreground, Brecht brings the stock market and the stockyards, the working places of capitalists and laborers. Derived from a Marxist view of capitalism, *Saint Joan of the Stockyards* employs an episodic structure based on two interconnected patterns.[19] One centers upon money: four shifts in economic relationships, each change heralded by a letter Mauler receives from his New York associates. The other centers upon morality: to help the suffering workers, Joan descends three times into what Brecht calls "THE DEPTHS," the world of the workers where in each instance disillusionment precedes learning. Although the two structures interrelate, their separation as patterns of action is a structural bifurcation that reflects Brecht's view of the bifurcation in capitalist society between the forces of money and morality.

Starting the monetary pattern, the first letter announces overproduction (too much merchandise on the market) and tariffs, newly enacted by South American countries, that remove former markets (fewer customers to buy). Prudently, Mauler contracts to sell his cattle at high prices before others discover the situation. Within four weeks, the bottom drops from the market. As a result, plant owners are destroyed, plants close, and unemployment rises. Furthermore, speculators become ruined, for they are in a bind: to pay Mauler the high prices they agreed to pay, they must sell what shares they own at prices that have lowered, and will lower further once they place their shares on the market.

Reminiscent of Undershaft's statement that the government does what his business requires, the second letter reveals that capitalists have bribed congressmen to vote to lower tariffs; thus, it hints, previously closed markets will reopen if countries to the south reciprocate. Buy before others learn of this development, advise Mauler's Wall Street associates. Although he claims to buy because the sight of the unemployed has stirred him (a moral justification), Mauler has already received the letter and made sure that the shares he has contracted to purchase are at current prices, which are low (a monetary reason). As before (when he sold), the moral reason is really a business ruse. Because of the unsold surplus created by overproduction, however, Mauler's decision does not affect unemployment. The plants remain closed.

19. See my commentary on this play in *Drama and Revolution*, pp. 307–11; and Darko Suvin, "*Saint Joan of the Slaughterhouses*: Structures of a Slaughterhouse World," in *Essays on Brecht: Theater and Politics*, ed. Siegfried Mews and Herbert Knust, pp. 114–40. *Schlachthöfe* translates as either *Stockyards* or *Slaughterhouses*.

The third letter announces that South American countries have lowered their tariffs. In the meantime, Mauler has cornered the market. As his broker Slift says, all of the cattle in Chicago belong to Mauler. When his associates at the stock exchange learn what has happened, prices rise. In order to take advantage of the reopened markets—that is, in order to conduct business—they must buy at the higher prices, which are still rising. From whom will they buy? Mauler. With livestock in demand at high prices, Mauler calls for delivery of the meat he contracted to buy at low prices. Those who have made these contracts and who do not have the cattle to deliver must therefore buy the meat from Mauler and, as Slift says, "it's expensive there." Both for those who would sell and for those who must deliver what they have sold, the result is ruin, since Mauler and his broker raise the price of the commodities they alone have for sale.

Through Mauler's victory, however, comes his (temporary) defeat. With the other capitalists ruined, they cannot buy from him. Thus, the market drops once more and Mauler too is ruined. The fourth letter advises him to reach a settlement with the stockbreeders that will limit the amount of livestock offered for sale and thereby rally prices. In other words, under Mauler's leadership, the capitalists create a cartel that sells a limited quantity of the product at high prices, which they control. Acting upon this advice, Mauler absorbs the other plants in a giant merger with their owners. To limit the amount of the product on the glutted market, he burns a third of the meat. Why not give it to the masses instead? Because they are among the potential customers. In order to maintain the high prices that a limited quantity of goods helps create, he orders the plants to operate at two-thirds capacity. Thus, only two-thirds of the workers will have jobs. Because three workers compete for every two jobs, the cartel lowers wages. Mauler triumphs. As Brecht's legend tells the audience, he "IS EXALTED." The overwhelming forces of money ignore the moral problem, the plight of the starving unemployed.

Linked to and affected by these economic crises are three personal crises, which create changes in Joan's moral viewpoint. Each, a "DESCENT INTO THE DEPTHS," follows roughly the same pattern. Every time, Joan receives a readymade interpretation of why the workers suffer. During each descent, she examines the evidence, learns that the interpretation is incorrect, reinterprets the evidence to reach a different conclusion, resolves upon a course of action, and then tries to act. She does not always succeed.

In her first descent, Joan subscribes to the doctrines of the Black Straw Hats. To the workers, she preaches that God mysteriously creates poverty and unemployment: "Trouble comes like the rain, that nobody maketh, and yet it comes." The workers' thoughts, she urges, should be on moral, not earthly matters: "Strive upward, not downward.... Those low pleasures you work so hard to get, a bite to eat, nice homes, the movies, are nothing but coarse sensual enjoyments, but God's word is a far finer, more intimate, more exquisite pleasure." To attain such goals, she pleads, the workers should abjure force, which immorally creates only destruction and chaos. The workers themselves know better. Having come to teach, Joan learns. The workers' troubles, they tell her, derive from the financial competition among meat packers, especially Mauler, who have closed their plants. Where can she find those responsible for low wages and unemployment? The workers direct her to the Livestock Exchange. Although the Black Straw Hats warn her not to become involved in earthly battles, which would destroy her moral purity, Joan is resolved to follow her path to its conclusion: "I want to know."

Before Joan's second descent among the workers, unemployed because of overproduction for a shrunken market, Mauler gives a different readymade interpretation of the cause of poverty, one that exonerates him. Neither heaven nor he is to blame, he asserts; the poor themselves are to blame, since they are immoral. Before one can change the world, the poor must change their immoral nature.

To demonstrate their wickedness, Mauler has Slift—his broker in this moral demonstration as in his stock market manipulations—accompany Joan to the stockyards, where, Slift tells her, he will prove that her pity is misplaced. To Mrs. Luckerniddle, the widow of the worker who fell into the bacon-making machine, he offers free lunches in the company canteen for three weeks, on condition that she abandon her inquiries about what happened to her husband. He offers food and money to a worker if he desensitizes himself and wears the dead man's clothes in front of the widow, then announces where he got them. Both the worker and the widow, who has not eaten for two days, accept the offer, and the widow does not change her mind after the worker carries out his part of the bargain. With Joan, whose values are basically those of a bourgeois liberal, to know is to forgive, and she understands that their motive is poverty. She forgives both. When Joan earlier says that Mauler is not wicked, Brecht tips off his audiences and readers that Joan's judgments are fallible and invites them to question her judgment on the widow and worker, who submissively accept and thereby perpetuate their social condition, despite other possible options (the widow, for instance, could take the food and then double-cross Slift, and later scenes hint at revolution as an option for both). Chiefly, however, Joan examines Slift's evidence but reaches a conclusion different from his. Not immorality but lack of money made the poor behave as they did. Brecht educates Joan one step at a time.

Next, Joan acts on her new understanding. To prove to Mauler that poverty is to blame for wickedness, and to awaken the consciences of the stock traders, she takes the poor to the Livestock Exchange. Confident that morality will prevail, she expresses her moral concerns in the monetary terms familiar to the capitalists she addresses, for she believes that she can thereby move them to humane action. She exhorts them to think of helping the poor in terms of serving customers. She appeals to their sense of morality and their sense of self-interest: "Immorality breeds down there in the slums, and revolution goes along with it. . . . My dear sirs, there is such a thing as moral purchasing power. Raise that and you'll get morality too. And by moral purchasing power I mean something very simple and natural: money. Wages." Although Mauler agrees to buy stocks—in order, he says, to create jobs for the unemployed and to get them out of his sight—Brecht soon indicates that his motive is really monetary: he has already received a letter from New York that advised him to buy.

From the sight of the poor, Mauler learns something: the imminence of revolution. Unless something is done, he recognizes, the system of buying and selling cannot continue, for the poor are too many and their numbers are increasing. Should they act, "Not one of us/will die in bed." Mauler does not fear God in his heaven above but the poor in their hell below. The latter, he predicts, "will/rise in the morning."

Since the capitalists wish to use religion to prevent the poor from helping themselves, they visit the mission of the Black Straw Hats, who are all too ready to assist the capitalists. More strongly and cynically than Shaw in *Major Barbara*, Brecht in *Saint Joan of the Stockyards* emphasizes that religious organizations sell themselves to the rich to maintain the status quo. Like Marx, Brecht demands the "abolition of religion," though unlike Marx (and Shaw) he regards religion not as "a protest against real wretchedness" or "the heart of a heartless world," but simply as a dispenser of opium to the people. More forcefully than Mrs. Baines, who refers only to anarchistic breaking of windows, Paulus Snyder—"*in the pulpit*"—reminds the rich who visit his mission that if unemployment continues, the workers will do something more meaningful, because it is more lasting, than destroy property; they will "take the factories away from you and say: 'We'll do as the Bolsheviks did. . . .'" The Black Straw Hats teach the poor that unhappiness falls like the rain from an unknown source, "that suffering is their fate and a reward for it awaits them," and that "the rich will be punished—when they're dead, of course." After Snyder and the capitalists haggle over the price, Brecht ensures that his audiences understand the impossibility of religious institutions being apolitical. "Where do you stand? This side of the barricades, or the other?" asks Slift. Snyder's response is pointed: "The Black Straw Hats stand above the battle, Mr. Slift. This side."

Joan recognizes that her attempt to help the poor through the rich was sheer folly. When she enters the Black Straw Hat mission, she dashes Snyder's hopes. Upon seeing the priests of Mammon in the temple of God, the representatives of money in what should be the home of morality, Joan expels them. "Out!" she cries. "Are you trying to turn God's house into a . . . second Livestock Exchange?" Although Mauler convinces her that religious institutions and capitalism share the same interests, and promises to give money to the Black Straw Hats, Joan refuses to ally herself with either the representatives of money or those of institutionalized morality. Mauler's financial aid will not help the people "who are offered nothing." Among them, in the stockyards, she declares, she will take her stand.

In her third descent, Joan dreams of herself as the moral leader of a band of marching revolutionaries. The dream is that of a bourgeoise in the process but not the conclusion of radical-

Money and Morality   131

ization. In her dream, she is at the head of the people, not among them. It is she who transforms, not the people themselves.

Reality partly reflects this aspect of her dream. "I'm for your cause, heart and soul," she tells a leader of the general strike that is set for the next day. "Our cause?" he asks. "So it isn't your cause?" Although Joan has determined to make the workers' cause her own, she has not yet shared their experiences or reached their conclusions. Anxious to help, Joan persuades the leaders to trust her to deliver an important letter that urges the workers not to break ranks in the general strike on the basis of deliberately misleading rumors. Yet she still believes that the use of force is immoral and cannot accomplish good. She asks a worker whether the communists incite people to crime. His monosyllabic negative response completely satisfies the naive Joan. When she hears the rumor that employment will resume because Mauler is selling livestock, Joan—still naive—believes it. The timely news symbolically corresponds to her hope in regard to the weather ("The ice has melted in their hearts"). On the basis of a supposedly moral principle, she does not deliver the letter. Consequently, the strike fails and immorality triumphs. Without a united front, the workers cannot resist their antagonists. Ironically, their antagonists succeed in preserving the status quo when they create a united front, a corporate merger under Mauler.

Too late, Joan recognizes the results of her inaction. Too late, she understands the system wherein the few on top are there because of the many below, whom those above must keep below if they are to remain on top. Her so-called morality, she perceives too late, was immoral, for it failed to help those who needed help. During her second descent, Joan pitied the widow, but while she herself went hungry longer than the widow did, she refuses to pity herself. As she now understands, pity is not a virtue when it becomes a substitute for action. "I did injury to the injured," she castigates herself, "and was useful to the injurers." Recognizing that knowledge without social consequences is useless knowledge, she concludes that nothing should be considered good or moral except what changes society, for society requires total transformation. Turning atheist, the erstwhile religionist demands that anyone who believes in God "should have his head banged on the pavement/until he croaks," for "only men help where men are." Embracing violence, the former proponent of nonviolence shouts, "Only force helps where force rules. . . ." What the representatives of money brand as immoral, she recognizes to be essentially moral.

In death as in life, the capitalists use her. With the aid of the Black Straw Hats, they canonize her Saint Joan of the Stockyards. With such biblical hosannas as "To him that hath shall be given!"[20] capitalists and religionists drown her out. With the "EXALTATION" of Mauler, who exemplifies the forces of money, comes Joan's "CANONIZATION," which is a mockery of morality. Yet Brecht derides Mauler's ascension as well. Loudspeakers interrupt the victors to announce the collapse of capitalist economy, clashes between unemployed workers and the police in capitalist societies, and the success of the Soviet Union's five-year plan. As the hypocritical litany of religionists and capitalists, who add Joan's name to their inventory, drowns out her voice, the news of larger events in the world casts doubt on the durability of their success. The triumphant note that concludes the play turns cynically upon its singers.

* * * *

In *An Enemy of the People*, the forces of money refuse to scrap their defective instruments and try to scrap the force of morality, which refuses to accept defeat. In *Major Barbara*, the force of morality scraps an ineffective instrument of morality, seizes an effective instrument, and unites with the forces of money to build a better world upon the achievements of the most enlightened portion of the status quo. In *Saint Joan of the Stockyards*, the force of morality decides to scrap utterly the monetary and religious forces of the status quo, but Joan is too late; those forces, scrapping morality, recycle her, as representative of morality, to serve them.

On which social group does each of the playwrights pin his hopes for social reformation? To Ibsen, it is the minority that transcends social classes. Individualist members of the professional classes—a doctor, assisted by a teacher and a sea captain—lead twelve disciples who come from all walks of life, proletarian included. Their individual regeneration is to precede society's regeneration. In *Major Barbara*, Shaw's hopes are pri-

---

20. Matthew 13:12 and 25:29; Mark 4:25; Luke 8:18 and 19:26.

marily on enlightened, educated individuals who, in Fabian fashion, will try to impose better social conditions, then socialism itself, from above. Simultaneously with socialist reformation of society from nonproletarian sources, however, comes individual regeneration among the proletariat, stimulated by a woman drawn from "the whole people." Unlike his playwriting predecessors, Brecht pins his hopes exclusively on the proletariat. Rejecting the status quo more forcefully than either of the other two plays, *Saint Joan of the Stockyards* suggests a different moral and social force to supplant it, communism, which Brecht brings onstage infrequently as personae with small roles in the play and as a faraway force whose achievements a loudspeaker reports. Brecht dramatizes not a successful proletarian revolution, but the desperate need for one. Unlike Ibsen and Shaw, he expects the job of social regeneration to be accomplished by one class of society, not several, and by the class that is lowest.

6

The Prospect of Revolution—Reactionaries, Liberals, and Radicals
Rosmersholm, *On the Rocks*, *The Mother*

The crumbling foundations of capitalist society—dramatized in *Pillars of Society*, *Heartbreak House*, and *Puntila and Matti, His Hired Man*—are in a more advanced state of collapse in *Rosmersholm*, *On the Rocks*, and *The Mother*, where the prospect of revolution is more imminent than in the former trio of plays. Indeed, it begins but is aborted in *On the Rocks* and it actually occurs in *The Mother*. In several important respects, the trio of plays that is the subject of this chapter begins where *An Enemy of the People*, *Major Barbara*, and *Saint Joan of the Stockyards* leave off. Before the start of *Rosmersholm*, Rosmer has arrived at conclusions similar to those reached by Dr. Stockmann at the end of *An Enemy of the People*, and Ibsen dramatizes Rosmer's brief entry into the political arena, where the cleavage between right and left appears to be greater than it was in the earlier play. At the end of *Major Barbara*, the intellectually astute Cusins enunciates what he believes must be done in order to move society toward socialism, and he accepts the power that he hopes will enable him to do it. Midway through *On the Rocks*, the protagonist becomes intellectually acute, formulates a specific plan to turn capitalist England into what he believes would be the beginning of a socialist state, and attempts to implement that plan. Between the composition of these plays the Russian Revolution of 1917 occurred, and when Shaw wrote *On the Rocks*, he saw the possibility that the time for peaceful change from capitalism to socialism may have run out. If it has, as he says in his preface to *Major Barbara*, the results in England and America might be "violent and sanguinary revolutions." This possibility, suggested in *Major Barbara*, is portrayed forcefully in *On the Rocks*. The realization reached by the title character of *Saint Joan of the Stockyards* at the conclusion of this play is reached by the title character of *The Mother* a third of the way through that play. Although the proletarian revolution in the former play fails, loudspeakers announce at the end that the class struggle continues: "BATTLE BETWEEN POLICE AND UNEMPLOYED OUTSIDE HENRY FORD'S PLANT IN DETROIT!" At the start of *The Mother*, working-class revolutionists prepare to act, and in the final scene, their actions succeed.

In *Rosmersholm*, *On the Rocks*, and *The Mother*—more prominently than in any of the plays analyzed so far—the radical authors focus on different aspects of political action. *Rosmersholm* revolves around the maneuvers of contending political factions in their efforts to win a convert and strengthen their position. *On the Rocks* centers upon cabinet meetings and confrontations between a prime minister and a working-class delegation. *The Mother* concerns radicalization and revolutionary action by the proletariat.

* * * *

More democratic than Dr. Stockmann in *An Enemy of the People*, John Rosmer of *Rosmersholm* wants to help not only an elite band of twelve but all his countrymen to become free, noble human beings. Whereas Dr. Stockmann is impetuous, quick-tempered, and ready to act upon the slightest provocation, Rosmer is a diffident, cool, ivory-towered intellectual who hesitates to enter the political arena. When he does so, he discovers that the methods employed by his reactionary opponents, who enunciate their political position more clearly than their counterparts in *An Enemy of the People*, are brutal and ruthless, and that the people he presumed were radical are really timorous liberals, opportunists who fear to move too far ahead of their supporters, lest they find themselves standing alone.

Shortly after the play begins, Kroll, who is headmaster of the local prep school, refers to a "civil war" that is raging between radicals and reactionaries like himself. Since Peter Mortensgaard's *Daily Beacon*, a paper he calls radical, has heaped what he terms "vile abuse" upon him, he has responded in kind. Vindictively, he determines to teach his opponents that he is not the type of person who turns the other cheek. What Kroll finds particularly galling is that the "revolutionary spirit has insinuated itself into the school," where it has influenced "all the brightest students. . . . It's only the numbskulls at the foot of the class who've kept out of it." Even more mortifying to Kroll, this spirit has infiltrated his very home and influenced his own children. Worse still, his son is "the ringleader of the conspiracy in school" and his wife, who for the first time in their marriage opposes him, blames him for the children's actions.

Although Kroll does not precisely identify the nature of this radicalism, or of the system he wishes to preserve, he more than hints at both when he says that his daughter has embroidered a *red* slipcase in which to hide her copies of the *Beacon*. He further indicates the nature of his own political cause when he claims that the country has "democracy enough!" According to him, it is plunging everyone "down into the muck and mire, where only the lowest of the low can thrive." Those who oppose his views are "the subversive elements in society," and he deplores the effect of Mortensgaard's paper on the "muddled masses," whom he later calls "barbarous scum."

Kroll tries to persuade Rosmer not to remain aloof from current politics, as he presently does, burying himself in historical research. Hesitant to become involved, Rosmer points out—with what later developments show to be an accurate assessment—that political action is not the proper kind of work for him and that he comprehends very little about politics. Kroll understands Rosmer's nature better in some respects, it turns out, than Rosmer does himself. What Kroll proposes is not that Rosmer become involved in the rough-and-tumble of public meetings, but that he assume the editorship of an opposition newspaper the reactionary forces are about to launch to counteract the effects of the *Beacon*. Not only are an editor's duties "more removed" than a political activist's, but now that Rosmer is no longer professionally occupied as pastor of the community, he has time to undertake such an obligation.

When Rosmer refuses, Kroll retreats to a fallback position: to persuade Rosmer to lend his name to the paper's masthead. Because Rosmer has always kept himself above political battles, because everyone in the county knows and values his integrity, because he still retains the respect he had held when he was a minister, and because of the aura of his family name—"the foremost family of the county"—his nominal support would be invaluable to Kroll's cause. Again, Rosmer refuses.

At first reluctant to do so, Rosmer finally explains his reason:

"I stand now . . . where your children stand." Aptly, Kroll calls him "an apostate." To Rosmer, what Kroll regards as "forces of decadence and corruption" are really "forces of liberation." Even in his apostasy, Rosmer reveals, he tries to remain aloof from actual battle, for he wishes not that one side will destroy the other, but that, in an effort to create the common good, both will reconcile with "peace and joy." As he explains, "I'm not committed to the spirit that destroys. Not to any faction. I want to bring people together from all sides. . . . I want democracy to assume its rightful role. . . . To elevate all our countrymen into noblemen. . . . By liberating their minds and tempering their wills." As an outside factor, he understands, he himself cannot liberate people; all he can do is try to arouse them so that they can liberate themselves. Perceptively, Kroll calls Rosmer a dreamer. Misunderstanding him, Rosmer announces that he will no longer dream in his ivory tower but will proclaim himself openly and test his powers. When Kroll refuses to meet him halfway, Rosmer proposes that if they must fight each other, they should do so honorably, a request Kroll unhesitatingly declines. "He who isn't with me in such matters . . . I owe . . . no consideration." Kroll also perceives that Rosmer is not the type of person who can stand alone. Whatever one thinks of Kroll's position, one must regard him as a political realist.

Whatever one thinks of Rosmer's position, one must regard him, since he is faced with Kroll's intransigence, as a naive utopian. However sympathetically Ibsen portrays the humane and noble ideals enunciated by Rosmer, Ibsen also shows Rosmer to lack sufficient understanding of the nature of a man he has known all his life. The spiritual regeneration that Rosmer conceives as an ideal fails to consider the unregenerate politicians against whom he will contend. Although Rosmer is an apostate in religion as well as political conviction, he still behaves like a pastor. He believes that uplifting sermons will, to use his word, *elevate* the opposing political factions he will address.

Again, Kroll demonstrates political astuteness. He suggests what amounts to another fallback position, that Rosmer keep quiet about his new ideas. If Rosmer will not join his reactionary faction, let him at least say nothing against it. Kroll argues that Rosmer has a duty to his family traditions. For ages, he continues, Rosmersholm has stood for everything that society has traditionally sanctioned and upheld. Now it is Rosmer's turn to reject Kroll's plea. According to Rosmer, his overriding duty is to shed light and happiness, which will replace the darkness and gloom for which Rosmersholm has stood for so long.

In act 1, Kroll urges Rosmer to climb down from his ivory tower to join him in fighting radicalism. In act 2, after it is clear that Rosmer will climb down to do the reverse, Kroll urges him to return to the tower and abandon politics. "It's not the work you were cut out for. You were made to live quietly, among books." Kroll's revised evaluation is correct, as Rosmer himself demonstrates when, after Kroll tells him that unless he withdraws from the political arena his friends will fight him to the end, Rosmer naively states, "They can't all be as fanatical as you." Later, Rebecca West reports that Rosmer had not anticipated that Kroll would be so fanatical and that Rosmer expected Kroll would sooner or later join him. To this admission, Kroll responds triumphantly: "That's how bad his judgment is when it comes to situations and people in real life!" As Rosmer should have foreseen, Kroll and his friends do what Kroll threatens. In their newspaper, they slander the sexually innocent relationship between Rosmer and Rebecca West.

From Kroll, Rosmer learns of reactionary politicians. From Mortensgaard, he learns of liberal politicians. Mortensgaard is delighted when Rosmer asks him to report in the *Beacon* that he has allied himself with liberal and progressive forces. He is less delighted when Rosmer adds that his self-liberation is absolute and unqualified. The former pastor has cut all his ties with the church; its doctrines now mean nothing to him. Mortensgaard will not print this news in the *Beacon*. If Rosmer openly announces his break with the church, he will hinder rather than help the politically liberal forces that are trying to attain sufficient respectability to persuade religious people to join them. While Mortensgaard himself has long held the position Rosmer now holds, he refuses as a matter of practical politics to risk supporting anyone who opposes religious doctrines. In other words, Mortensgaard will do nothing to flaunt public opinion and will lead only as far as he dares. To achieve his goals, he will compromise when necessary. Although his policy is practical, it is also opportunistic.

Caught between the uncompromising convictions of reactionary forces and the malleable convictions of liberal forces which their reactionary opponents call radical, Rosmer collapses. Although he vows, "I won't have my way of life dictated, either by the living or—anyone else," his resolution comes to nothing. The fears of his dead wife Beata provide Kroll's newspaper with the opportunity to slander him. Her death still exerts a hold on him, as do Rosmersholm's traditions, despite his verbal renunciation of them. Faced with the newspaper's slander, all he does is to call it the work of dishonorable men, lament that "all the best in humanity will go down if this sort of thing is condoned," and cry that it must be stopped. He paints a glowing image of what life would become if he could teach people to unite "in tolerance—in love. . . . Oh, what joy it would be then to live. No more brutal conflicts. Only friendly competition. All eyes converging on the same goal. Every will, every mind striving onward and upward—each following out its own natural path. Happiness for all—created through all." While he recognizes that he is incapable of bringing this dream to fruition, he fails to recognize that such a dream cannot materialize at all from present politics and those engaged in them. Because the interests of Kroll and Mortensgaard are diametrically opposed, their eyes inevitably focus on different goals, their wills on different objectives; if one moves onward and upward, the other inevitably moves backward and downward; and happiness for one is, inevitably, unhappiness for the other.

According to Rosmer, inner purity must precede social regeneration. His self-doubts weaken him. As Kroll perceives, Rosmer lacks the stamina for the sort of fight he has undertaken. When Rebecca confesses that she manipulated both Rosmer and Beata, his collapse is complete. "I've been like putty in your hands," he says in despair. If Rebecca is guilty, moreover, what does her guilt make the ideals to which she led him? It does not occur to Rosmer to divorce social and political ideas from those who espouse them. He fails to consider that just as Rebecca's personal purity would not validate her social and political convictions, neither would her personal deficiencies invalidate them. Instead, like Kroll, he links persons and ideas. Personal corruption must mean social and political corruption, and the reverse. Thinking this way, it is logical that Rosmer would return to the fold. Having been manipulated by the living Rebecca, Rosmer chooses to be manipulated by the moribund Rosmersholm tradition.

"The Rosmer way of life ennobles," says Rebecca, who adds, "but it kills happiness." She would be more accurate if she were to say that while the Rosmer way of life may ennoble, it does so in social isolation, with the result that it drains energy and prevents both happiness and meaning by divorcing such ennoblement from a social context. Not only does the Rosmer way of life kill happiness, it kills life itself. Rosmer and his wife had no children. As Rebecca recognizes, he "isn't cut out to deal with crying children." But living children are crying children—and laughing children as well. Traditionally at Rosmersholm, the housekeeper tells Rebecca, children do not cry, and after they grow up, they do not laugh. Rosmer is unable to deal with life, as suggested in this play by the political arena, where ways of life do battle. The Rosmersholm tradition—with children as with ideas—shuts off life. Consequently, what it regards as ennoblement leads to death. How can Rosmer fight to ennoble others when he has lost faith in himself? Who can determine whether or not he has ennobled Rebecca? "There is no higher judgment than ours," he decrees, "so we have to carry out justice ourselves." In Rosmersholm, the noble ideal of justice is personal, divorced from societal responsibility. To prove their nobility, Rosmer and Rebecca commit suicide together. What such expiation really proves is not their ennoblement but their social irresponsibility,[1] a fit conclusion to Rosmer's ideals, which though humane are naive and divorced from the social reality of the world in which he lives.

Paralleling Rosmer is Ulrik Brendel, his former tutor, who—perniciously—did his job well. As numerous critics observe, the two appearances of Brendel cast light upon Rosmer. In connection with the relationship of the idealist Rosmer and the practical world, these appearances are particularly significant. When Brendel appears in the first act, before Rosmer informs Kroll of his changed values, he foreshadows the attitudes and fate of his former pupil. Brendel, says Kroll, filled Rosmer's head with radical notions. Soon, Rosmer will tell Kroll of his radical notions. Brendel recognizes Kroll as "one of those bullyboys of virtue that had me booted out of the Debating Club." So will Kroll and

---

1. In "The Quintessence of Ibsenism," Shaw suggests this when he calls expiation by sacrifice a superstition (Bernard Shaw, *Major Critical Essays*, p. 82). F. W. Kaufmann is more explicit. As he points out, Rosmer deceives both himself and Rebecca when he calls their suicide atonement, whereas the action really is an escape from responsibility. See "Ibsen's Conception of Truth," in *Ibsen*, ed. Rolf Fjelde, p. 27.

his reactionary colleagues try to boot Rosmer out of political debate and respectable society. As Rosmer will reveal, Brendel reveals that he believes in the aristocracy of intellect and spirit, though unlike his former pupil Brendel is aristocratically classconscious: he calls Mortensgaard an idiot because his name sounds plebeian. Brendel announces that "the time has come to put on the new man—to cast off that delicate reticence I've displayed till now." He will enter the public arena and offer a series of lectures. Like Rosmer—as Rosmer discloses after Brendel departs—he has done nothing about his liberated ideals but is about to do so. His great ideas "remain unwritten. . . . I love to savor things in solitude. . . . But now they're going on the block." To emphasize the resemblances between them, Ibsen has Rosmer give Brendel his own clothes to wear to town: a clean dress shirt, a topcoat, and a pair of shoes.

Had Ibsen made Brendel enter after Rosmer discloses his ideas and goals, the scene would be trite, for it would obviously underscore aspects of the protagonist. However, Ibsen cleverly places this scene before Rosmer's disclosure. It serves not only to anticipate what Rosmer will do, but also enables one to perceive retrospectively and by inference that Rosmer's goals are as incapable of realization as those of Brendel,[2] who is unmistakably pretentious (he sprinkles German and French phrases in his speech), threadbare (clothes symbolize the man), and a windbag.

Following Rosmer's capitulation, Brendel reappears. Not only does his degradation suggest that Rosmer's surrender is also degrading, Brendel indicates part of the reason for Rosmer's failure. Like Rosmer, Brendel has lost his ideals. What of Brendel's unwritten works? "For twenty-five years I've sat like a miser on his chest of gold. And then yesterday—when I opened it up to take out the treasure—there was nothing." With Rosmer too, the preciously stored ideas evaporate in the light of reality. Not only is he incapable, like Brendel, of putting them into practice in real life, but also like Brendel, the ideas themselves are without reality to begin with. Whereas Brendel could not even enunciate his ideas, Rosmer's enunciation of his own—in such terms as *joy* and *onward and upward*—demonstrates their fuzziness

---

2. Thomas F. Van Laan goes further. According to him, the very oddness of Brendel discredits Rosmer and what he plans to do. See *The Idiom of Drama*, p. 356.

and divorce from real life. Brendel leaves, spiritually impoverished. Also spiritually impoverished, Rosmer commits suicide, but when he does so he deceives himself that the action is spiritually ennobling.

In *Rosmersholm*, the naive idealist, incapable of translating social ideas into political action, enacts the consequence of impotent idealism. He kills himself. Just as Rosmer is childless, so are his political ideals without issue. He represents the last of his line, and his ideas reach the end of their line. In dramatizing the weakness of Rosmer, Ibsen makes the progress of the play swerve in order to conform to the type of collapse its central character undergoes. The play begins with social questions, but these fade into the background as personal questions assume prominence. Incapable of dealing with social questions, Rosmer withdraws from the political battlefield into a personal combat zone. Although Ibsen does not withdraw from these issues— pointedly, the final act has Brendel remind Rosmer that the political future is in the hands of liberal opportunists like Mortensgaard—the play's structure parallels Rosmer's withdrawal by changing course to focus on the related but different personal problems at Rosmersholm.

* * * *

Like *Rosmersholm*, *On the Rocks* has as its central character an ineffectual reformer. Unlike Ibsen's Rosmer, however, Shaw's Sir Arthur Chavender is in the innermost part of the political arena. He is prime minister of England. In the first half of Shaw's play, Chavender, like Rosmer, has no practical measures to improve society. In the second half, he does. Yet like Rosmer, he lacks sufficient stamina to fight them through.

During the almost half century that separates these plays, Europe engaged in a major war and communists seized power in Russia. When Shaw wrote *On the Rocks* in 1933, only two years after his visit to the Soviet Union, Europe and America were in the midst of the Great Depression and the Fabian-influenced British Labour party had proved ineffective in Parliament.[3] At this time, fascist dictatorships were strengthening themselves in Germany and Italy, and in capitalist democracies the prospect of revolution seemed imminent. Recalling Shot-

3. See James W. Hulse, *Revolutionists in London*, pp. 227–28.

over's observation in *Heartbreak House*, that the ships of drunken skippers may run on the rocks, is the very title of Shaw's later play. Also recalling that observation is a statement, with a significantly different tense from that used by Shotover, that the country's skipper, the prime minister, has already "piloted England on to the rocks." *On the Rocks* dramatizes the failure of capitalism and parliamentary democracy as presently constituted to deal satisfactorily with problems of massive unemployment, explicitly proposes socialism as the remedy to capitalism's failure, just as clearly insists that the accomplishment of this solution might result from its imposition by a dictatorial leader rather than through parliamentary means, and suggests that, failing this method, the masses might revolt.

The first few speeches indicate the problem of widespread unemployment, potentially revolutionary masses whose present purposelessness vitiates effective and meaningful action, and the incapacity of parliamentary government to function effectively in their behalf. Because the crowds of unemployed have made the streets impassable, the prime minister's secretary arrives late for work. All the unemployed do, however, is walk "aimlessly about Westminster and the public offices." All Prime Minister Chavender does is sit aimlessly in his office, complain that it is business's job, not his, to create employment, and fidget with his papers. Although he is a liberal, he resembles the conservatives in that he shows no comprehension of the lot of the unemployed workers. Also like them, he does nothing to solve the unemployment problem. Like them, he waits for the improvement of trade—profit-oriented actions by the capitalists—to provide a solution. As a character later puts it, the only distinction between liberals and conservatives seems to be that liberals make speeches "about Progress and Liberty instead of about King and Country."

As prime minister, Chavender is the leader of the House of Commons, but "what is the use of leading the House," his secretary frustratedly asks, "if it never goes anywhere?" Although he remained there the previous night in a session that lasted until three in the morning, its parliamentary business was irrelevant to the problems facing the country. According to Lady Chavender, who like his secretary displays no admiration for Parliament, neither her husband nor anyone else governs England. "The country isnt governed: it just slummocks along anyhow."

In a statement suggestive of speeches by Mortensgaard in *Rosmersholm* and Hovstad in *An Enemy of the People*, Chavender laments, "I cannot go faster than our voters will let me." Shaw's prime minister, one may infer, suggests how Ibsen's liberal newspapermen might act, or fail to act, if they held political office. Lady Chavender has as little admiration for the electoral process as she has for Parliament. The voters, she declares, know nothing about government, their real interests are football, prizefighting, and war, which they regard more as a movie than as something that causes real deaths and mutilation.

To the chief commissioner of police, aptly named Sir Broadfoot Basham, mass meetings are effective safety valves that prevent disruptive action by the unemployed. While a crowd is listening to speeches, he says, it will never *do* anything. Although the government does not give the people enough *panem*, it provides plenty of *circenses*. In a devastating observation, Basham hints at Chavender's failure later in the play: "the fellows who make the speeches can be depended on never to do anything else. In the first place, they dont know how. In the second, they are afraid."

Chavender further reveals his and Parliament's incapacities when he receives a deputation from the Isle of Cats. Although Chavender seems incapable of doing anything to solve the unemployment problem, says the mayor of the Isle, something must be done. After he insists that he really cares about the suffering of the poor, Chavender makes the claim that he and everyone else are "in the grip of economic forces that are beyond human control," a claim he later recognizes to be nonsense. As the deputation complains, the government has not adequately taxed the capitalists, who do not appear to have suffered seriously, but instead has tried to stretch the public relief budget by cutting unemployment compensation and imposing a means test in order to make fewer people eligible to receive it.

All but one member of the deputation leave in disgust. Old Hipney, who remains, tries to negotiate off the record with the prime minister. An old hand in such matters, Hipney acts decisively on his own, bypasses the usual activities of his other democratically elected colleagues, and thus foreshadows what Chavender will attempt to do. Conferences and debates, says

The Prospect of Revolution

Hipney, echoing Chavender's secretary, do no good. Nor has the presence in Parliament of "Labor men that started as red-hot Socialists." When Chavender proposes educating the voters as a solution, Hipney explodes that notion, for "you cant teach people anything they dont want to know." Although Karl Marx thought that when he had explained capitalism to the working classes they would rise and overthrow it, says Hipney, they instead, fifty years after he founded the Red International, rose and killed each other in a large war, as if Marx had never been born. Prophetically, Hipney adds, "And theyd do it again tomorrow if they was set on to do it." Once more, Chavender attempts to calm the troubled waters by references to the inability of the government to interfere in the economics of supply and demand and to "the inexorable laws of political economy." "No use, Srarthur," Hipney interrupts. "That game is up." Although he himself has not read Marx, he suggests that Chavender do so.

Before the second and final act, he does—and Lenin, Trotsky, and Stalin as well. As a result, he is converted to socialism. Previously, he recognizes, he did nothing but whitewash the slums with speeches that were "all hot air." Whereas he once thought he could do nothing about the nation's problems, he now perceives what he can do and how he can do it.

In the second act, he outlines a program that characters variously call a "dose of boiling Socialism," an "outburst of Bolshevism," and "first rate Platonic Communism." He demands the nationalization or municipalization of land rents, banks, collieries, transportation, urban land, the building trade, and the fertilizer industries, with governmental compensation to their present owners; the removal of death duties, together with a hundred percent increase in the surtax on unearned income; the institution of compulsory public service for all social classes, plus the augmentation of police and naval forces; the illegalization of strikes; the establishment of collective farming; and the prohibition of foreign trade in protected industries, with the substitution of imports by the state, which will sell them at regulated prices.

Because various interest groups find something for themselves in this program, they initially agree to support Chavender.

Nevertheless, his proposals suffer defeat. Opposed to him from the start is a coalition of reactionary politicians and representatives of labor. Racism alienates some supporters; Chavender's unparliamentary methods, others.

A reactionary and a fascist, Sir Dexter Rightside, whose given name and surname both symbolize his right-wing affiliation, correctly identifies Chavender's program as the abolition of private property in England. Unless Chavender withdraws his proposals, Rightside threatens to organize a Union Jack equivalent of the Nazi brownshirts and the Italian blackshirts. A rascist too, he calls a Cingalese capitalist who supports Chavender "a silly nigger," which prompts the Asian plutocrat to leave, with a threat to make India withdraw from the Empire. When Chavender calls Rightside a fool for having said what he did, the First Lord of the Admiralty, also a rascist, switches his allegiance to Rightside. "After all," says he, "we are white men" and an Englishman has a right to call a heathen a nigger.

Making common cause with the reactionary forces are the workers. "Trade Unionism is not Socialism," says Shaw in *The Intelligent Woman's Guide to Socialism, Capitalism, Sovietism, and Fascism*, which he revised the year before he wrote *On the Rocks*, "it is the Capitalism of the Proletariat."[4] In *On the Rocks*, organized labor not only refuses to revolt, it refuses to accept socialism when it is handed to them. As the Duke of Domesday observes, "Chained dogs are the fiercest guardians of property; and those who attempt to unchain them are the first to be bitten." Aloysia, the Marxist member of the Isle of Cats delegation, which returns in the second act, maintains, "The Class War is a fact." It is not a fact, argues Chavender; rather, the working class is divided against itself. In actuality, the delegation confirms his view. Among them, the "revolutionary socialist" Hipney and the communist Barking (who unlike Hipney is a viscount, not a proletarian) support him. The unionists and the Marxist do not. Although the rich live on the poor, says Chavender, the poor also live on the rich. Shopkeepers and shopworkers, parsons and portrait painters, gardeners and gatekeepers, are among many with a vested interest in the rich, who enable them to earn a living. As Shaw says, the line sepa-

---

4. Bernard Shaw, *The Intelligent Woman's Guide to Socialism, Capitalism, Sovietism, and Fascism*, p. 186.

rating those who would maintain capitalism from those who would replace it with socialism "is a line drawn not between rich and poor, capitalist and proletarian, but right down through the middle of the proletariat to the bottom of the very poorest section. In a civil war for the maintenance of Capitalism the capitalists would therefore find masses of supporters in all ranks of the community. . . ."[5] As Chavender asserts in the play, the dividing line is not between capitalists and workers, but between Rightside's view of the world and his. The war is not between classes, but between those who exist for what they can get from the world and those who exist in order to make the world a better place for everyone.

Despite large-scale unemployment, most of the workers' representatives distrust Chavender's principle of compulsory public service for everyone. Although he explains that those who already have jobs will not be compelled to work elsewhere, but that only those without—the unemployed and the idle rich—will be affected, he fails to persuade the Isle of Cats delegates. As one of them says, Chavender will make the real workers slaves for the sake of making a few idlers go to work. Unimpressed by Chavender's argument that the right to strike is "the right to starve on your enemy's doorstep and set the whole public against you," another delegate tells him that the British worker will refuse to support any program that would remove his hard-won right to strike.

Unwaveringly, the majority of the delegation rejects the plan to compensate owners of nationalized and municipalized property, for it appears to them to consist of removing something from one pocket only to put it into another, more sleight-of-hand to deceive workers to whom government officials have lied for years. Despite the Duke of Domesday's explanation that those who receive compensation will have to pay taxes on it, so that ultimately the people will get both the land and the money, the Isle of Cats Labor Party firmly opposes compensation.

Finally, liberal views of democracy—held by labor, Rightside's Conservative Party, and Chavender's own Liberal Party—defeat the prime minister. No matter how often politicians tell the people that democracy makes them the real government of the country, Chavender argues, they know very well that they are

5. Ibid., p. 373.

not. They know too that whatever party label the government may bear, it always supports profitmaking and nothing else. The people are sick of hearing cant about liberty when they know they have none, sick of living idly on unemployment relief when they are not drudging for salaries too low to pay the rent for anything better than an overcrowded one-room flat in a slum, and sick of all politicians. What the people want, insists Chavender, are decent jobs and the destruction of those who, despite massive hunger, burn food because they cannot sell it profitably. They also want, he claims, justifying an aspect of his program that resembles the fascist corporate state, rulers who will organize the populace, discipline them, and dictatorially set matters right. To accomplish these objectives, he aims to bypass parliamentary democracy by having the King adjourn Parliament, then establish new tribunals and special commissions composed of officials upon whom he can rely (thus, he will sidetrack the courts and obstructionist civil servants), and after he achieves all his goals, get Parliament to pass an act of indemnity to legitimize what he has accomplished. Although the liberal politician admits that normal parliamentary action would result in thousands of watering-down amendments to Chavender's program and take at least fifty years to get through, he refuses to support unparliamentary action. Labor declares itself to be against what it calls dictatorship. It supports "the will of the people . . . the referendum . . . the initiative." The reactionary Rightside also opposes Chavender's attempt "to play fast and loose with democracy" and this, he vows, "both the people and the governing class of this country are determined you shall not do," an inadvertent admission that the two are separate groups.

Old Hipney is no more surprised by liberal opposition than he is by right-wing and labor opposition. Long ago, he concluded that members of Parliament would never do a thing, and that "the only man that ever had a proper understanding of Parliament was old Guy Fawkes" (who tried to blow it up with gunpowder). On 25 November 1932, less than two and a half months before he began to write *On the Rocks*, Shaw gave a lecture under the auspices of the Fabian Society, "In Praise of Guy Fawkes." In his own person, he made statements similar to those of Hipney. Realistically and historically, said Shaw, the only function of Parliament in England is "to prevent anything being done by endlessly talking about it," or, put differently, "to prevent the Government from governing."[6]

Nevertheless, *On the Rocks* is not antidemocratic. Instead, it opposes what Shaw regards as the illusory appearance of democracy in what is really a government controlled by the plutocracy, which as he said in his preface to *The Apple Cart* a few years earlier "has bought and swallowed democracy. Money talks: money prints: money broadcasts: money reigns," and Shaw compared democracy as England knows it to "a big balloon, filled with gas or hot air, and sent up so that you shall be kept looking up at the sky whilst other people are picking your pockets." To remove democracy as a remedy for the ills of capitalism, however, as Chavender emphasizes in *On the Rocks*, is to throw out the baby with the bathwater. The people must have a voice in the government, he insists, and a choice of who will govern them. As Shaw says in his "Guy Fawkes" speech, the only real security the people have against a dictatorial leader's "abuse of his powers is to establish in his mind a certainty that if he does not prove himself a capable rider he will be thrown off [his horse] ignominiously."[7] After a strong man imposes socialism from above, the play argues, Fabianly, true democracy should be instituted. Contrasting real democracy with the present system that goes by its name, Hipney declares, Shavianly, that the people should have what they do not at present have, both a voice and a choice. "But let it be a voice to squeal with when theyre hurt, and not to pretend they know more than God Almighty does. Give em a choice between qualified men . . . and not windbags and movie stars and soldiers and rich swankers and lawyers on the make." At present, the people have a choice among the latter, not the former. As Shaw says in his preface to *The Apple Cart*, "if the last dozen parliaments had consisted of the candidates who were at the foot of the poll instead of those who were at the head of it there is no reason to suppose that we should have been a step more or less advanced than we are today."

Like Ibsen's Rosmer, Shaw's Chavender lacks the stamina to inaugurate the society whose need he has come to recognize.

---

6. Bernard Shaw, *Platform and Pulpit*, pp. 235–36, 240.
7. Ibid., p. 246.

Although he sees what must be done, he knows he is incapable of doing it. Basham is astonished: "You cant chalk up a program like that and then run away." Yet he can, and he does. Recalling Basham's observation about speechmakers early in the play, Chavender perceives that he is a talker, not a man of action. An old dog who has learned what the new tricks are, he is nevertheless unable to perform them. Instead, leaving the job to others, he resigns himself to wait until "the men of action clear out the talkers. . . ." To have Chavender do otherwise—override his opposition—would not only be untrue to the character, a middle-aged compromiser who, though aroused, can muster only limited strength for a type of battle to which he is totally unsuited; it would also be melodramatic.

But Chavender's withdrawal from the battle does not conclude the play. Like Chavender, Shaw is a talker. As he recognizes in the "Guy Fawkes" lecture: "For fortyeight years I have been addressing speeches to the Fabian Society and to other assemblies in this country. So far as I can make out, those speeches have not produced any effect whatever."[8] Shaw calls for action. In the first act of *On the Rocks*, he dramatizes the need for action and the inability of present parliamentary democracy to act effectively for the public good. In the bulk of the second act, he dramatizes the failure of a man to make himself dictator in order to impose socialism on England. The conclusion of that act, and of the play, presents another alternative.

Earlier in the second act, the Marxist Aloysia, in the name of the workers, tells the assembled representatives of the landowning and capitalist classes that what the workers want, they themselves will have to take. *On the Rocks* ends with what might be the start of the fulfillment of her warning. From offstage come the shouts of a mob of unemployed workers who surge into the streets, and the sounds of breaking glass and police whistles. Chavender's secretary announces that the unemployed have broken into Downing Street, where the prime minister resides, but are smashing windows on the wrong side of the street. Says Chavender, "they always break the wrong windows, poor devils." His adverb may be inaccurate. At the end of the play, the behavior of the unemployed differs from their behavior at the beginning. In the first act, they form an inert mass, aimlessly milling about. Here, they begin to do something. Their next ac-

---

8. Ibid., p. 235.

tion, which Shaw does not dramatize, might focus on the right target.

Through the prime minister's windows, the characters observe mounted police ride into the mob and club them. Defiantly, the unemployed sing "England, arise" and Chavender's secretary, a worker for the present parliamentary government, rushes out (in visual terms, leaves this place of work) to join them (in their work). *"Unemployed England, however, can do nothing but continue to sing,"* says Shaw in a concluding stage direction, which audiences do not read. Instead, they hear the song and Chavender's comment, the play's final, ambiguous line, "Suppose England really did arise!"—not a certainty, but a possibility that, with the emphasis on the first word, might be a hope, perhaps even a prophecy.

Paralleling Chavender's efforts to cope with the problems of the country are his efforts to cope with those of his family,[9] whose appearances in *On the Rocks* resemble those of Brendel in *Rosmersholm*.[10] As in the case of Brendel, it casts light on the problems of the principal characters. As Brendel first appears before Rosmer and Kroll confront each other over the issue that separates them, Chavender's family first appears before Chavender and the Isle of Cats delegation confront each other over the issue that separates them. As Brendel reappears after the defeat of Rosmer, Chavender's family reappears after his defeat.

The family first appears when Chavender tries, with little success, to compose a speech on, of all things, the family as the foundation of the British Empire, which he soon extends to all human society. As they barge in, one at a time, they interrupt his work. It becomes clear that his family, like England itself, is in disarray and that he is unable to cope with his son and daughter. Chavender himself makes the analogy between family and nation explicit when he says that the talking of his children is like the talking in the House of Commons, except that his children's speeches are shorter.

In the second act, after he has perceived how to solve the

9. Frederick P. W. McDowell points out that "the instability and confusion in his family parallel the disorganization present in society at large." See "Crisis and Unreason: Shaw's *On the Rocks*," *Educational Theatre Journal*, p. 195.

10. Margery M. Morgan asserts, but provides no evidence, that it is Old Hipney whose appearances parallel Brendel's. See *The Shavian Playground*, p. 281.

problems of the country, the problems of his family begin to sort themselves out. Significantly, however, since the domestic arena continues to reflect the political, Chavender himself resolves nothing. The first problem concerns his daughter and the blue-blooded laborite from the Isle of Cats, whose hand she has refused. "Make her marry me," the young man tells her father. "Certainly," says Chavender. "I'll order her to marry you if you think that will get you further." So much for this problem. On the domestic level, as on the political level, Chavender only proposes to behave like a dictator. In the domestic arena, he knows that his order will not have the slightest effect. His daughter will obey him if she wants the excuse to marry her young man, or disobey him if she does not. It is Aloysia who resolves the second, more difficult problem. She determines to marry Chavender's son David. As Lady Chavender observes, Aloysia is resolute and successful, whereas David is irresolute and unsuccessful; if she has decided to marry him, she probably will. But Lady Chavender warns that Aloysia will have to support him. "I shall expect him to work for his living," says Aloysia. Lady Chavender is unfazed: "Marriage seldom fulfils all our expectations." Neither is Aloysia fazed: "I will find him a job and see that he does it." On the domestic level, Aloysia sets out to enact two aspects of Chavender's political program, which he was unable to enact. She assumes the role of dictator, and she aims to provide compulsory labor for an idler.

At the end of *On the Rocks*, the status quo remains. Yet its foundations have shaken. In a revolutionary and dictatorial manner, the Marxist Aloysia seizes command of her new family. In a potentially revolutionary manner, the unemployed workers begin to act.

* * * *

Like *Rosmersholm* and *On the Rocks*, the subject of *The Mother* is radicalization. In Ibsen's play, reactionary forces defeat a radicalized intellectual. In Shaw's play, reactionary forces defeat a radicalized liberal. In Brecht's play, a radicalized working-class woman, in concert with other members of the proletariat, defeats the forces of reaction. *The Mother* dramatizes both the process of radicalization and the successful results of a radicalized proletariat, exemplified by its title character. Neither Ibsen's nor Shaw's play has a title character. Ibsen's title suggests reactionary forces whose hold on the protagonist prevents him from breaking away and drags him to his death. Shaw's title suggests the societal problem to which radical action is a solution. Literally, Brecht's title points to the play's main character. Symbolically, it suggests birth and nurture. The mother's own son has become a radical—a communist, in fact. She herself becomes radicalized—giving birth to new ideas, as it were—and then nurtures the communist cause until, in the Russian Revolution of 1917, it matures as a new state.

The Mother is as much a morality play as *Everyman*. The medieval play dramatizes Everyman's road to spiritual salvation; Brecht's dramatizes Everyproletarian's road to earthly salvation. In morality plays, the contending forces are godly conservatism and the evil that began with Satan's revolt against God. Although angelic and diabolical forces do battle in Brecht's play, the angelic forces are revolutionary (communism) and the diabolical forces conservative (capitalism). Like Everyman, Brecht's Everyproletarian learns what to reject, what to accept, and what to do for salvation. *The Mother* is a schematic play, for among its aims is the portrayal of radicalism as process.

The opening scene establishes a working-class family—mother and son, for unlike Maxim Gorky's novel, from which it derives, the play begins with the father already dead (Brecht may have deleted Gorky's unsympathetic father because he did not wish to diminish the spectators' sympathy for the working class by showing one of its members in a bad light). This family lives in wretched poverty. Such a family and such a condition constitute code words for virtue. The son, who unlike his parents reads books, regards his lot, exemplified by his inadequate food, as insufficient. When he refuses his soup, symbolic of his refusal to accept his lot, the mother is unhappy. As a chorus relates, the alienation inside the house, between mother and son (she prepares food, he rejects it), derives from political and economic alienation outside the house, between workers and politico-economic forces that affect their lives. At this early stage in the mother's path to secular salvation, she fails to see what can be done. In this scene, Brecht presents the problem, which the chorus abstracts: "Your spot is desperate/and getting worse./ Things can't go on this way/but what can you do?"[11]

Next, Brecht presents the first phase of the solution. With revolutionary workers, the son plans to distribute propaganda leaflets to their fellow workers and, at a factory meeting, to press for a strike unless the owners agree to restore a recent wage cut. Disturbed by these activities, the mother fears they will result in her son's losing his job. Besides, she argues, such activities will not help to pay the rent. One of the revolutionists tells the son, but not the mother, "She finds it very difficult to understand that we must do this here just so she can . . . pay her rent." Avoiding dialectical discourse, the stratagem of Shaw's *On the Rocks*, Brecht provides audiences and readers, but not the title character, with a reason. Instead of explaining to the mother that the solution to her household problems lies outside her household, another worker sings slogans to her: "If you have an empty plate/how do you expect to sup?/It's up to you to take the state/ and turn it over, bottoms up,/till you have filled your plate." Needless to say, the song does not convince the mother.

What begins to convince her is action—not by the revolutionists, but by their antagonists, the police, agents of the reactionaries, who raid her house. In striking contrast to the friendliness of the revolutionary workers, the first words of the police are, "Halt! Anyone who moves, I'll shoot!" Insulting in his words, the police commissioner is brutally destructive in his actions. He tears open the divan, smashes the mirror, overturns a chest of drawers, drops a pot of lard on the floor, and rips down the curtains. As in a morality play, the antagonistic exemplars of evil and good speak in terms that connote their own abstract qualities. The commissioner asks the mother, "why must you tangle with us bloodhounds in your old age?" and tells the son, "you are going to learn your place." The son tells him, "You don't find any rubles in there, do you? That's because we are workers and do not earn very much. . . . In the breadbox there isn't much bread . . . and in the jar there isn't much tea."

After the police leave, the mother is confused. Forces of law and order, which she has been taught to respect, "do not do the right thing." Not for her, but for the audience, a chorus provides

---

11. All quotations from this play are from the translation by Lee Baxandall.

the moral. One cannot detach the practitioners from the practice. Evil people serve evil causes, not good causes; evil causes result in evil people who behave in an evil way. "So never say the state is good that treats you badly. . . ."

When the mother agrees to distribute revolutionary leaflets, it is not because of convincing arguments by the revolutionary workers. After all, they have employed slogans rather than arguments, and the police have blamed them for their own actions. Since she cannot read, she does not even know what the leaflets say. As Walter Benjamin points out, her motive is emotional, maternal: she wants to protect her son, whose activities the police observe.[12] They will pay no attention to her, a presumably harmless old lady. Although Brecht does not put it in so many words, the mother's behavior contrasts with that of the police. Whereas they, serving a bad cause, behave reprehensibly, the mother, serving a good cause, behaves humanely.

The next lesson in this primer of revolution is the rejection of the liberal position, negotiation with capitalists. The result of a bargaining session between labor and management is not restoration of the wage cut but the owner's agreement to use the money to drain nearby swamps, which are a health hazard to the workers' children. However, health is neither the sole nor even the primary reason for the owner's decision. He intends to expand his factory on the reclaimed land. "New jobs would emerge from this," the workers' negotiator reports him as saying. No doubt as a veiled threat against a strike, the owner also stated that with a nearby factory closing, seven hundred workers will become available for jobs. The negotiator concludes, "We believe in the lesser evil." The revolutionists reject this solution in favor of a strike on the first of May, and they will try to persuade workers at other plants to join them. Brecht does not mention whether the workers' negotiator proposed restoration of the wage cut and drainage of the swamp at the owner's expense, to be regarded as part of capital outlay that first profits from the expanded factory would restore. Brecht's interest is not nuances about collective bargaining, but either/or: the presentation of the two essential alternatives, negotiation and confrontation. Categorically rejecting negotiation, Brecht urges the recogni-

---

12. Walter Benjamin, *Understanding Brecht*, trans. Anna Bostock, p. 34.

tion of class warfare as the only viable method to benefit the workers.

In a major phase of the mother's radicalization, rational arguments persuade her that the actions of the revolutionary workers are not immoral, and they plant the seeds for her recognition that the actions of their antagonists are immoral. Cannot the factory owner do as he wishes with his factory, since it belongs to him, just as she can do as she wishes with her table, since it belongs to her? There is a difference, one of the workers explains: "He can use his property to use us." Unless he uses the workers, another worker points out, the factory is useless to him. He therefore needs the workers so that he may use his property. If one person tells him this, he will laugh in that person's face. If eight hundred tell him—as they will do by striking—he will not laugh. The mother is relieved, because she thought the strike would be violent, and she opposes violence. Since the strikers plan a peaceful demonstration, she concludes, the police will not trouble them. Unsuccessfully, one of the revolutionists tries to disabuse her of this notion. Like the title character of *Saint Joan of the Stockyards*, the mother later reverses her opinion about violence. At this stage, Brecht plants the seeds of that reversal.

Based on the premises just displayed, the next step is the mother's radicalization. When the police, employing violence in behalf of the factory owner, fire upon the peacefully demonstrating workers, and shoot one who holds a red flag, she takes the flag from him. In doing so, she also takes his place. "All of this must be changed!" she concludes.

The radicalized mother now wants to spread the gospel. To a group of workers, she sings "Praise of Communism," which consists of a series of maxims, for instance: "The stupid call it stupid, and the rotten call it rotten/it's against what's rotten, and against stupidity./The exploiters call it a crime./But we know/it is the end of crime."

Because she also wants to learn more, she persuades an apolitical teacher, whose house she keeps (since the May Day disturbance resulted in her son's arrest, she did not have the money for rent and was evicted), to teach her and her worker friends how to read. As she learns, she teaches the teacher—and therefore Brecht's audience—that one should not divorce learning from social utility. Whereas Brecht's Galileo, in the work Brecht had not yet written, learns this only at the end of the play, Brecht's proletarian mother understands it early in the game. Because learning plays a role in social development, she recognizes, its divorce from a social context retards such development. Although the teacher tries to teach spelling by using such words as *branch*, *nest*, and *fish*, the mother insists that he employ words more socially relevant to factory laborers, such as *worker* and *class struggle*. Even reading, says she, is a part of the class struggle. After she and the other workers learn it, they can write their own pamphlets and become leaders in that struggle. In a song, "In Praise of Learning," she explains the workers' need to prepare themselves to take command. Education involves questioning, she sings, and workers must learn to question. "What you yourself don't learn," she adds, "you don't know"—an analogy to the Marxist doctrine that what the workers do not get for themselves, they will not get at all.

As a result of her radicalization, the mother—employing folksy cunning—actively engages in radical activity. Having learned how to read, she and her fellow workers become the leaders to which she alludes in the teaching scene: they print their own writings about the class struggle. In an early scene the revolutionists agree to let her deliver pamphlets in order to protect her son, whom the police know; in a later scene they prevent her from accompanying her son—who has escaped from Siberia and is fleeing to Finland—to the railroad station, since the police know her. While in the first scene mother and son are alienated from each other, in a later scene they are united in a common cause, at which both actively work. Brecht makes this union visual: the son joins her to work at a printing press.

Paralleling the May Day demonstration scene, which ends when the mother picks up the red flag from the hands of a fallen comrade, the play's final scene concerns another demonstration, in which she carries the red flag from the start. In the winter of 1916–1917, says a character, a quarter of a million striking workers rallied to the Bolsheviks. As the revolutionary activities peak, the mother declares, "The victims of today will be the victors of tomorrow/And Never is changed into Today." As finale to the scene, a projection shows the words "THE RUSSIAN PROLETARIAT SEIZED POWER IN NOVEMBER 1917." *The*

Mother begins with a statement of the problem and ends with a statement of the revolutionary solution to the problem.

* * * *

Rosmersholm portrays a political conflict, but without a revolutionary force sufficiently strong to act, let alone to effect social equality. Its contending forces are a naive idealist who is unable to translate his radical ideas into social action, a liberal political opportunist who values expedience more than he does his ideals, and a reactionary who does not hesitate to use any means to achieve his goals. At the end, the reactionary wins and impotent radical idealism turns suicidal. In *On the Rocks*, a liberal politician becomes radicalized but is defeated chiefly by a coalition led by a reactionary politician and labor leaders. At the end, the unemployed masses, ignoring their political and labor representatives, begin to act on their own—fumblingly at first, but with potential power. Unlike these plays, *The Mother* ends with the victory of political radicals. In it, the revolutionary working class has direction, acquires power, and uses it.

In *Rosmersholm*, Ibsen dramatizes his political themes with both explicit and implicit methods. In *On the Rocks*, Shaw is usually explicit, though at crucial points—notably, the end—he relies on implicit means, and employs dialectical argument wherein opposing forces present their cases as strongly as possible. *The Mother* is not only explicit almost throughout (the views of the communists represent those of the author), its leading character is exemplary, its dialogue for the most part and its songs entirely employ slogans rather than dialectical argument, and its dramatic development is schematic. Culminating in a successful revolution, Brecht's play is a dramatic primer about revolutionary action.

Although Ibsen, Shaw, and Brecht did not write *Rosmersholm*, *On the Rocks*, and *The Mother* in chronological sequence (the first performance of *The Mother* was in January 1932, over a year before Shaw began to write *On the Rocks*),[13] the three plays correspond to three successive stages in political clashes among reactionaries, liberals, and radicals. Are *all* of these stages necessary for the radical transformation of society?

---

13. Lee Baxandall, Introduction to *The Mother*, p. 9; Shaw, *The Bodley Head Bernard Shaw*, 6:572.

The Prospect of Revolution

A Marxist like Brecht, who pins his hopes on the last, might think so. Ibsen, who inclines toward anarchy, sees the first two as futile, and though he does not pin all his hopes on a single class, as Brecht does, he believes—as quoted earlier in the analysis of *An Enemy of the People*—that the aristocracy of mind and spirit, which might improve society, may derive from women and working classes. Although Shaw would prefer the less sanguinary second step, he recognizes the final phase as necessary if the second is unsuccessful. To a Marxist, Brecht's play is clearly the most radical of the three. To a non-Marxist, however, Brecht's play might be merely a depiction of one form of successful radicalism.

7.

Money and Politics in Ibsen, Shaw, and Brecht

As everyone knows, money talks. The preceding chapter quotes Shaw's preface to *The Apple Cart*, which points out that money talks from the printed page and from the airwaves. When it changes hands or is withheld, it is also vocal. Because it talks, it buys: politicians, among other commodities. Thus, "money reigns."

In capitalist societies—which are the societies about which Ibsen, Shaw, and Brecht write—money underlies virtually all human activities. Partly for this reason, it is a prominent factor in each of the plays analyzed in this book. Not only does money talk, but in these plays people talk about money. Nora Helmer needs it, and it is her husband's very business (banking); it is the excuse for Henry Higgins's undertaking (a bet) and the prospect of being able to earn more of it is the reason Liza tolerates his bullying lessons; Mother Courage is a tradeswoman whose buying and selling activities form integral elements of the fabric of the play partly named for her. To working men and women, and to members of the professional classes, money is a vital factor. Carpenters, servants, prostitutes, and laborers earn it. Neither master builder nor architect builds houses without a commission; doctors sell their services at the going rates in different parts of the community, as artists sell their art; and while the scientist sells what business demands, he tries to earn time to do the research his profession demands. Among the pillars of the social system are bank accounts, and the money contained in them is often divorced from morality. In these societies, money turns people into commodities to be bought, sold, or rented—exploited, in a world that Ibsen, Shaw, and Brecht variously view as a brothel, exemplified most vividly, perhaps, by Kitty Warren's profession; or as a market, exemplified most vividly, perhaps, by the stock exchange and the stockyards, where Pierpont Mauler and the forces he represents turn people into commodities, which they buy and sell as they buy and sell stocks and cattle, for indeed people become cattle, whose value, which rises or falls, is expressed in monetary terms. Such clichés as "that person is worth millions" and "he isn't worth a plugged nickel" might serve as epigraphs for *Saint Joan of the Stockyards* and several other plays examined in this book. Through such characters as Pastor Manders, Mrs. Baines, and Paulus Snyder, Ibsen, Shaw, and Brecht portray organized religion's connection with the forces of money. "To him that hath shall be given!" Brecht reminds his audiences, some of whom may recognize the phrase's biblical sources, but he also perceives the gap between him that hath and him that hath not, and both he and Shaw remind audiences that the person who hath not may take from him that hath.

Money reigns. It informs the political process in capitalist societies, even democratic societies. To ensure that those who have will keep what they have, Mayor Stockmann uses money as one of the levers to mold public opinion, while Kroll and his political colleagues, all wealthy, have no difficulty in financing a newspaper, also to mold public opinion. Because Undershaft pays the piper, he calls the tune and therefore is himself the real government of his country. As Mauler learns, Wall Street buys American congressmen. Not only in the plays in which these characters and actions figure prominently, but in most of the plays analyzed in this book, politics is an important factor. Sometimes politics comes onstage, notably in *On the Rocks*, where a prime minister meets members of his coalition cabinet and also a labor delegation, and in *The Mother*, which portrays politically revolutionary actions by communists. Where politics does not directly make its appearance, it remains an offstage force that characters discuss—in *Mother Courage and Her Children*, for instance, where small fry who do not make a large profit from war recognize that kings do, and in *Heartbreak House*, where a businessman in a democratic society explains that he was a member of the government without having to go through the bother of an election.

Although these three radical playwrights form what I have called an apostolic succession, this phrase does not necessarily connote progress. Let us avoid the evolutionary fallacy that would evaluate them as good, better, and best; or indicate a trend from less radical to more radical to most radical; or suggest that the more radical the play, the better the play. None of these is the case.

For various reasons, Marxist critics tend to debit Ibsen's form of radicalism. His solutions are too general, they claim, and lack socially constructive ideas; he retreats from practical politics, which he distrusts, to impractical ethics; he fails to recognize the Norwegian working class as the major factor in social progress; and so forth and so on.[1] To some extent, all such criticisms are valid. To a greater extent, they are irrelevant. Why should an artist define his social thoughts along anyone's established political lines when these lines might confine, distort, or falsify, and thus fail to represent, his thoughts? Ibsen's refusal to dramatize his ideas along such political lines constitutes a challenge to political sects to expand or redefine their ideas and policies to embrace his. Time has demonstrated the wisdom of Ibsen's distrust of politics and politicians, radical as well as reactionary. Although *A Doll House* and *Ghosts* exemplify every so-called deficiency just cited, they are no less revolutionary on that account. In attacking moribund social institutions, and the forces of what today are called the Establishment, which support these institutions, his plays represent an onslaught against the very foundations of society. Ibsen's contemporaries certainly thought so. While one might regard his refusal to spell out specific, practical solutions to the problems he dramatizes as a failure, a deficiency, and a convenient, idealistic excuse not to dirty his hands in practical politics, one might also regard it as a daring challenge to his audiences to work out their own solutions. As Brecht puts it in *The Mother*, though not in connection with Ibsen, what people do not learn for themselves, they do not truly know. Moreover, Ibsen himself—through the character of Rosmer—casts an unfavorable light on those who retreat from the political arena into either an ivory tower or a watery grave, both of which separate them from life. Ibsen's plays are radical engagements and confrontations with life and society, not retreats from them.

Do the Shavian and Fabian notions of socialism result in non-

---

1. See, for example, Angel Flores, ed., *Ibsen*, pp. 18, 30–31, 62, 80–81; John Howard Lawson, *Theory and Technique of Playwriting*, pp. 63, 79.

radicalism and nonsocialism, as Shaw's Marxist critics claim? Based on Marxist premises, they often do. But since when have the Marxists cornered the market on what constitutes either radicalism or socialism? In the years since Shaw wrote most of his plays, different Marxist governments have testified that Marxism itself contains what the head of one such government (Tito of Yugoslavia) calls different roads to socialism. And would anyone but politicians with vested interests in the status quo, at times not even such politicians, maintain that democratic governments as presently constituted are the most ideal form of representative democracy?

Brecht's Marxism does not make him more radical than Ibsen or Shaw, just different from them. Is *Mother Courage and Her Children* more radical than *A Doll House*, *The Good Person of Szechwan* more radical than *Mrs. Warren's Profession*? Mother Courage lived a few centuries before Marx (therefore, no Marxist she), and in *Mrs. Warren's Profession*, Sir George Crofts explains—more clearly than anyone in *The Good Person of Szechwan* does—the relationship between capitalism and prostitution. As Brecht says in one of his theoretical works, lack of faith can move mountains.[2] In regarding what for a long time was the world's only communist country, the Soviet Union, Brecht did not abandon his skepticism. "By looking at the Gestapo," the Marxist critic Walter Benjamin reports him as saying in 1934,[3] "you can see what may become of the Cheka" (the Soviet secret police). In 1953, as Esslin relates, after the suppression of a workers' uprising in East Germany, Brecht composed a wry poem, "The Solution," which proposed that since the government had lost confidence in the people, it might dissolve the people and elect another.[4] His responses to political realities—in Stalinist Russia, communist Germany, and elsewhere—were thoughtful, not knee-jerk.

If a play is explicitly radical, it does not thereby become a better play than one that employs implicit methods. Although Ibsen provokes questions, he refuses to provide specific, practical answers. The same is usually true of Shaw, whose *On the*

2. Bertolt Brecht, *Brecht on Theatre*, trans. John Willett, p. 189.
3. Walter Benjamin, *Understanding Brecht*, trans. Anna Bostock, p. 111.
4. Martin Esslin, *Brecht: The Man and His Work*, p. 195.

Rocks is among the few exceptions in the Shavian canon in that it proposes clear-cut solutions. Compared to *The Mother*, however, Shaw's play is a very model of subtlety. In this play, whose explicit solution is just as exceptional in the Brechtian canon as *On the Rocks* is in the Shavian (as evidence, compare it with the other plays analyzed here), Brecht is not interested in subtlety. As he himself says, in a Note on the play, *The Mother* "has no intention of handing over the spectator to a 'suggestive' theatre experience. Rather its concern is to teach the spectator a most definite practical conduct that is intended to change the world. . . ."[5]

Unlike the teaching methodology in his other plays, Brecht in *The Mother* employs elementary lecturing, *tableaux vivants* and *parlants* that show and tell, assertions, slogans, and rigged arguments. The very end of the play is a rigged, upbeat finale, probably designed to encourage willing workers of the cause. Imposed by the author, rather than a logical culmination of developments within the play itself, the historical fact of 1917 does not satisfactorily resolve the dramatic issue of *The Mother*. One might end it as Gorky ends his 1906 novel, with the police seizing and brutalizing the mother while she distributes leaflets of the speech her son made during the trial which condemned him to exile—a conclusion that develops from her radicalization and connects directly to the actions of her son, who initiates her radicalization. One might even end the play as Brecht does, but in order to make such a conclusion dramatically satisfactory, one would, throughout the play, have to do something similar to what Brecht does in *Saint Joan of the Stockyards*: dramatize the larger revolutionary forces, factors, and people involved in what culminated in the 1917 revolution. To do so would obviously result in a very different play, whose focus might be the meaning of 1917.

As this analysis suggests, the more explicit the drama, the more *un*successful it usually is. Do sloganeering and name-calling convert the unconverted? As to the already converted, some might ask, "What else is new?" Others, however, might find in the play what they but not the playwright put there. Again, take

---

5. Bertolt Brecht, *The Mother*, p. 133. As Martin Esslin states, this play represents Brecht's "nearest approach to an orthodox Communist propaganda play" (*Brecht: The Man and His Work*, p. 167).

The Mother. According to Walter Benjamin, the title character, "'widow of a worker and mother of a worker,' is therefore someone who is doubly exploited: first, as a member of the working class, and second, as a woman and mother."[6] A good dramatic conception, this. Unfortunately, Brecht does not dramatize it in this play. Perhaps Benjamin brings to Brecht's play his familiarity with Gorky's novel, which executes this conception.

What applies to Brecht applies to Ibsen and Shaw as well. Take their plays analyzed in this book (and these, like Brecht's, are representative dramatizations of their radical ideas). Whatever the virtues of those plays wherein each is most explicit about his own ideas, *Pillars of Society* and *On the Rocks*, both are dramatically more clear-cut than the others. In *Pillars of Society*, Ibsen spells out the deficiencies of both his protagonist and his protagonist's society; he has this protagonist see the light, confess his guilt publicly, and take what remedial steps he is capable of taking; and the playwright provides a pithy moral to the tale, that the spirits of truth and freedom should become the real pillars of society. Shaw—whose title, *On the Rocks*, is as thematically clear as Ibsen's—spells out the deficiencies of his protagonist and his protagonist's society, which has drifted onto the rocks; he has this protagonist see the light and provide comprehensive solutions to society's problems, then gives specific reasons why various social classes first accept, then reject these solutions, or why they reject them from the outset; and he indicates what might happen when these solutions are rejected. This is not to say that the radical ideas in the other plays of these writers are less dramatically forceful than in these plays. It is to say, however, that those in the other plays are more difficult to summarize. Which means, ultimately, that they have more contact with reality, which stubbornly resists reduction to simple summaries.

At their best, the dramatized radicalism of Ibsen, Shaw, and Brecht is very stubborn indeed. To what extent, for example, is Nora to blame, Helmer to be exonerated, for what occurs in *A Doll House*? To what extent should one applaud the assertions and exhortations of Captain Shotover in *Heartbreak House*? In *The Good Person of Szechwan*, what is the dialectic that gener-

6. Benjamin, *Understanding Brecht*, p. 34.

ally results in audiences' and readers' greater dislike of the family that leeches off Shen Teh than their dislike of Shui Ta, although Shui Ta creates more social harm than the family? Since, in *Life of Galileo*, seventeenth-century Padua and Florence serve, among other uses, as analogies for twentieth-century capitalist West and communist East, would Galileo have ultimately put science to the service of humanity if he had stayed in Padua? Although none of these questions—or similar questions about these and other plays—is easy to answer, the difficulty does not deradicalize the plays. Rather, it enriches this and other aspects of them.

Bibliography

(1) By Henrik Ibsen

The Complete Major Prose Plays. Translated by Rolf Fjelde. New York: Plume Books, 1978.
Ibsen: Letters and Speeches. Edited by Evert Sprinchorn. New York: Hill and Wang, 1964.
The Oxford Ibsen. Edited by James Walter McFarlane, 8 vols. (1 and 4 in collaboration with Graham Orton). London: Oxford University Press, 1970–1977.

(2) By Bernard Shaw

The Bodley Head Bernard Shaw: Collected Plays with Their Prefaces. 7 vols. London: Bodley Head, 1970–1974.
Collected Letters 1898–1910. Edited by Dan H. Laurence. London: Max Reinhardt, 1972.
"Discarded Pages of Paper on Ibsen Not Included in *Quintessence.*" British Library 50661.
"The Doctor's Dilemma." Holograph manuscript. British Library 50619.
Essays in Fabian Socialism. London: Constable, 1949.
The Intelligent Woman's Guide to Socialism, Capitalism, Sovietism, and Fascism. London: Constable, 1949.
Major Critical Essays. London: Constable, 1948.
The Matter with Ireland. Edited by David H. Greene and Dan H. Laurence. New York: Hill and Wang, 1962.
"Notes for a Fabian Lecture." 1914. British Library 50687.
Our Theatres in the Nineties. 3 vols. London: Constable, 1954.
Platform and Pulpit. Edited by Dan H. Laurence. New York: Hill and Wang, 1961.
Report on Fabian Policy: Fabian Tract No. 70. London: Fabian Society, 1896.
The Road to Equality. Edited by Louis Crompton with the assistance of Hilayne Cavanaugh. Boston: Beacon Press, 1971.
Shaw: An Exhibit. Edited by Dan H. Laurence. Austin: Humanities Research Center, University of Texas, 1978.
Shaw on Theatre. Edited by E. J. West. New York: Hill and Wang, 1958.
Sixteen Self-Sketches. London: Constable, 1949.
"Socialism at the International Congress." *Cosmopolis* 3 (September 1896). British Library.

(3) By Bertolt Brecht

Aufbau eine Rolle: Laughtons Galilei. Berlin: Henschelverlag Kunst und Gesellschaft, 1956.
Brecht on Theatre. Translated by John Willett. London: Methuen, 1964.
Collected Plays. Vols. 1, 2, 5, 6, 7, and 9. Edited by Ralph Manheim and John Willett. New York: Vintage Books, 1971–1977.
The Messingkauf Dialogues. Translated by John Willett. London: Methuen, 1965.
The Mother. Translated by Lee Baxandall. New York: Grove Press, 1965.
Saint Joan of the Stockyards. Translated by Frank Jones. Bloomington: Indiana University Press, 1969.

(4) Ibsen, Shaw, and Brecht: Works by Others

Bentley, Eric. *Theatre of War*. New York: Viking Press, 1972.
Brustein, Robert. *The Theatre of Revolt*. Boston: Little, Brown, 1964.
Dukore, Bernard F. "Brecht's Shavian Saint." *Quarterly Journal of Speech* 50(1964): 136–39.
Friedell, Egon. *A Cultural History of the Modern Age*. 3 vols. Translated by Charles Francis Atkinson. New York: Knopf, 1932.
Lawson, John Howard. *Theory and Technique of Playwriting*. New York: Hill and Wang, 1964.

(5) Ibsen: Works by Others

Bradbury, Malcolm, and James McFarlane, eds. *Modernism 1890–1930*. Harmondsworth: Penguin Books, 1978.
Clurman, Harold. *Ibsen*. New York: Collier Books, 1977.
Downs, Brian W. *Ibsen: The Intellectual Background*. Cambridge: Cambridge University Press, 1948.
―――. *A Study of Six Plays by Ibsen*. Cambridge: Cambridge University Press, 1950.
Dukore, Bernard F., ed. *Dramatic Theory and Criticism*. New York: Holt, Rinehart and Winston, 1974.
Egan, Michael, ed. *Ibsen: The Critical Heritage*. London: Routledge and Kegan Paul, 1972.
Fjelde, Rolf, ed. *Ibsen*. Englewood Cliffs, N.J.: Prentice-Hall, 1965.
Flores, Angel, ed. *Ibsen*. New York: Haskell House, 1966.
Gray, Ronald. *Ibsen—A Dissenting View*. Cambridge: Cambridge University Press, 1977.
Hardwicke, Elizabeth. *Seduction and Betrayal*. New York: Random House, 1974.
Kapp, Yvonne. *Eleanor Marx*, vol. 2. New York: Pantheon, 1976.
Meyer, Michael. *Ibsen: A Biography*. Garden City, N.Y.: Doubleday, 1971.
Nordau, Max. *Degeneration*. Translator anonymous. New York: Howard Fertig, 1968.

Northam, John. *Ibsen: A Critical Study*. Cambridge: Cambridge University Press, 1973.
Strindberg, August. *Getting Married*. Translated by Mary Sandbach. New York: Viking Press, 1972.
Valency, Maurice. *The Flower and the Castle*. New York: Macmillan, 1963.
Van Laan, Thomas F. *The Idiom of Drama*. Ithaca: Cornell University Press, 1970.
Weigand, Hermann J. *The Modern Ibsen*. New York: Dutton, 1960.

(6) Shaw: Works by Others

Albert, Sidney P. "The Price of Salvation: Moral Economics in *Major Barbara*." *Modern Drama*, 14 (1971): 307–23.
Bentley, Eric. *Bernard Shaw 1856–1950*. New York: New Directions, 1957.
Berst, Charles A. *Bernard Shaw and the Art of the Drama*. Urbana: University of Illinois Press, 1973.
Boxill, Roger. *Shaw and the Doctors*. New York: Basic Books, 1969.
Carpenter, Charles A. *Bernard Shaw and the Art of Destroying Ideals*. Madison: University of Wisconsin Press, 1969.
Caudwell, Christopher. "George Bernard Shaw: A Study of the Bourgeois Superman," in *Five Approaches of Literary Criticism*. Edited by Wilbur Scott. New York: Collier Books, 1962.
Chesterton, G. K. *Irish Impressions*. New York: John Lane, 1920.
Crompton, Louis. *Shaw the Dramatist*. Lincoln: University of Nebraska Press, 1969.
Dukore, Bernard F. *Bernard Shaw, Playwright*. Columbia: University of Missouri Press, 1973.
―――. "The Undershaft Maxims." *Modern Drama*, 9 (1966): 90–100.
Frank, Joseph. "Internal vs. External Combustion: Dickens' *Bleak House* and Shaw's *Major Barbara* and *Heartbreak House*." *The Shaw Review*, 20 (1977): 126–34.
Gibbs, A. M. *Shaw*. London: Oliver and Boyd, 1969.
Goldman, Emma. *The Social Significance of Modern Drama*. Boston: Badger, 1914.
Heilman, Robert B. *The Ways of the World*. Seattle: University of Washington Press, 1978.
Henderson, Archibald. *George Bernard Shaw: Man of the Century*. New York: Appleton-Century-Crofts, 1956.
Hulse, James W. *Revolutionists in London*. Oxford: Clarendon Press, 1970.
Marx, Karl. *Critique of Hegel's "Philosophy of Right."* Translated by Annette Jolin and Joseph O'Malley. Cambridge: Cambridge University Press, 1970.
McDowell, Frederick P. W. "Crisis and Unreason: Shaw's *On the Rocks*." *Educational Theatre Journal*, 13 (1961): 192–200.
―――. "Technique, Symbol, and Theme in *Heartbreak House*." *PMLA*, 68 (1953): 335–56.

Morgan, Margery M. *The Shavian Playground*. London: Methuen, 1972.
Nethercot, Arthur H. *Men and Supermen*. New York: Benjamin Blom, 1954.
Rosenblood, Norman, ed. *Shaw: Seven Critical Essays*. Toronto: University of Toronto Press, 1971.
Scherbina, Vladimir. *Lenin and Problems of Literature*. Moscow: Progress Publishers, 1974.
Stanton, Stephen S., ed. *A Casebook on* Candida. New York: Crowell, 1962.
Strauss, E. *Bernard Shaw: Art and Socialism*. London: Gollancz, 1942.
Turco, Alfred, Jr. *Shaw's Moral Vision: The Self and Salvation*. Ithaca: Cornell University Press, 1976.
Webb, Beatrice. *Our Partnership*. Edited by Barbara Drake and Margaret I. Cole. London: Longmans, Green, 1948.
West, Alick. "*A Good Man Fallen Among Fabians.*" London: Lawrence and Wishart, 1950.
Wisenthal, J. L. *The Marriage of Contraries*. Cambridge: Harvard University Press, 1974.

(7) **Brecht: Works by Others**

Benjamin, Walter. *Understanding Brecht*. Translated by Anna Bostock. London: NLB, 1973.
Demetz, Peter, ed. *Brecht*. Englewood Cliffs, N.J.: Prentice-Hall, 1962.
Dukore, Bernard F., ed. *Drama and Revolution*. New York: Holt, Rinehart and Winston, 1971.
Esslin, Martin. *Brecht: The Man and His Work*. New York: W. W. Norton, 1974.
Ewen, Frederic. *Bertolt Brecht: His Life, His Art, and His Times*. New York: Citadel Press, 1967.
Fuegi, John, ed. *Brecht Heute/Brecht Today*, vol. 2. Frankfurt: Athenäum, 1974.
———. *The Essential Brecht*. Los Angeles: Hennessey and Ingalls, 1972.
Gorky, Maxim. *Mother*. Translated by Margaret Wettlin. Moscow: Foreign Languages Publishing House, n.d.
Gray, Ronald. *Brecht the Dramatist*. Cambridge: Cambridge University Press, 1977.
Mews, Siegfried, and Herbert Knust, eds. *Essays on Brecht: Theater and Politics*. Chapel Hill: University of North Carolina Press, 1974.
Morley, Michael. *Brecht: A Study*. London: Heinemann, 1977.
Wekwerth, Manfred. "Brecht Today." *The Drama Review*, 12 (1967): 118–24.
White, Alfred D. *Bertolt Brecht's Great Plays*. New York: Barnes and Noble, 1978.
Williams, Raymond. *Modern Tragedy*. Stanford: Stanford University Press, 1967.

Index

A

Albert, Sidney P.: on *Major Barbara*, 114
Aveling, Edward, xvi*n*

B

Benjamin, Walter, 163; on *The Mother*, 155, 165
Bentley, Eric: on Brecht, xix; on *Good Person of Szechwan*, 27*n*; on *Life of Galileo*, 71*n*; on *Major Barbara* and *Saint Joan of the Stockyards*, 122*n*; on Shaw, xvii*n*, xviii*n*
Berkeley Repertory Theatre: its *Major Barbara* production, 113*n*
Berst, Charles A.: on *Mrs. Warren's Profession*, 35*n*; on Pygmalion, 9*n*
Booth, Gen. William, 173
Brandes, Georg, xii, xiv; on Ibsen, xv
Brecht, Bertolt, xi–xiv, xix–xxi, xxii, 160–66; *Galileo*, 63*n*, 71*n*, 72; his collaboration on American production of *Galileo*, 71*n*; *Good Person of Szechwan*, xix–xx, xxi, 27–28, 40–49, 92, 93, 160, 163, 165–66; his Marxism, xix–xx, 163; his production of *Mother Courage and Her Children*, 20*n*, 24*n*, 25*n*; *Life of Galileo*, xxi, 50, 63–74, 157, 160, 166; *Messingkauf Dialogues*, xiii; *Mother*, xxi, 134–35, 152–59, 161, 162, 164–65; *Mother Courage and Her Children*, xxi, 1–2, 18–26, 91, 160, 161, 163; *Puntila and Matti, His Hired Man*, xxi, 75–76, 90–99; *Saint Joan of the Stockyards*, xii, xxi, 100, 122–33, 134–35, 156, 160–61, 164; on Shaw, xii; "The Solution," 163
Brustein, Robert: on *Enemy of the People*, 108*n*; on *Mother Courage and Her Children*, 24*n*
Bunton, George, 54*n*

C

Caudwell, Christopher: on Shaw, xviii

Chesterton, G. K., 84*n*
Crompton, Louis: on *Doctor's Dilemma*, 59*n*

E

Engels, Friedrich, xvi*n*, xvii; on Ibsen, xv–xvi, xix
Esslin, Martin: on Brecht, xix, 70*n*, 163; on *Mother*, 164*n*
Everyman, 153

F

Fabianism and the Fabian Society, xiv, xvi–xviii, xvii*n*, xix
Fjelde, Rolf: on *Doll House*, 2*n*
Frank, Joseph: on *Heartbreak House*, 85*n*
Friedell, Egon: on Shaw, xviii*n*
Fuegi, John: on *Good Person of Szechwan*, 44*n*

G

Gibbs, A. M.: on *Heartbreak House*, 84*n*
Goldman, Emma: on *Major Barbara*, 119*n*
Gorky, Maxim: *Mother*, 153, 164–65

H

Heilman, Robert B.: on *Doctor's Dilemma*, 59*n*

I

Ibsen, Henrik, xi–xvi, xix, xx–xxii, 160–65; his anarchism, xiv–xv; *Doll House*, xi, xvi, xxi, 1–9, 18–19, 25–26, 160, 162, 163, 165; *Enemy of the People*, xvi, xxi, 100–110, 117, 122, 132–33, 134, 135, 144, 159, 161; *Ghosts*, xxi, 27–34, 39, 40, 44, 45, 48–49, 160, 161, 162; *Lady from the Sea*, xi; *Master Builder*, xxi, 50–54, 72–73, 160; *Pillars of Society*, xxi, 75–82, 90–91, 98–99, 165; *Rosmersholm*, xxi, xxii*n*, 134–42, 144, 149, 152, 158–59, 161; on Shaw, xiv; on socialism, xiv

K

Kaufmann, F. W.: on *Rosmersholm*, 140*n*

L

Laughton, Charles, 63*n*, 71*n*, 72
Lenin, V. I.: on Shaw, xix

M

Mangan, James Clarence, 84*n*
Marat, Jean-Paul, xv
Marx, Karl, xvii, xix, 115–16, 130, 145, 163
Marx-Aveling, Eleanor, xvi, xvii*n*
Marxists: on Ibsen, 162; on Shaw, xvi, xvii–xix, 37, 115, 162–63. *See also* Caudwell, Christopher; Strauss, E.; West, Alick
McDowell, Frederick P. W.: on *Heartbreak House*, 84*n*; on *On the Rocks*, 151*n*
McFarlane, James: on *Enemy of the People*, 105*n*
Morgan, Margery M.: on *On the Rocks* and *Rosmersholm*, 151*n*

N

Nethercot, Arthur: on *Heartbreak House*, 85
Nordau, Max: on Ibsen, xv

P

Proudhon, Pierre Joseph, xv, 85

R

Reinhardt, Max, xii

S

Shakespeare, William: *As You Like It*, 27

Shaw, Bernard, xi–xiv, xvi–xxii, 160–65; *Apple Cart*, 149, 160; *Arms and the Man*, 39; *Candida*, xi; *Doctor's Dilemma*, xvii, xxi, 50, 54–63, 72–73, 160; *Heartbreak House*, xxi, 75, 82–92, 98–99, 143, 161, 165; "In Praise of Guy Fawkes," 148–49, 150; *Intelligent Woman's Guide to Socialism, Capitalism, Sovietism, and Fascism*, 146; *Major Barbara*, xii, xiii, xvii, xxi, 100, 109–22, 124, 130, 132–33, 134, 161; *Man and Superman*, 88; *Mrs. Warren's Profession*, xxi, 27–28, 34–41, 44, 45, 48–49, 160, 163; *On the Rocks*, xviii, xxi, 134–35, 142–53, 158–59, 161, 163–64, 165; *Pygmalion*, xxi, 1–2, 9–18, 25–26, 160; *Quintessence of Ibsenism*, xi, xiv, xvi, xxii, 140*n*; on *Rosmersholm*, 140*n*; *Saint Joan*, xii; *Sanity of Art*, 58; *Widowers' Houses*, xi. *See also* Fabianism and the Fabian Society
Strauss, E.: on Shaw, xviii
Strindberg, August: on *Doll House*, 6*n*

T

Tito, Josip Broz, 163

V

Valency, Maurice: on *Enemy of the People*, 108*n*
Van Laan, Thomas F.: on *Rosmersholm*, 141*n*

W

Webb, Beatrice, 116*n*
Webb, Sidney, xvii*n*
Weigand, Hermann J.: on *Pillars of Society*, 78*n*
Weigel, Helene: as Mother Courage, 20*n*, 24*n*
West, Alick: on Shaw, xvii, xviii, xix
Wisenthal, J. L.: on *Doctor's Dilemma*, 59*n*; on *Heartbreak House*, 89*n*